Rightsizing for Corporate Survival

An IS Manager's Guide

by Robert Massoudi, Astrid Julienne,
Bob Millradt, and Reed Hornberger

SunSoft Press
A Prentice Hall Title

The products described in this book may be protected by one or more U.S. patents, foreign patents, or pending applications.

TRADEMARKS—Sun, Sun Microsystems, the Sun logo, Sun Microsystems Computer Company, SunSoft, the SunSoft logo, Solaris, SunOS, SunLink, Sun Integration Services, and ToolTalk are trademarks or registered trademarks of Sun Microsystems, Inc. in the U.S. and certain other countries. UNIX is a registered trademark in the United States and other countries, exclusively licensed through X/Open Company, Ltd. OPEN LOOK and NetWare are registered trademarks of Novell, Inc. PostScript and Display PostScript are registered trademarks of Adobe Systems, Inc.

IBM, DB2, and OS/2 are registered trademarks of International Business Machines Corp. Apple, LocalTalk, Macintosh, and AppleShare are registered trademarks of Apple Computer, Inc. DEC, DECnet, and Rdb are trademarks or registered trademarks of Digital Equipment Corp. Informix is a registered trademark of Informix Software, Inc. dBASE is a registered trademark of Borland International, Inc. HP is a registered trademark of Hewlett-Packard Co. X Window System is a trademark of X Consortium, Inc. Microsoft and MS-DOS are registered trademarks of Microsoft Corporation.

All other product names mentioned herein are the trademarks of their respective owners.

All SPARC trademarks, including the SCD Compliant Logo, are trademarks or registered trademarks of SPARC International, Inc. SPARCstation, SPARCserver, SPARCengine, SPARCstorage, SPARCware, SPARCcenter, SPARCclassic, SPARCcluster, SPARCdesign, SPARC811, SPARCprinter, UltraSPARC, microSPARC, SPARCworks, and SPARCompiler are licensed exclusively to Sun Microsystems, Inc. Products bearing SPARC trademarks are based upon an architecture developed by Sun Microsystems, Inc.

The publisher offers discounts on this book when ordered in bulk quantities. For more information, contact: Corporate Sales Department, Prentice Hall PTR, 113 Sylvan Avenue, Englewood Cliffs, NJ 07632. Phone: 800-382-3419 or 201-592-2498, Fax: 201-592-2249, email: dan_rush@prenhall.com

Printed in the United States of America.

Cover designer: *M & K Design, Palo Alto, California*
Cover photo: *Imtek/Masterfile*
Manufacturing manager: *Alexis R. Heydt*
Acquisitions editor: *Gregory G. Doench*

10 9 8 7 6 5 4 3 2 1

ISBN 0-13-123126-X

SunSoft Press
A Prentice Hall Title

Dedication

My love and thanks to my best friend Maria for her support, love and understanding, and to my father who is my intellectual icon. Special thanks to all the hardworking people at Sun who contributed significantly to the knowledge and material contained in this book and to those who were my mentors over the years. My deepest thanks and appreciation to all.

— Robert

Much love and appreciation to my daughter Shelby and to my special friend Joseph for their continued love and support of me. Also, special thanks to Steve Uhlir—one of the best managers I've ever worked with—for the support and encouragement he has given me during my tenure with his engineering organization.

— Astrid

I am very grateful to all of the talented people at Sun who contributed to this book and without whom this book would not have been possible. Special thanks to Reed Hornberger and Gary Steele who have been a source of motivation and inspiration for me and who have given me so much support over the years.

— Bob

I owe a great deal of thanks to Bob Millradt and Gary Steele for their continuing support, creativity, and guidance in getting these ideas and concepts to paper and evolving them over the past three years. And to my wife, Carolyn, and sons, Myles and Christopher, thank you for your support and encouragement during the late nights and weeks of travel developing this information and writing the book itself.

— Reed

Table of Contents

Rightsizing for Corporate Survival

Acknowledgments

Very special thanks to the following companies and organizations for contributing their personal experiences in rightsizing their business, without which this book could not have been written:

ADCO	National Vulcan Insurance
Andersen Consulting	Naval Air Warfare Center
Banc One	New Zealand Inland Revenue Department
Burlington Coat Factory	Northwest Airlines
Eastman Kodak	Smith Foods
EDS	Sun Microsystems, Inc.
Ehapa Verlag GmbH	U.S. Department of Defense
GfK	Wells Fargo Bank
Gulf Canada Resources	WorldCorp
Meeschaert Roussel	

Very special thanks and much appreciation to Gary Steele for his support and for providing significant contribution to the concepts and ideas contained in this book.

Special thanks to industry rightsizing specialist Larry DeBoever (of DeBoever Architectures, Acton, MA) for conducting research on the phases of rightsizing.

Special thanks to Kevin O'Neill and Claudia Hanlin of Business Research Group for conducting research on the economics of rightsizing.

Special thanks to Ovum Ltd. for contributing technical research. Ovum Ltd. is an international consulting firm specializing in supplier strategies and markets for leading-edge technologies in computing and telecommunications. To publish this book, we used information from Ovum's 1992 research report *Rightsizing: Strategies, Tools, and Markets*. (Additional information can be obtained by contacting Ovum Ltd., 1 Mortimer St., London W1N 7RH, England; telephone 071-255-2670.)

Special thanks to Tucker Network Technologies, Inc. for contributing technical consulting. Tucker Network Technologies focuses on the architecture, design, and engineering of distributed network computing systems and applications. (Additional information can be obtained by contacting Tucker Network Technologies, Inc., 30 Washington St., South Norwalk, CT 06856; telephone 203-857-0080.)

Special thanks to Scott McNealy and Bill Raduchel for their contributions and support of this book.

Thanks to Jennifer Callison, Carl Cargill, Dr. R. G. G. "Rick" Cattell, David Ditzell, Maura McNulty, Karen Lusardi Richards, Marty Robins, and Laurie Yoler for their source contributions.

Thanks to Marsha Cavanagh, Kathy Patterson of Patterson and Associates, and Penny Johnson for their perseverance in managing the collection, production, and validation of information used in this book.

Thanks to the following team members for their unending support in building and spreading the message of rightsizing to audiences worldwide: Steve O'Brien, Lisa Sieker, Carl Stolle, Maria Geenen, Vicki Morris, Jeff Bates, Donna Prlich, Thelma Bataille, and Denise Casey.

Thanks to Doug Allgodd (Boerringer-Mannheim), John Ameling, G. Phil Clark (Kodak Imaging), Dennis Courtney (Dunlop Tire), Mark S. Gilbert (Sterling Pharmaceutical), Martin Hardee (SunSoft), Don Karmazin (Chicago Board Trade), Terrance J. Laber (Mead Data Central), Al Pappas (Adobe), Roy Sherman (Home Savings), and Ed Taylor (Sun Microsystems) for their independent reviews of this book.

Thanks to Mary Lou Nohr for copy-editing the manuscript.

Thanks to Phyllis Eve Bregman, our Prentice Hall editor when we started this book, Karin Ellison, our SunSoft Press publisher, and Greg Doench, our Prentice Hall editor as we went to press, for their enthusiasm and support of this project.

About the Authors

Robert Massoudi is the manager of SunSoft's Intercontinental Sales Engineering Organization which spans all of Asia, South Pacific, Australia, Japan, as well as Central and South America. ICON Sales Engineering is responsible for all pre-sales technical activity including enabling, enthusing, and empowering key and strategic distributors, OEMs, and end-user customers. Leveraging the combined experience of this organization and his previous position as the ISV Engineering Manager for commercial markets, Mr. Massoudi and his team have produced and published several porting guides, including the *Solaris Porting Guide, Writing Applications for the Solaris Environment: A Guide for Windows Programmers*, and *Writing Applications for the Sun Environment: A Guide for Macintosh Programmers*. Between 1989 and 1992, three of Mr. Massoudi's articles were published in *SunWorld Magazine*, where he also served as a member of both the technical review board and the editorial staff.

Astrid Julienne is a senior technical writer in the Object Products Group at SunSoft™, a Sun Microsystems Inc. company, located in Mountain View, California. A writer in the industry for more than 10 years, Ms. Julienne's technical portfolio includes authoring *The ToolTalk Service: An Inter-Operability Solution* and *ToolTalk and Open Protocols: Inter-Application Communication*, and developing and producing the final version of *Rightsizing the New Enterprise: The Proof, Not the Hype*.

Bob Millradt is the manager of the Rightsizing group in Sun Microsystems Computer Company (SMCC) Product Marketing. Prior to this, he was responsible for defining Sun's software development strategy in SMCC Market Development. Mr. Millradt has spent over three years creating and defining SMCC's rightsizing program. In this capacity, he worked with Sun's customers, addressing management issues such as how to identify rightsizing opportunities, how to transition to client-server, and how to financially justify rightsizing. Before joining Sun, he spent five years at Hewlett-Packard in both product marketing and engineering positions to provide solutions to application developers.

Reed Hornberger is responsible for Software Development Marketing within Sun's Market Development Department. In this position, he has responsibility for a team working on strategy development, education, and evaluation materials to help customers transition to client-server software development on UNIX. Prior to this current responsibilities, Mr. Hornberger spent three years building and defining Sun's rightsizing strategy and helping customers understand—and implement—Sun client-server rightsizing solutions.

Prior to joining Sun, Mr. Hornberger spent 10 years at Hewlett-Packard in various marketing positions, including hardware and software product marketing, sales support, and market communications. He also co-developed HP's application development plan for its proprietary mini-computer family, the HP3000.

Foreword

Recently, I attended a CIO conference and heard Tom Peters speak. He said, in effect, that in the 1990s, successful organizations will be chaotic by design—I was sure he was speaking about my company, Sun Microsystems. However, as I looked around the room at all the nodding heads, I realized that all of us in IT have the same challenge: building an IT infrastructure to support business needs that not only are unknown but are *unknowable*. That is a long way from the systems development methodologies I learned twenty years ago.

Surviving as a CIO is the challenge today. We are all struggling with technological changes and economic changes. And the competitive landscape has never been more demanding. All this is true for me, as CIO of Sun, just as it is for other CIOs. Maybe I have some advantages, in that I know just how cheap the computer technology is going to become—and just how much more powerful. And I know more about how and when object technology will be deployed in the real world. And about 64-bit environments. And all the implications of ATM networking technology, which is hugely important and being deployed right now. However, all this means is that my business partners are very knowledgeable about what technology can do.

A year ago, we were pretty smug about our network. We had integrated our mainframe and minicomputer-based environments, our professional (mainly Research and Development) workstation environment, our UNIX-based business applications, and all of our standard desktops into one global, TCP/IP-based network. More than 22,000 desktops. Over 3,000 servers. We ran the company on the network. We used email to do our work. What we had is what many of our customers are building. At Sun, the network is not just the computer. The network *is* our organization; it *is* our business. So we felt good.

Today, we realize the daily efforts needed to stay ahead of business change and the new corporate environment. As a business, we have to support our employees working at home and while traveling. We understand that in the future, we will have to have all of our customers and our suppliers linked to us electronically. While the Internet does some of this, we need more. And the Internet and similar networks pose a whole new set of challenges for us. The corporate network is no longer neat and tidy. We have whole new challenges of security and copyright and inter-operability. In these challenges, I find myself right there with many of our customers as we struggle to find the answers we need today with the technology available today.

At the same time, the types of applications are changing rapidly. We tend to think about communications as being an adjunct to the network that runs our business applications. As I look to the future, I realize that the applications will be an adjunct to a network whose principal value probably will be supporting communications. Not just text but audio, graphics, full-motion video as well. Not just one-to-one but one-to-many and many-to-many. Real-time and delayed. With powerful tools to get more from those communications. Publisher. Communications carrier. Educator. New roles. Powerful roles. Roles, however, that today are not fully developed or understood. Bandwidth may be free tomorrow, but it is not free today. Especially internationally. Or in the last 100 meters. The result is even greater strain on IT. And on the relationships between IT and its business partners.

An old boss taught me that business was always three things: here, there, and getting there. Well, for IT, the 'here' is getting worse day-by-day as our current application environment falls further behind current business needs. At the same time, the 'there'—where we all would like to go—keeps moving out because of the new technology. And the pace of technology change is increasing. The result is the IT stretch: getting from 'here' to 'there' is becoming harder every day. On top of it all, competitive pressures mean there is less money to make it happen.

Where do you start?

Talk with business colleagues and read books such as this one which contains five years' worth of experience by talented individuals at Sun who have worked side-by-side in the field with customers, helping them to rightsize their organizations. This book contains the actual customer case studies and insights learned during those rightsizing efforts. The "do's" and the "don't's." The processes, costs, benefits, and successes.

I highly recommend this book as an excellent source of information for the CIO or MIS manager who needs to gain a better understanding on the subject of rightsizing and on the planning needed to get 'there' from 'here'.

This book can ease your rightsizing efforts.

Bill Raduchel
Chief Information Officer, Sun Microsystems, Inc.

Preface

In recent years, there has been explosive growth in desktop systems, local area networks (LANs), and client-server computing. Responding to competitive challenges and cost pressures, information systems are being redeployed from centralized to distributed environments in record numbers in a phenomenon often referred to as *rightsizing*. But despite the pressure to do something "different" and the many praised benefits of distributed computing, most IS (Information Systems) managers are still concerned about the risks of change. They are asking themselves questions such as:

- What is rightsizing all about?
- Why do I want to rightsize?
- What are the new technologies involved with rightsizing and how do I use them?
- Where should I start?
- How much will it cost?
- What results can I expect?
- What is the process to rightsize an information system?
- How do I manage the transition?

Furthermore, before staking their business on a new paradigm, most IS managers want to know who other companies are that have already made these kinds of changes, and they want to learn from the successes and mistakes of these companies.

Rightsizing for Corporate Survival is written to provide you with answers to these and other questions you may have regarding rightsizing. The book is written for IS managers who are considering undertaking a rightsizing effort and are looking for "hands-on" guidance for developing a rightsizing strategy and implementing initial projects. *Rightsizing for Corporate Survival* is based on primary research conducted through visits to several multi-national corporations worldwide. It details the experience and insights of IS professionals at these companies regarding the many processes, methods, and considerations they deemed critical to a successful rightsizing venture. Throughout the text, you will find case studies and "lessons learned" from these companies who have successfully rightsized.

Through the process of creating this book, we have found that rightsizing, when carefully planned and implemented correctly, enables IS organizations to operate more effectively and to use information to achieve sustainable competitive advantage. *Rightsizing for Corporate Survival* was written and published to help you accomplish these improvements for your business.

Note – All of the companies researched for the material used in this book were customers of Sun Microsystems Computer Company. However, the use of Sun® equipment in each of the configurations is *not* meant to imply that rightsizing can only be achieved by using Sun equipment.

How Is This Book Organized?

Rightsizing for Corporate Survival is organized as follows:

Chapter 1, "Rightsizing: The Corporate Solution," defines rightsizing, outlines why companies are rightsizing to survive, and discusses the results that companies are achieving by rightsizing.

Chapter 2, "Rightsizing Technologies," defines the key technologies being used in rightsizing efforts and explains why they are important. These concepts will help you to understand the architectures and configurations discussed throughout the remainder of the book.

Chapter 3, "Rightsizing Opportunities," answers the question of "Where to begin?" by identifying excellent starting points for rightsizing projects. It identifies common target areas that corporations are choosing for initial projects. Each opportunity identified includes a conceptual discussion followed by an actual case study. The case study details the business issues that drove the company to rightsize, the changes they made to their computing environments, and the benefits they achieved.

Chapter 4, "Economics of Rightsizing," discusses the major factors that affect the return on investment of a rightsizing project. It outlines where costs and returns often occur, and suggests how to minimize the costs and maximize the returns. The chapter also includes several actual case studies documenting the economic analysis performed by customers who have benefited from rightsizing. The analysis compares the cost of ownership of the old system to the new system and identifies where costs increased and decreased.

Chapter 5, "The Rightsizing Process," outlines a six-phase process for rightsizing an information system. This process is a collection of the steps that the customers interviewed for this book experienced during their rightsizing effort. For each phase, the activities, key decisions, and expected outcomes are defined and discussed. The chapter also contains many "lessons learned" from the contributing customers.

Appendix A, "Case Studies Summary," contains a synopsis of each of the case studies included in this book.

Appendix B, "Application Scoring Model," provides a model using a "scoring" system for selecting initial applications to rightsize.

Appendix C, "Cost/Benefit Model," provides a model to allow you to perform your own cost/benefit analysis of potential rightsizing projects. Its objective is to create a side-by-side comparison of all the relevant costs and benefits of your current system and those of each of your alternatives.

Appendix D, "Open Systems Checklist," provides a sample checklist to evaluate open systems technologies.

Appendix E, "Vendor-Selection Criteria," provides a sample list of criteria to evaluate vendors of rightsizing technologies.

Appendix F, "Sun's Perspective of Rightsizing," briefly describes Sun Microsystems®' internal rightsizing story and some of the lessons the company learned in the process.

Appendix G, "Recommended Reading," contains a list of other suggested books and papers on rightsizing and related technologies.

Rightsizing for Corporate Survival

Rightsizing: The Corporate Solution

"Many companies have spent the last 20 years building centralized pools of information. Rightsizing is about tapping those central information pools and flowing that information to the users who need it the most." [1]

Rapidly changing business conditions have placed tremendous pressure on corporations in the past decade. Many businesses have grown to become large multi-national corporations competing in worldwide markets. To continue to be successful in these markets, these companies need to understand the requirements, expectations, and competition in each local market in which they compete. Daily decisions made by people at all levels impact the development and delivery of products and services all over the world. Furthermore, consumers worldwide continue to demand more and better products sooner. In the past, products lived 5–10 year life cycles; today, many products are obsolete in two years or less.

To meet these challenges, businesses are experiencing an ever-increasing need for information. They need information to be processed faster, accessed more efficiently, and used more effectively. Consequently, they need information systems to do more than complete transactions. They need information systems that supply competitive advantage and reduce the cost of operating the business. In short, the information systems of a business are becoming the *key* to corporate survival.

Furthermore, to obtain competitive advantage, many corporations are changing structurally, moving to flatter organizations and cutting layers out of the traditional hierarchy. Functional barriers that had existed between business operations are being removed, and "cross-functional" teams are becoming the common method of operation, as illustrated in Figure 1-1. Working in far less structured environments, these cross-functional users are requiring information access across traditional departmental boundaries.

---

1. Excerpted from a speech given by Bill Raducel, CIO of Sun Microsystems, Inc., at 1994 CIO Conference.

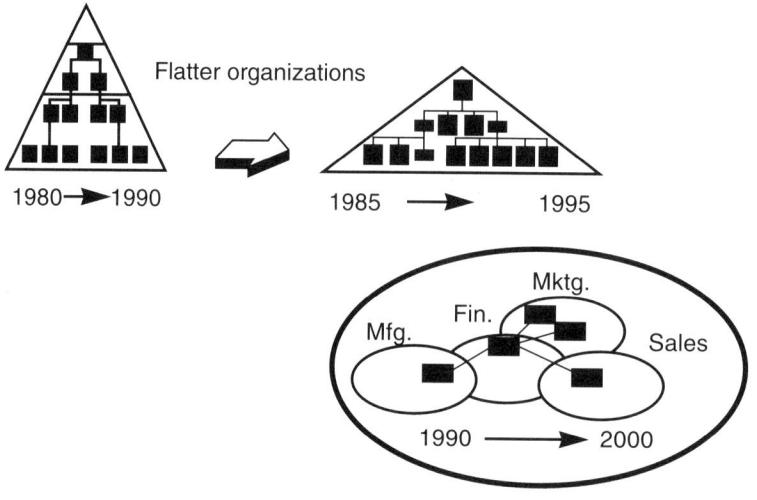

Figure 1-1   Flattened Organizations Are Resulting in Cross-Functional Teams

However, while business conditions and corporate organizations have changed rapidly, computing systems have not. Legacy applications written using technologies such as hierarchical databases and COBOL and running in centralized, time-shared environments have not provided the flexibility and adaptability to respond rapidly to change. As a result, IS managers have been struggling to meet the demands placed on them by the marketplace and their executive management teams.

Faced with these issues, many IS organizations have begun to look at alternative platforms such as distributed computing environments composed of PCs or UNIX® workstations and servers on which to run information systems. With ever-increasing processing power, disk capacity, and user capacity, these platforms look increasingly appealing to IS managers. Through distributed computing, they are enabling the use of new information systems that can increase a business's flexibility while, at the same time, reducing its operating costs or increasing its profits.

Today, the movement of information systems from traditional, centralized environments to distributed computing is sweeping the business world in a phenomenon often referred to as *rightsizing*.

What Is Rightsizing?

Rightsizing is the process of re-evaluating IS resources to see how they meet current business requirements and then evolving those resources to maximize cost effectiveness and maintain the business's competitive advantage.

Rightsizing is a general term that describes an overall process companies undertake to re-evaluate and assess their IS resources against their current business requirements. Rightsizing is not a discrete activity but rather a gradual process. The process of rightsizing is as much a business exercise as it is a technology exercise. Companies do not rightsize computers—they rightsize business functions. As a result of this process, a company may choose to modify its computing architecture, business processes, company policies, or reward structure—or a combination of these factors.

In general, the rightsizing phenomenon describes the *business factors* that have driven the movement of information systems away from centralized mainframes and independent PC LANs to enterprise-wide distributed systems. In particular, it describes the movement to network-based client-server environments, as illustrated in Figure 1-2.

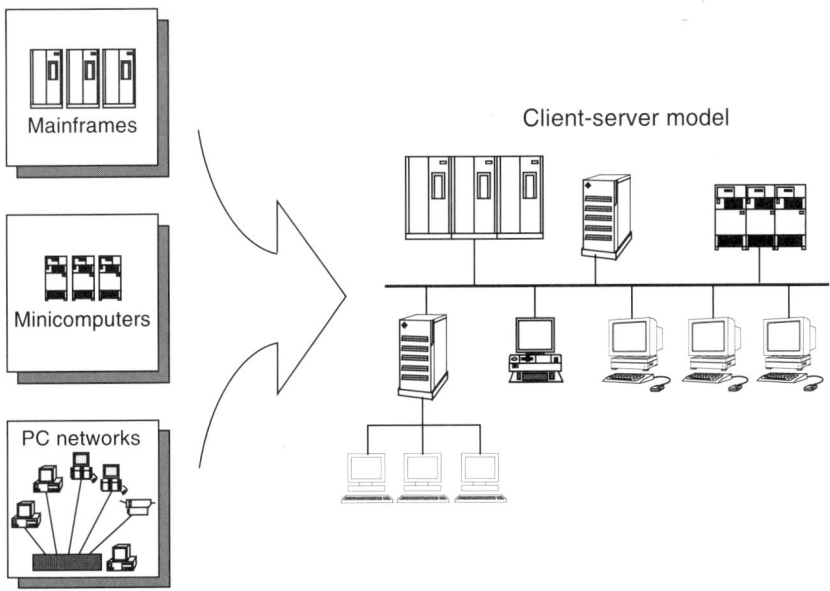

Figure 1-2   Moving Information Systems Away from Centralized Mainframes and Independent PC LAN

Clearly, rightsizing is *not* about replacing mainframes, minicomputers, or PCs. As the case studies in this book will show, the equipment that hompanies choose to use or replace depends on their business objectives and the technology requirements driven by those objectives. In some cases, entire applications are moved to newer, lower-cost platforms; in other cases, application components are split across existing computer resources. Some companies rightsize without adding any new equipment.

At the core of most companies' rightsizing projects lies the client-server model of computing, centered around open, high-performance workstations, servers, and networks. Client-server computing moves processing to users' desktops while maintaining access to shared resources, thus reducing the load on these centralized resources. Because client-server is a hardware-independent, open-systems model, applications in rightsizing projects can inter-operate across different hardware platforms, from low-cost desktop systems to mainframes. Client-server technology supplies a more flexible IS architecture that enables cost-effective distributed computing. Clients can be PCs, terminal servers, or workstations; servers can be mini-computers, mainframes, or super-computers.

Client-server computing is being accepted at a rapid pace: it is growing at a compounded annual rate of more than 58 percent in the United States and more than 79 percent in Europe[1].

Although no single case study can address all aspects of your individual challenges, several key points emerge from a review of companies that have successfully implemented rightsizing strategies:

- Rightsizing technologies centered around client-server computing are proven and commercially available at an attractive price/performance point.

- The tools to port, develop, and maintain client-server applications are established and available.

- Early adopters are satisfied that rightsizing technologies have met their unique requirements and are now moving to more ambitious projects. At the same time, many traditional IS organizations are initiating rightsizing strategies, using open systems and client-server computing models.

---

1. source: Ovum Research Ltd.

Why Do Companies Rightsize?

Generally, companies rightsize for two reasons: to reduce IS costs or to gain competitive advantage.

Business driver	Cost reduction	Gain competitive advantage
Project focus	Lower-cost platform scaling	Business process re-engineering
Business theme	Reduce processing costs Decrease development costs	Reduce cycle time Improve decision making

Rightsizing to reduce IS costs usually occurs by scaling applications to lower-cost technology. Corporations generally choose this path when the current application and information flows are adequate but the costs of running the application have become prohibitive. In these cases, the applications are transferred from the existing platform to the new platform. This transition is accomplished by using conversion software (such as COBOL/CICS emulators) which is available in the market today, or by transitioning applications that are generally platform-portable (such as applications written in SAS, Oracle®, and SAP). The benefit of starting with these quick migration projects is that rightsizing is quickly validated, CPU cycles are freed up on legacy systems, and users require little retraining or experience little disruption.

Rightsizing for competitive advantage, however, is the path companies take when their fundamental business processes and information systems are *not* meeting their current needs. Usually encompassing a broader set of changes to a business area, these projects take users and IS through a process known as *business process re-engineering* (BPR). Roy W. Camblin, Senior Vice President, Wholesale Services Operations, Operations & Development, Wells Fargo Bank, San Francisco noted this in the November 9, 1992, issue *Information Week*: "The benefits of the project are undeniable because of the cost savings it generated. However, it is the chance to re-engineer the business processes and create an entirely new way of thinking that makes the long trek worthwhile."

> *Business process re-engineering involves an evaluation of the policies, procedures, and work routines against business objectives.*

The goal of BPR is to improve cycle time through efficient business processes and effective information delivery.

The term BPR has been overused and is frequently associated with companies that "completely reinvent themselves." For the most part, the companies referenced in this book did not radically reinvent themselves but rather evolved their business processes to take advantage of new technologies. Companies who have successfully re-engineered processes understand the importance of balancing IS changes with policy, procedure, and workflow improvements, as illustrated by Figure 1-3.

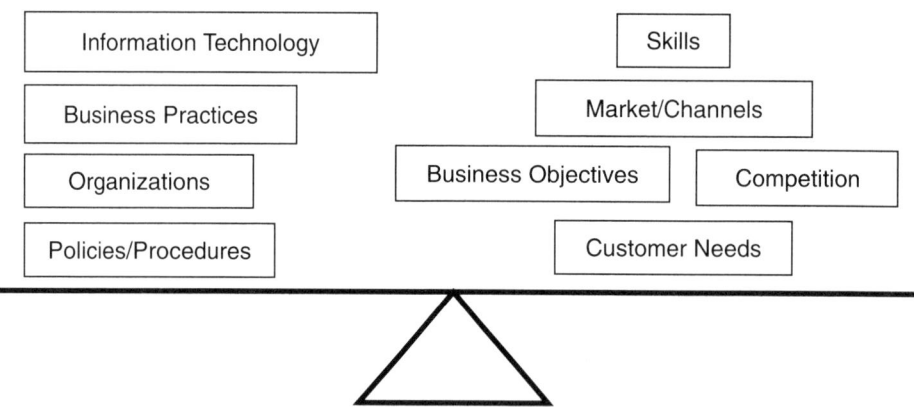

Figure 1-3   Striving to Achieve Balance Across a Broad Set of Constantly Changing Business Parameters

Whatever path is taken—cost reduction or competitive advantage—rightsizing asks end-users and IS managers to evaluate where information is generated, how it is used, how timely it is, and how it is delivered. Based on the answers to these questions, IS managers can then determine how workloads, databases, and applications can be restructured and restaged throughout the enterprise to improve information flows and decision making.

Throughout this book, the term *rightsizing* is used to refer to both scaling and re-engineering projects.

Rightsizing for Cost Reduction

Over the past decade, IS expenditures have been steadily increasing. In some industries, IS budgets now represent more than 50 percent of a company's annual capital expenditures. With the downturn in the world's economies, many businesses must find new ways to make IS resources more cost-effective. Companies most often seek cost improvements in two areas: *reducing IS processing costs* and *reducing application development costs*.

Business driver	**Cost reduction**	Gain competitive advantage
Project focus	**Lower-cost platform scaling**	Business process re-engineering
Business theme	**Reduce processing costs** **Decrease development costs**	Reduce cycle time Improve decision making

Reducing IS Processing Costs

Companies seeking to reduce processing costs are finding that powerful reduced instruction set computer (RISC) processors deliver transaction throughput equivalent to mainframes at 10 to 20 percent of the cost. Similar discoveries are occurring when companies compare the relative costs of memory, storage, and software. For example, the monthly charge for a DB2™ database on a mainframe nearly equals the *entire* license fee of an equivalent relational database management system (RDBMS) running on a UNIX server.

Examples of the cost reductions that can be achieved by using RISC/UNIX technology include the following:

- RISC desktop systems provide a powerful end-user environment with 50–70 MIPS of processing power for about $2995[1] or more powerful systems with 100 MIPS of power for about $3,995.

- RISC data center systems capable of 700–900 transactions per second are available at a cost of point of $250 per MIPS.

(For more information about RISC systems and their specifications, see Chapter 2, "Rightsizing Technologies.")

---

1. Unless noted otherwise, all costs are stated in US dollars.

Table 1-1 summarizes some key price points of RISC/UNIX desktop and data center systems that can be used as a baseline for evaluating the savings that can be realized by replacing traditional mainframes and minicomputers.

Table 1-1   A Comparison of UNIX Desktop and Data Center Server Price Points

	Entry Desktop System	Mid-Range Desktop System	Data Center Server
MIPS	59	100	1,670
Cost/MIPS [1]	$51	$45	$250
Cost/MByte Memory [1]	$78	$78	$84
Cost/MByte Disk [1]	$1.00	$1.00	$1.00
Database Software [2]	$2,500 – $5,000	$6,400 – $51,200	$76,800 – $307,200

[1] Sun Microsystems' Hardware Pricing Guide, August 1994.

[2] Third-party Database Software, User-based Pricing.

Companies are saving millions of dollars in hardware and software costs by migrating applications from mainframes to more cost-effective processor technology:

➤ *The Computer Sciences Directorate of the Naval Air Warfare Center Aircraft Division* will reduce its operating budget by $6.5 million over 5 years by replacing two mainframes with UNIX systems.

Other companies are pursuing a strategy of simply off-loading a portion of the mainframe's processing. This strategy allows companies to improve processing throughput to mainframe users and avoid expensive, multi-million-dollar upgrades to the mainframe.

➤ *Gulf Canada Resources Ltd. of Calgary, Alberta, Canada* redirected the deployment of three new applications— originally targeted for the mainframe—to a server system. The action avoided $1.2 million in mainframe upgrades over three years and saved an estimated $1 million per year in data center costs. It also provided strategic positioning in the client-server commercial application environment, leading to future opportunities for rightsizing, improved client services, and associated cost savings.

Reducing Application Development Costs

Traditionally, companies have developed applications on the same platforms on which they are deployed; that is, terminal-based mainframes or minicomputers. Using these platforms for development has proved to be costly. Many companies are substantially cutting their IS budgets by off-loading development to more cost-effective, productive platforms.

By off-loading development, companies are also reducing costs because developers can create applications more quickly. In using client-server development environments, applications can be developed as much as four to ten times faster than in traditional environments, as illustrated in Figure 1-4.

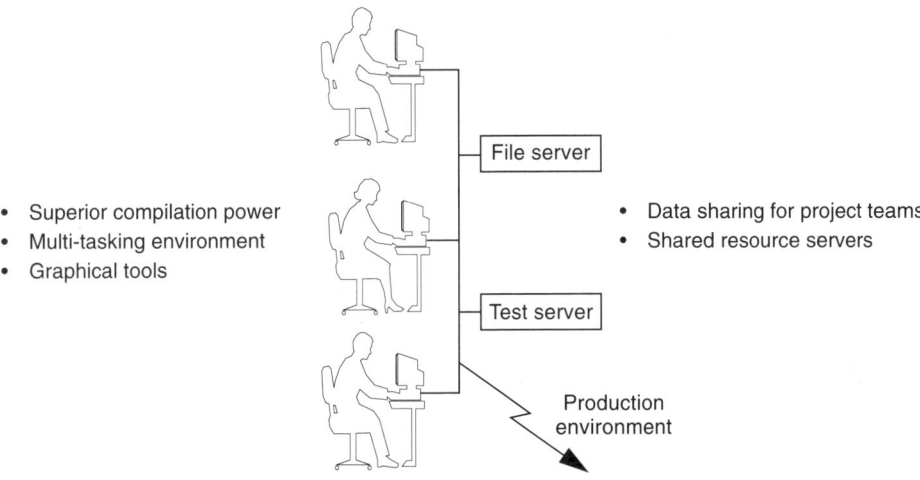

Figure 1-4   UNIX Development Enables Advanced Programming Techniques

Tworeasons why companies can obtain these results are:

- Client-server is a more productive development platform.
  Compiles and other CPU-intensive tasks are "queued up" on mainframes, resulting in unpredictable response times for developers. Local, dedicated servers increase available processing power by an order of magnitude and deliver predictable response time to developers. On the desktop, workstations or PCs provide many advantages over traditional terminals, including graphical user interfaces, dedicated processing, and multi-tasking. The result is reduced wait time and increased productivity.

- More-productive development tools are enabled by client-server.
  Graphical, interactive development environments enable more-productive development approaches that are a major improvement over line-oriented editors and batch compiles. By using approaches such as rapid application development, developers can interactively build user interfaces or reports with end-users. These tools can reduce development time and produce applications that better meet user requirements.

  > *Gulf Resources Ltd. of Calgary, Alberta, Canada* cited a savings of more than $100,000 in application development costs for its applications, compared to their traditional method.

For a more in-depth analysis of the factors that affect cost reduction, refer to Chapter 4, "Economics of Rightsizing."

Rightsizing for Competitive Advantage

Many companies are rightsizing to achieve benefits for their business. They are trying to achieve competitive advantage by re-evaluating business processes, policies, and structures.

Business driver	Cost reduction	**Gain competitive advantage**
Project focus	Lower-cost platform scaling	**Business process re-engineering**
Business theme	Reduce processing costs Decrease development costs	**Reduce cycle time Improve decision making**

To gain competitive advantage, companies typically use business process re-engineering to fundamentally change their core business processes and the information systems that service them. The goal of business process re-engineering is to cut time from business cycles by creating efficient processes and making effective use of IS resources. Enterprises with successful re-engineering programs save money, improve product quality, and achieve higher customer satisfaction. Roy W. Camblin, Senior Vice President, Wholesale Services Operations & Development, Wells Fargo Bank, San Francisco, summarized the importance of BPR in a 1992 interview with *OPEN Finance*: "The new technologies alone will not give us the payback we are looking for; it is a matter of rethinking various processes and then re-engineering the business around the technologies that are now available."

Companies are discovering that many of the business processes in use today are ineffective: Some processes were designed before the availability of current information technology or before the availability of computers. In addition, the business policies and practices that support these processes were defined in an era when *computers* were expensive and *personnel* was inexpensive. For example, at one time it was acceptable to route computer reports daily through the mail room—a practice companies can no longer afford in terms of time and labor. Processes such as these are candidates for close re-evaluation.

Reduce Cycle Time

Due to rapid changes in technology, product/service cycles, and the economy, companies in every industry are demanding ever-shorter, more-effective business cycles. To remove information-processing delays and unnecessary steps from their business cycles, companies are exploiting client-server computing. For example, they are moving time-critical applications from batch to on-line processing, removing the latency periods associated with batch processing. They are off-loading, or replicating, data from the mainframe and placing it on dedicated local servers where business units can access it without delay, as illustrated in Figure 1-5.

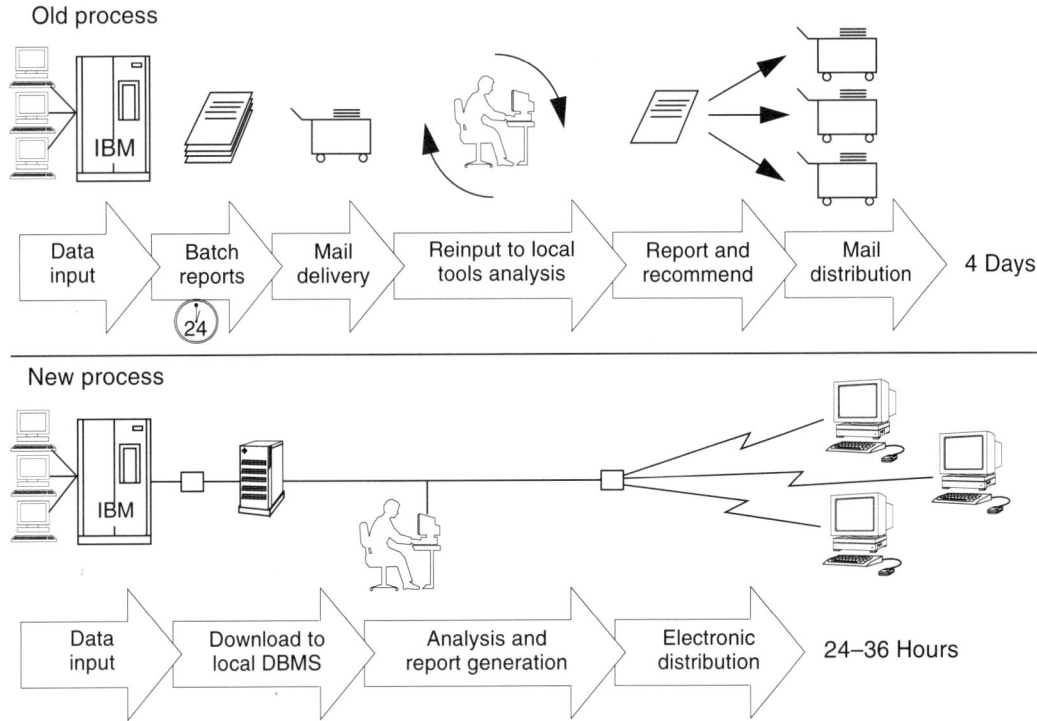

Figure 1-5   Removing Process and Technology Bottlenecks

Companies that have benefited from exploiting client-server computing include:

➤ *The New Zealand Inland Revenue Department, Wellington* re-engineered its operations by redeploying its mainframes to function as nodes in a client-server network. Critical applications such as a security system, automated data entry, and an RDBMS now run on UNIX servers. This strategy reduced tax return processing cycles from three to four months to less than six weeks. The $300 million project has been completely self-funded and pays for itself every year.

➤ *Sun Microsystems of Mountain View, California* integrated its purchasing, inventory, and order-processing systems to reduce its capital commitment cycle (the number of days that capital is committed to serve a customer's order) from 274 days to 174 days. During three years, this improvement has added $700 million in cash to the balance sheet.

Many companies are also using business process re-engineering to integrate business processes across systems so that a business event automatically initiates other events. Event automation shortens response time, reduces human error, and improves quality. By introducing new technologies (such as imaging), processes that were once precluded from automation because the type of data being managed could not be stored electronically can now be streamlined. This type of automation improves not only processing and handling costs but also quality checks and audits.

➤ *Northwest Airlines of Minneapolis, Minnesota* is saving millions of dollars annually by changing the process of auditing passenger revenues. Their system uses image technology to scan sales receipts and flight coupons and electronically matches them for accuracy.

➤ *Andersen Consulting/CSCOE of Minneapolis, Minnesota* developed the Passenger Revenue Accounting (PRA) system in conjunction with Northwest Airlines. The company purchased from Northwest the rights to resell the PRA application and has evolved this solution into a business (*PRA Solutions*) that now processes a significant percentage of the airline tickets in North America. Through economies of scale, automation of manual tasks, and effective use of imaging technology, it is believed that PRA Solutions services could result in operating cost reductions of 10–30 percent, while revenues could increase by 0.5–1 percent without a single additional ticket being sold.

Improved Decision-Making

Traditionally, users received information from the mainframe in the form of "canned"—or pre-defined format— reports. The mainframe was so overloaded with transaction processing during the workday that reports were restricted to nightly batch jobs. Reports were printed and distributed to users, who then reentered some of the data into spreadsheets for analysis. Users seldom issued requests for custom reports because of the time—as much as several weeks—it took IS to develop and run them. These limitations forced users to perform their jobs with limited data, making educated guesses when they lacked sufficient information.

Enterprises are removing these barriers and improving the accessibility and delivery of information to improve decision-making. By downloading data into relational databases, users can directly access information and no longer need to wait for batch reports.

➤ *Bank One Columbus (a subsidiary of Banc One)* improved access to account information that resulted in better, more-informed risk management decisions—and increased profits by $6–7 million annually. In addition, the enhanced analytical capabilities of their solution have reduced delinquency write-offs, resulting in an additional projected savings of $4 million annually.

Many companies are also using relational databases to give end-users control and to facilitate responsiveness and data accessibility, as illustrated in Figure 1-6. With relational databases, IS programmers seldom need to code custom reports because end users can handle their own ad hoc requests, using easy-to-use query tools. In fact, many of these tools use English-like statements or graphical icons.

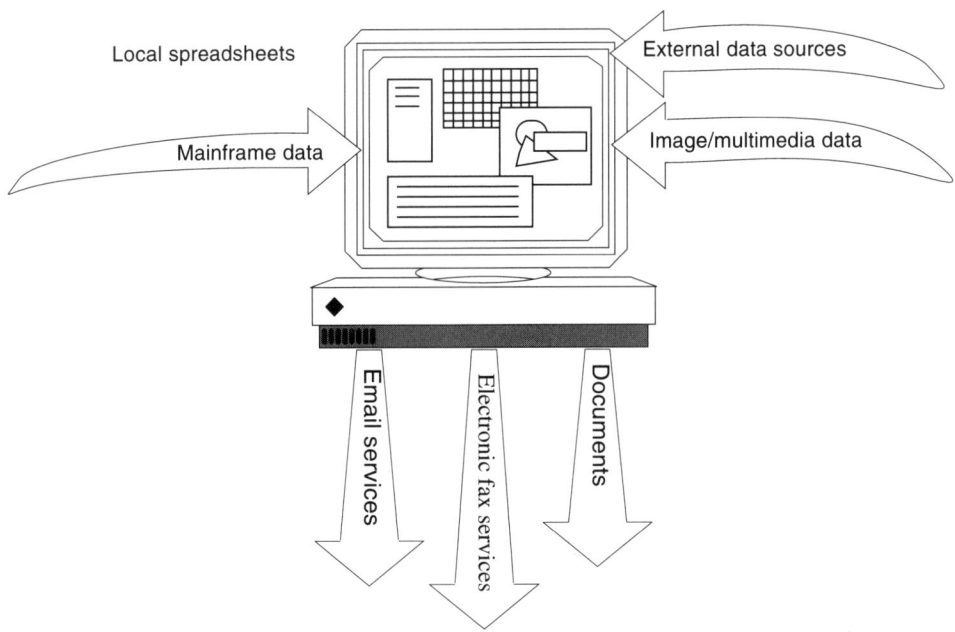

Figure 1-6   UNIX Systems Improve Access, Delivery, and Analysis of Information

Enterprises are also reaping benefits by providing decision-makers with windowed environments (instead of single-screen terminals) which allow users to view multiple data sources online, speeding comparisons. In this environment, information can also be shared across windows. For example, results from a database query can be moved into tools data analysis and decision support tools such as those from SAS. These results can later be "cut-and-pasted" into an email message and communicated electronically. Each of these steps saves time and avoids human error, allowing users to spend more time on analysis rather than on data gathering.

Rightsizing Benefits

Beyond cost reduction and competitive advantage, companies are finding many other benefits from rightsizing. This section briefly describes a few of these results.

IS Organizations "Map" to the Business Structure

A frequent outcome of rightsizing efforts is that the IS organizational structure is more closely aligned with the corporate business structure. Total IS resources are seldom reduced in rightsizing projects. Typically, they are redeployed from central IS organizations into the corporation's business units. Through redeployment, IS resources become more responsive to local operational needs and more efficient at user communication. At the same time, IS costs are more directly aligned with the business units being served.

In addition, the skill sets required in the new jobs change slightly as the alignment takes place. Most notably, coding and programming skills are de-emphasized in favor of stronger communication and conceptual skills—most companies feel that it is more important to have an IS staff that can communicate and relate conceptual ideas to end users.

A central IS staff usually is still maintained to support functions common to all of the business units, such as technology evaluation and architecture definition.

IS Investments are Preserved

Companies that are rightsizing are adopting new technologies while taking advantage of their existing hardware, software, and networking investments, as illustrated in Figure 1-7 on page 15. Investments in hierarchical databases are still used for transaction-based systems, while the data is replicated in relational database technologies to allow decision-makers to more directly access data. At the same time, legacy data can be accessed by using "middleware" technologies.

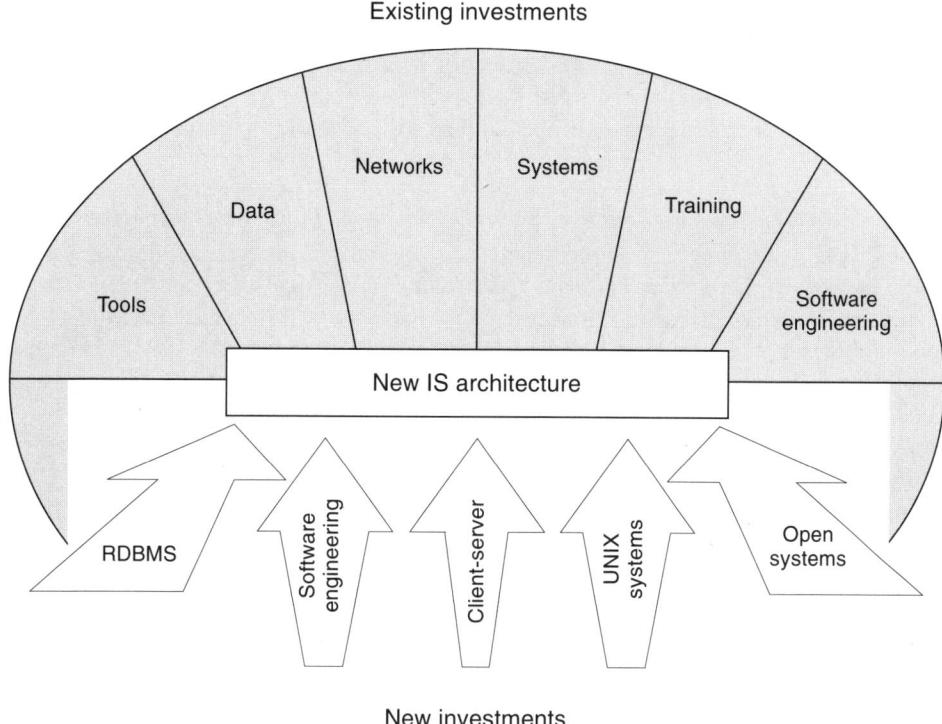

Figure 1-7   Using Existing Investments and Enabling the Adoption of New Technologies

Many companies are concerned about adopting new technologies that make their investments in desktop resources obsolete. By adopting a hardware-independent application architecture, companies can use desktop investments such as PCs, Macintosh®, and UNIX workstations as clients. In many cases, companies are even still using terminals in client-server environments (in this case, terminals are connected to terminal severs that act as "logical clients"). As a result, desktop investments are preserved, users use the products that best meet their needs, and the company still realizes the benefits of client-server computing.

Similarly, large systems—mainframes and minicomputers—once used for general-purpose processing are being reconfigured and tuned for file, database, or batch services. The repositioning of these resources to specific tasks enhances their value because they are more closely aligned to a specific need of the business while still playing a key role in the new architecture.

Access to previously incompatible networks is now possible: Connectivity limitations no longer preclude companies from implementing process or technology improvements. For example, companies can improve information delivery to end users with technology that enables access to legacy data. A broad variety of products in the UNIX market provide access to and interoperability with SNA, DECnet®, Apple®, Novell®, LAN Manager®, and other networks, enabling investments in current networks to be preserved and fully utilized.

×××

"Kodak runs every type of computer hardware imaginable. Sun's networking strategy helps us to centralize billing statement distribution operations while preserving the company's existing hardware investment. The Sun architecture has enabled Kodak Imaging Services to extend output processing capabilities to virtually any statement application. We now provide checking/savings statement processing and Material Safety Data Sheet output, as well as on-demand printing services for both Kodak and non-Kodak customers. Sun's architecture makes this possible ... and cost-effective."
—Phil Clark, Director, Applications Development and Integration, Kodak Imaging Services, Rochester, NY.

Software tools once available only on mainframes and minicomputers are now available on UNIX or PC systems. Companies can redeploy applications written with these tools to reduce costs while preserving their investments in software, training, and engineering. The same concept applies if a company is decentralizing operations—the company can replicate sites/services more cost-effectively on UNIX or PC platforms while maintaining the software investments.

See Appendix G, "Recommended Reading," for additional information on the wide variety of compatible software tools that are available for migration or redevelopment of systems to client-server platforms.

More Satisfied End-Users

Many IS departments report that end-user satisfaction increases from rightsizing initiatives. End-users feel more successful, especially if they have participated in the design, development, and measurement of the systems' effectiveness. The advanced tools and design methodologies make it easier to collect, conceptualize, and validate user requirements. As a team working with IS, the users can align business policies, practices, and processes with the technologies necessary to access information and make decisions that positively impact their jobs. They also feel they have control over the local IS resources to help them manage their business in a unique fashion.

More Adaptive IS Infrastructure

In rightsized environments, processing power for shared resources is often localized to the workgroup level, whereas desktop processing is localized to the user level. Imaging systems, optical scanners, and bar code readers may be integrated into the infrastructure to trap business transactions at their inception. High-speed networks may be used to quickly deploy necessary information to decision-makers. Manual events and business rules can be built into the application system logic, reducing human intervention and error. Event-driven environments process business events in real time, enabling specific business events to trigger new events.

Such systems are inherently adaptive, designed to support quick changes in response to new business requirements. The architecture can be quickly modified; for example, bandwidth can be modified by redeploying servers to handle different operations or by dividing user activity among multiple servers.

Adaptive systems are an important benefit that can result from business process re-engineering and rightsizing. If IS resources need to be re-engineered to adjust to current business conditions, market forces will probably require further re-engineering to meet future business conditions. By implementing a more resilient infrastructure that can adapt to changing business conditions, many companies believe that rightsizing has enabled them to get ahead of the "change curve."

≡ 1

Rightsizing for Corporate Survival

Rightsizing Technologies 2 ≡

Before initiating a rightsizing project, companies need to familiarize themselves with currently available technology. This familiarity helps evaluators identify areas in which new technology may provide significant gains. It also furnishes an information base from which to assess existing technologies. This chapter reviews the technologies that IS managers have identified as crucial for their rightsizing projects. This is not a detailed technology discussion—rather, it is designed to give an overview of the technologies that IS managers may find critical to their projects. The chapter provides a brief explanation of the following technologies and their relation to rightsizing projects:

- Open Systems/Standards
- Client-Server Architecture
- Operating Systems
- Processor Architecture
- Database Technologies
- Enterprise Networking
- Enterprise Management
- Application Development
- Electronic Imaging

For more detailed reviews, see Appendix G, "Recommended Reading."

Note – If you are already familiar with these technologies, you may want to skip this chapter and proceed with Chapter 3, "Rightsizing Opportunities."

Open Systems/Standards

Companies are becoming less tolerant of being locked into a single hardware vendor. Proprietary information systems cost too much, do not inter-operate, and can hold IS managers "hostage" when new technologies and upgrades are delayed by suppliers. IS managers need to install new technologies while preserving their investments in software and data. They need to streamline application development costs—they can no longer afford to have their programmers spending a majority of their time building custom interfaces to legacy systems. Software from multiple vendors has to inter-operate.

While there is no panacea for these issues, many companies are making substantial headway by adopting an open systems strategy. What are open systems and how can they help an IS organization?

> *Open systems are computing architectures based on freely available, vendor-neutral interface standards that offer users a wide range of product choices from multiple sources.*

To provide users with a wide range of choices from multiple vendors, open systems should meet these criteria:

- Have a published interface that allows multiple vendors to easily create their own implementation of the system

- Have a specification that is accessible without legal encumbrances

- Have an interface supported by an independent organization that conducts branding and compatibility testing

Open systems that meet these criteria enable:

- The development of portable applications that run on hardware platforms from different vendors without modification

- The use of scalable interfaces to run the same application across multiple platforms, from desktop systems to supercomputers

- The development of inter-operable systems that interact seamlessly

Open systems do not guarantee the delivery of these results. Rather, these results are attained only when customers demand systems that meet the criteria of openness and vendors adhere to and deliver on these criteria.

Open systems enable IS organizations to make hardware and software decisions independently and then to revisit those decisions as business conditions demand—without paying a penalty. Because open systems allow existing systems to be integrated with newer technology, IS organizations can preserve their software and engineering investments. Open systems can also eliminate the need for platform-specific development teams.

The goal of open systems is to provide companies with choices: the ability to select multiple products from multiple vendors and integrate them seamlessly across the enterprise. History shows that giving buyers more choices has always produced better products and lowers prices. Figure 2-1 is a representation of this model.

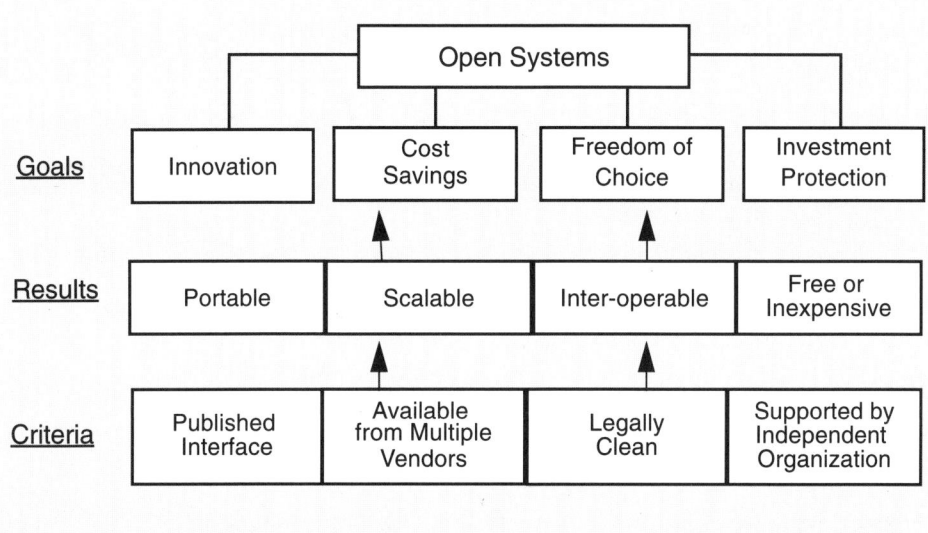

Figure 2-1   The Goal of Open Systems

To assess open systems, you can use a checklist to isolate and define the criteria by which technologies meet your goals of openness. One checklist is shown in Table 2-1.

Table 2-1   Checklist of for Open Systems

✓ Published interface	At a minimum, an open specification must be well-written and published to allow other vendors to easily create their own value-added implementations of the interface. For example, the published specification for UNIX System V Release 4, which is being used by more than 250 companies.
✓ Multi-vendor	Implementations of the interface must be available from multiple vendors.
✓ Legally Clean	Users should be able to access and use the specification without the threat of a lawsuit.
✓ Supported by independent organization	Ideally, the interface is supported by an independent organization that conducts branding and compatibility testing of implementations.
✓ Free or inexpensive	The specification should be accessible without exorbitant royalties or fees for its use.
✓ Portable	The software should be able to run on multiple hardware platforms without having to be recompiled.
✓ Scalable	The software should be able to run on any hardware—from PCs to mainframes to supercomputers.
✓ Inter-operable	A system should seamlessly share data and applications with systems made by different vendors.
✓ Reference of the implementation	Although references are not a formal requirement of openness, it is easier to build a car after seeing an example of one.

One mistake IS managers frequently make is believing that the key to open systems is standards. This is not true. A standard is, by definition, *an acknowledged basis for comparing or measuring*. In many cases, standards are set by volume sales, *not* necessarily because they are "open." A difference between closed and open systems is that closed systems have specifications too, but they are not freely available to multiple vendors. Simply buying a "standard" product does not ensure the benefits of openness. For example, the Microsoft® Windows operating system is not an open system (since the interface specifications are not freely available from multiple sources), but it has become a volume standard in the industry.

The key to achieving the benefits of open systems is to focus on standard definitions and interfaces. These interfaces tie computer systems together, linking users with software, software with hardware, and systems with other systems. Virtually all parts of a system—the microprocessor architecture, the system bus, the operating system, networking software, window system, and the graphical user environment—have interfaces that make the underlying system elements accessible. Therefore, making specifications—or blueprints—for the interfaces open allows different vendors to create compatible implementations of that interface. Figure 2-2 illustrates the benefits of open systems through standard interfaces.

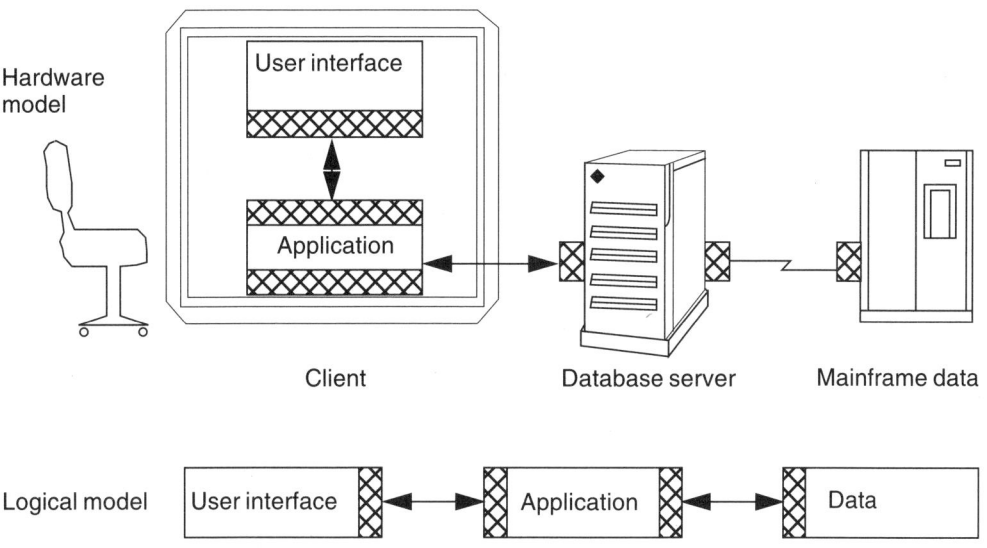

Figure 2-2   Standard Interfaces Connect User to Software, Software to Hardware, and Systems to Other Systems (Used with permission of Ovum Ltd., 1993)

Standards are not defined and set in any one place or by any one governing body. There are generally three areas from which standards are generated:

- Standards Organizations
  Organizations chartered to evaluate, define, and communicate standards. Examples include the International Standards Organization (ISO), which has set and defined the OSI model for networking and communication layers, and the American National Standards Institute (ANSI), which has set standards for languages and other technologies.

- Standards Consortiums
  Groups with some common business interest, such as X/Open™, which has defined the X1170 UNIX operating system specification, and the Object Management Group (OMG™), which has defined specifications to enable distributed object management across heterogeneous hardware platforms.

- Volume Standards
Usually set by a vendor with dominant market volume, such as Microsoft Windows or the IBM® Systems Network Architecture (SNA).

Table 2-2 contains some examples of standard organizations.

Table 2-2   Examples of Standard Organizations

Standard Body	Type	Definition	Area
SQL Access Group	Consortium	SQL-92	Relational data access
X/Open	Consortium	X1170, XPG3	UNIX operating system
X/Open	Consortium	MIT X-11	User interface
POSIX	Consortium	SVID, SVR4	UNIX operating system
ANSI	Standard organization	FORTRAN, C, COBOL	Compilers
IEEE	Standard organization	P1754	RISC hardware
OSI	Standard organization	X.25	X.25 packet communication
OMG	Consortium	CORBA	Object management
COSE	Consortium	CDE	Common desktop environment
Microsoft	Volume standard	Microsoft Windows	Operating systems
Intel®	Volume standard	80x86	Processors

Note – This list is not a complete representation of the many standards bodies in existence today.

The following sections contain brief descriptions of some standards-based organizations listed in Table 2-2.

cose – The Common Open Software Environment

The Common Open Software Environment (cose) effort has been referred to as the "Unification of UNIX" and is a significant example of standards developed by a consortium of vendors.

In March 1993, worldwide UNIX system leaders Sun Microsystems, Hewlett-Packard®, IBM Corporation, The Santa Cruz Operation, Inc. (SCO®), Univel™, and UNIX System Laboratories, Inc. (USL™) announced their intent to deliver a common open software environment across their UNIX system platforms. This response came from increasing customer demand for consistent interfaces across multiple platforms to provide greater technology choice and enable developers to create applications that would run across multiple UNIX platforms without change.

The first implementation of COSE is the common desktop environment (referred to in this book as "CDE"). This environment includes aspects of the HP Visual User Environment (VUE), the IBM Common User Access™ Model and Workspace Shell, the OSF Motif® toolkit and Window Manager, the SunSoft Deskset Productivity tools, andthe SunSoft ToolTalk® messaging service, as well as a set of core APIs.

OMG – The Object Management Group

The OMG was founded in April 1989 specifically to define the standards required to facilitate development and use of distributed object applications in heterogeneous environments. The OMG now includes over 300 members—including platform vendors, object-oriented database vendors, development tool vendors, applications vendors, and corporate developers. The goal of the OMG is the definition of the Object Management Architecture, which will include the Object Request Broker (ORB) specification, Object Services, Common Facilities, and Application Objects.

The SQL Access Group

SQL is the de facto industry standard for data access; however, each database vendor uses a variation of the standard. The purpose of the SQL Access Group (SAG) is to overcome these variations with its call-level interface (CLI), which allows any client software or application to access any server's data.

The SAG has worked to allow heterogeneous data access via accepted standards. It influences the establishment of standards by developing new technology, improving its quality, and cutting development time. The 40-vendor consortium has recently finished work on a new standard SQL specification for inter-operable portable applications called SQL-92.

Client-Server Architectures

Client-server is a modular, hardware-independent, application model that describes the location of an application's components and how they communicate. By using the client-server model, IS organizations can begin rightsizing efforts without sacrificing existing investments in equipment. Rightsizing can increase the value and placement of the existing resources so that they better serve business requirements.

Business applications typically have three distinct parts: the database, the application (logic), and the user interface (screens). All three components traditionally reside on a central processor and are highly integrated. Although this integration tightly links the components, it also makes them virtually inseparable and tied to a single processor. When one centralized processor must handle all processing requirements for all users, contention for central resources such as CPUs, disks, and network interfaces becomes a problem.

With client-server computing, applications are separated into components that run on different machines and communicate with one another through inter-process communications. For example, the user interface may run on a desktop client system, the application on a multi-user server, and the database on a mainframe. Client-server implementations improve processing efficiency by using multiple systems to process an application. The components communicate with each other as peers, as illustrated in Figure 2-3 on page 27.

Peer-to-peer communication differentiates client-server computing and provides IS with more flexibility to designate any computer resource as a client or server, regardless of system type, size, or location. Clients can be PCs, Macintosh systems, or multi-user systems. Servers can be minicomputers, mainframes, or PCs. Systems can act as servers for one process and as clients to another process.

The peer-to-peer model is more flexible than the typical client-server (master-slave) relationship in which terminals and PCs are logically (and physically) linked to a specific system. Access to system resources is fixed and predefined, processing is restricted to a central machine, and access to remote machines usually entails overhead processing on the assigned master system. The fixed requirements typical of master-slave approaches significantly restrict the ability of IS organizations to resolve processing bottlenecks and localize resource distribution.

Client-server computing gives IS organizations the flexibility to use existing equipment to creatively define and segment the services needed by the business. This benefit, coupled with powerful desktop systems and high-speed LANs, makes client-server computing practical for workgroups and large organizations.

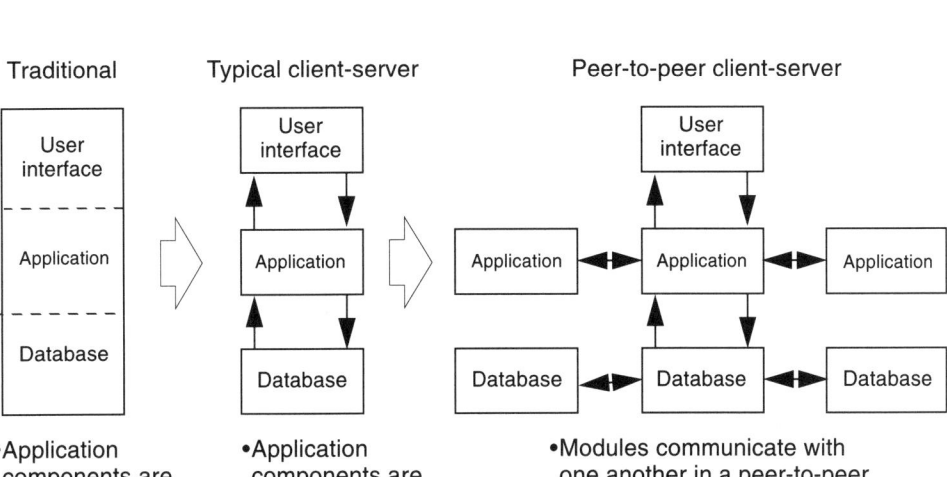

Figure 2-3   *Application Components Placed on Separate Processing Resources*

Improving Information Flow

While cheaper hardware enables companies to distribute processors cost-effectively to business locations, client-server technology enables effective application resource distribution, improving processing efficiency and information flows.

Client-server computing moves processing work to users' desktops, reducing the overhead on centralized resources. This reduction frees centralized resources to service user requests. These resources can then be adapted to specific computing tasks such as database services, file services, electronic mail, network services, and batch services, as illustrated in Figure 2-4.

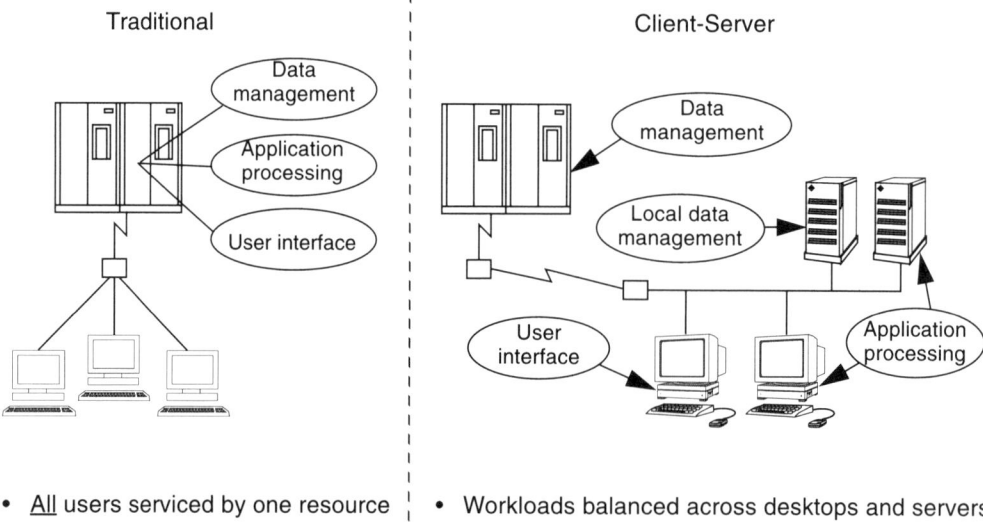

Figure 2-4   *Comparison of Traditional Application Processing to Client-Server Environments*

Client-server computing allows companies to position application resources closer to business operations. Applications are distributed to local sites and run at LAN speeds instead of overloading central mainframes or WANs. Data moves to low-cost local servers for decision support. Servers are specialized for database requests, speeding information delivery.

Information is no longer centralized; users no longer compete for a single resource. Information is collected and processed locally but is available to anyone on the network. With IS resources properly staged, information flow improves and better matches business needs.

Bringing Adaptability to IS

One of the benefits frequently cited by IS organizations that have completed rightsizing projects is that their IS infrastructure is more "adaptive." A large portion of this adaptability comes from the client-server computing model, which gives IS organizations more choices to solve their problems. For example, with client-server architectures, companies have the freedom to identify and cost-effectively upgrade a specific resource to match the business needs, compared to traditional environments in which upgrades had to occur in much larger increments. To increase application throughput, IS organizations have several options:

1. Add or upgrade desktop processors to improve application performance.

2. Upgrade or add servers to improve database services.

3. Increase LAN or WAN bandwidth to improve communications speed.

Figure 2-5 illustrates these options.

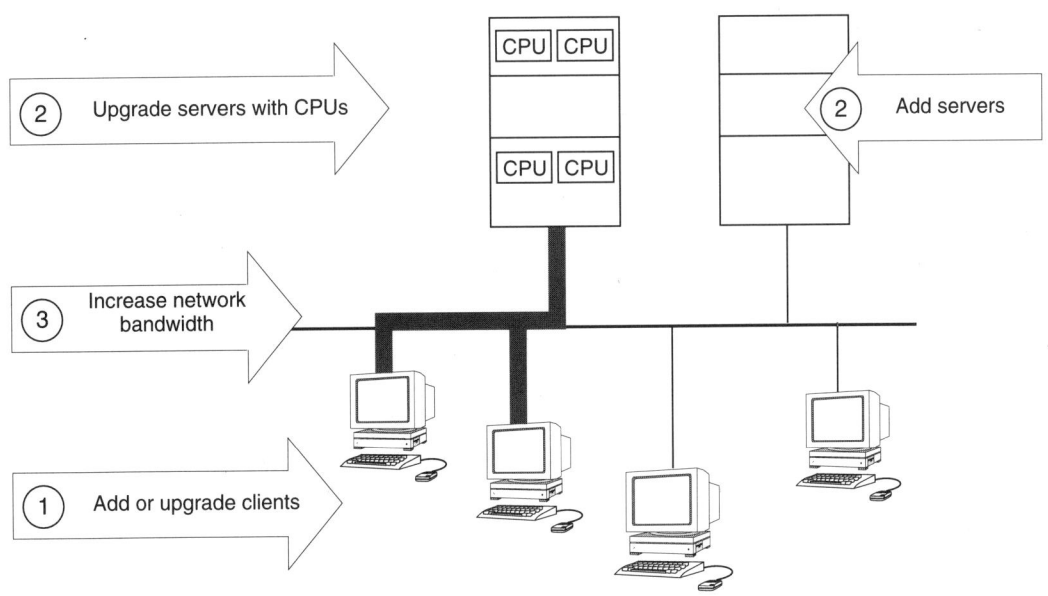

Figure 2-5   Client-Server Gives IS Options to Upgrade Only Specific Services

Graphical User Interfaces (GUI)

Companies that transition to client-server architectures, particularly from terminal-based mainframe environments, are also realizing substantial gains in productivity from a more productive GUI. While client-server computing gives users access to more distributed resources, graphical user interfaces give them a more productive delivery vehicle for data analysis and decision-support. Users can compare data from several sources, move the data into single desktop tool for analysis, and communicate decisions or recommendations from one logical environment. For end-users, GUIs boost productivity by supplying an intuitive interface in which to collect and complete business transactions. Applications with well-designed GUIs may offer:

- 20 to 30 percent productivity improvements
- Shorter learning curves
- High transaction accuracy
- Higher end-user satisfaction

Companies are finding this technology particularly beneficial in customer service applications.

Operating Systems

Companies that are moving to client-server to solve their business problems are evaluating operating system technology to assess its ability to operate and manage a distributed, heterogenous computing architecture. As a result, many companies are evaluating a variety of operating systems, including Micorosft Windows, Windows NT™, and MS-DOS® and UNIX operating systems from a number of vendors. Surprisingly, UNIX, which originally gained popularity in the technical marketplace, has gained significant popularity as an operating system for rightsizing projects. Companies are finding the advanced facilities of the UNIX operating system very well suited to supporting rightsizing projects for the following reasons:

- Superior COnnectivity
  By easing the programming effort to access a broad range of systems, UNIX provides the technological "glue" that fuses data centers and desktop environments, enabling better information flow.

- Portability/SCAlability
  With an industry-standard Application Binary Interface (ABI), UNIX applications can be built to run on systems ranging from desktop to data center or across different vendors' platforms. Standard ABIs offer the portability that many rightsizing projects demand.

- Advanced Performance Features
  Using new technologies, such as multi-processing, UNIX can provide significant throughput improvements.

Although there are numerous UNIX versions in the market today, implementations based on UNIX System V Release 4 (SVR4, which is Spec 1170-compliant) are becoming the preferred operating system standard. The SVR4 specification is the result of a unification of the UNIX marketplace into one common operating system definition. AT&T—which invented UNIX in the late '60s—began a standardization program in 1984: the System V Interface Definition (SVID) program. Shortly after releasing the first System V Interface Definition, AT&T embarked on a joint venture with Sun Microsystems to develop a version of System V that would incorporate the best features of today's leading UNIX operating systems: AT&T System V, Sun Microsystems' SunOS, Berkeley Systems Distribution (BSD), and Microsoft's XENIX®. The result of this project, the SVR4 specification, unites over 80 percent of the 10 million UNIX systems installed today. Figure 2-6 shows the evolution of the UNIX operating system.

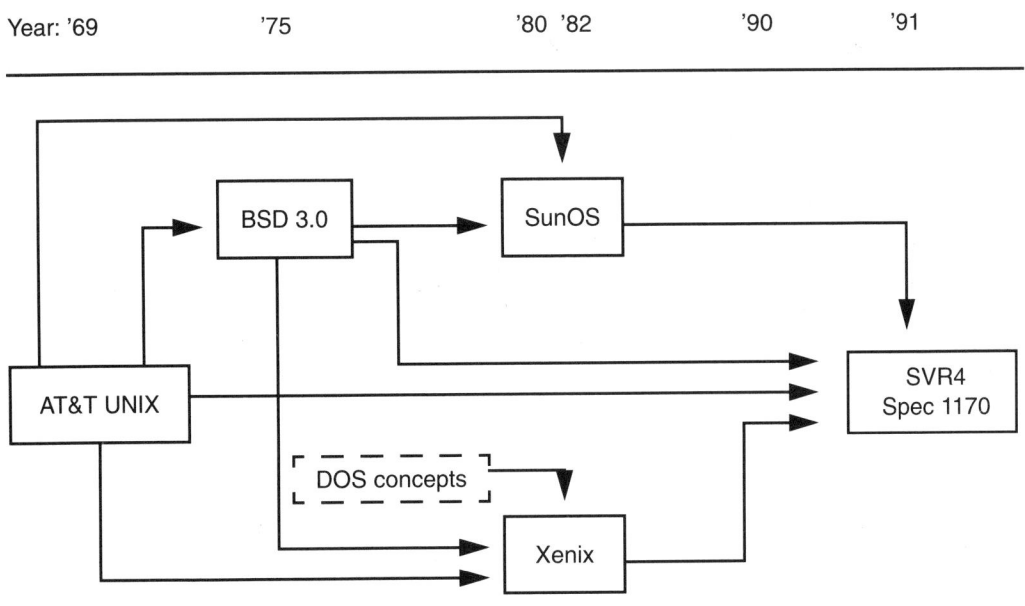

Figure 2-6   Evolution of the UNIX Operating System

Performance Advances: Multi-tasking, Multi-threading, Multi-processing

The UNIX operating system is a multi-tasking operating system, meaning that it can manage multiple requests or activities concurrently. Multi-tasking is extremely beneficial on the desktop becauseusers are accessing data through multiple windows in parallel rather than serially. Multi-tasking provides similar benefits in a LAN environment where multiple users are accessing a variety of network services on a single host server.

The SVR4 implementation includes a wealth of new operating system capabilities to handle multi-processing implementations. The goal of multi-processing is to improve a system's throughout by adding more processors. To support multi-processing, SVR4 uses advanced scheduling mechanisms to manage workloads across multiple CPUs. The scheduler separates tasks and allocates each one to a separate processor, which significantly increases throughout.

Further advances in throughput are accomplished with SVR4 through multi-threading, where the operating system splits each task into separate "threads" and then allocates each thread to its own processor, as shown in Figure 2-7 on page 32.

Together, these features of SVR4 enable companies to increase system performance by simply adding more processors, enabling more work to be performed across the additional CPUs.

Two Methods of UNIX Multi-processing

Traditional Multi-processing   Multi-threading

Computer
with multiple
processors

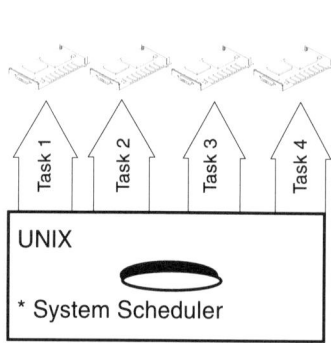

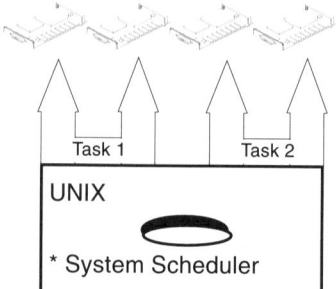

A separate task is allocated to each processor.

Tasks are split into threads, which can run on separate processors to boost speed.

Figure 2-7   Advances to the UNIX Operating System Manage Workloads Across Multiple CPUs

Portability/Scalability

One of the chief design criteria for SVR4 (Spec 1170) is to provide a single, consistent ABI thatdefines the interface between applications and the operating environment. This interface was built to assure software developers that software written for this ABI would be portable across all ABI-compliant platforms.

Software that is ABI-compliant for a particular architecture will run unchanged in its binary form on any machine of that architecture. As an example, SunSoft's SVR4-compliant Solaris® operating system provides binary compatibility across its family from desktop to data center—applications developed for Solaris are developed once and can be deployed to any Solaris system without recompiling. It is the SVR4 ABI that provides this scalability.

Additionally, ABI-compliant software will be source compliant with any other ABI-compliant system and will run unchanged, after recompilation, on the target system. As an example, software developed on SunSoft's Solaris could be recompiled and run on any other SVR4 -compliant system such as those from NCR®, Siemens/Nixdorf, or Fujitsu. This compliance frees users from being tied to a particular system vendor and provides the portability that rightsizing projects frequently require.

Connectivity Strengths

One reason UNIX is gaining such acceptance for business applications is the diversity of connectivity options supported. One of the most widely used options is the Sun NFS® distributed computing file system. It has been adopted by more than 30 systems vendors and has over 100 implementations available today. Any system with an NFS implementation can be transparently accessed by any other system with an NFS implementation. For example, the NFS environment is available today for MVS systems, allowing transparent distributed access to MVS files from a UNIX system.

By supporting a wide range of inter-process communications facilities such as Remote Procedure Calls (RPCs), named pipes, streams, and Transport Level Interface (TLI), UNIX has been a great relief for systems programmers charged with integrating disparate systems. These facilities provide a means for communication between the operating system and an application. Using these facilities, programmers can distribute applications across networks.

UNIX is often regarded as providing fast, transparent access to distributed systems. One of the reasons for this regard is that the TCP/IP protocols are integrated into the UNIX kernel. Furthermore, the SVR4 version now includes integrated OSI protocols, allowing transmission of data transparently over TCP/IP-based or OSI-based networks. These networking strengths, combined with the multi-tasking capabilities described earlier, enable UNIX systems to run TCP/IP protocols simultaneously with other protocols. As a result, many companies are using UNIX to integrate various systems and networks to improve information flow across the enterprise.

Connectivity Options for UNIX

❑ UNIX systems can access multiple databases and distribute applications over a network. UNIX can run MS-DOS as a task, allowing users to access DOS and UNIX applications simultaneously

❑ All types of hardware can reside on a single backbone network by means of using standard protocols.

❑ UNIX supports many communications facilities: Remote Procedure Calls (rpc), streams, pipes, named pipes, and Transport Level Interface (TLI).

❑ With multi-tasking, a UNIX system can run TCP/IP and a variety of other protocols simultaneously.

Processor Architectures

Complex Instruction Set Computers (CISC) have been the mainstream of processor technology for nearly 40 years. By most forecasts, CISC processors will continue to play a key role for many years to come. Within the last several years, however, there has been a growing interest in Reduced Instruction Set Computers (RISC) as an alternative processor architecture. Both of these processor architectures are vital to enterprise computing. Nevertheless, it is important to understand why there is a growing interest in RISC technology and how RISC technology provides unique value to rightsizing.

CISC processors deliver power through complex instruction sets, but these instructions often result in slower executable code. In contrast, RISC processors have fewer instructions than CISC processors, typically run at faster clock speeds, require fewer clock cycles to complete instructions, and hence usually deliver better performance than CISC processors.

These attributes of RISC processor technology enable simple, high-performance hardware implementations. As a result, a number of benefits are attained that are critical to rightsizing:

• Direct performance gains
  With RISC processors, the average number of clock cycles to execute an instruction is almost 1, as opposed to CISC processors in which it is almost 10. Performance increases can more directly result from improvements in CPU cycle times—which

translate directly into overall application performance gains. As a result, RISC processors provide performance for business and technical applications that once could only be delivered by mainframes or supercomputers.

- Simpler designs and implementations.
  RISC architectures are simpler than CISC architectures, requiring far fewer gates on a specific chip. Designs can be completed in a shorter amount of time—which translates into shorter design and manufacturing cycles, enabling more focus on innovation with the technology. These factors have driven the costs of RISC systems down to the point that companies can afford to distribute processing power to a more granular level throughout their organizations. In addition, RISC systems require less space and have far fewer environmental requirements (such as heat dissipation, air conditioning, and water cooling) than most CISC systems.

RISC technology provides the performance necessary to drive distributed transaction processing applications, decision-support systems, and large RDBMSs. In the past, successes with distributed systems were unsuccessful because using multiple mainframes to achieve distributed systems was too expensive, andlow-end minicomputers generally lacked the performance and functionality to do the job. Now that RISC systems are proven and widely available, a great deal of processing power can be applied to serve the needs of distributed business operations for rightsizing projects.

RISC technology enables upgrades in small, cost-effective increments, allowing information architectures to match business requirements as tightly as possible—a critical factor in rightsizing projects. It also avoids waste. Upgrades are quick, and the costs are small in comparison to the costs associated with mainframe upgrades. For example, adding 160 MIPS of additional processing power to a UNIX server can cost as little as $21,000 and can be completed in minutes.

Database Technologies

Decision-making in the traditional mainframe environment is often slowed by impenetrable database models. Many of these databases are driven by batch updates that restrict access to daily reports. Still others require the help of a programmer to build a simple ad hoc query. Relational database technology benefits rightsizing by reducing the access time to data, eliminating the custom coding that was once required for ad hoc reports.

Relational databases are advanced data models well suited for delivering information to business decision-makers. Data is stored in tables, much like spreadsheets, that are intuitive for end-users. A broad range of tools assist end users in gaining direct access to this information, as illustrated in Figure 2-8.

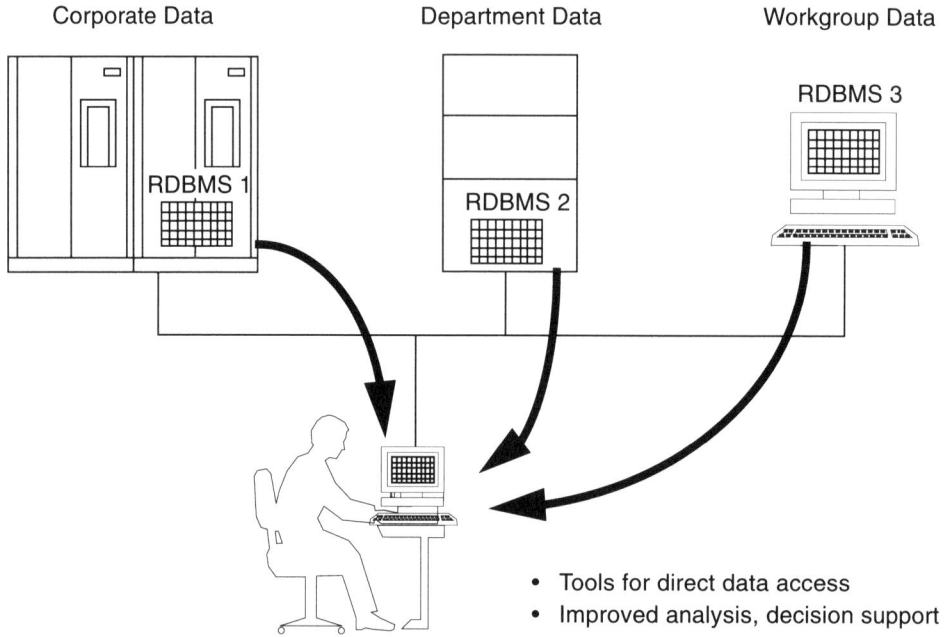

Figure 2-8   Transparent Information Delivery in Distributed Environments

Recently, several advances in relational DBMS technology have been made that are particularly well suited for client-server environments: distributed database technology and replicated database technology. Distributed databases can give users access to data in multiple locations that make up one logical DBMS; replicated databases can give users access to multiple copies of the data, which is coordinated by one DBMS.

Using these technologies with the client-server model dramatically extends the capabilities of relational technology by allowing end users to access different tables on different databases, even on different systems (as illustrated in Figure 2-8 on page 36). Consequently, data is stored local to the business unit, yet is accessible by others in the network as a shared resource. These features, coupled with the lower cost of relational technology on RISC systems, enable companies to provide more local, accessible data resources.

Both distributed and replicated database technologies give businesses alternatives to improve data access services for end users. With these technologies, companies can reduce or remove access bottlenecks inherent in centralized databases, replicate and reposition data resources closer to business operations, and at the same time, provide enterprise-wide access to all information. In addition, local users feel they have more autonomy and control over the data they need to do their job.

Distributed Database

A distributed database management system is a collection of independent databases physically located on different servers over local- or wide-area networks that appear to users as a single, logical database.

For example, a company may store its inventory data in one database, its payroll in another database at a separate location, and its accounting data in yet another database at a third location. With a distributed database system, a user can query data pulled from any or all of these locations without knowing where the data is located. Although there are several physical DBMSs, the system operates and manages the data as if it were one logical DBMS, as illustrated in Figure 2-9.

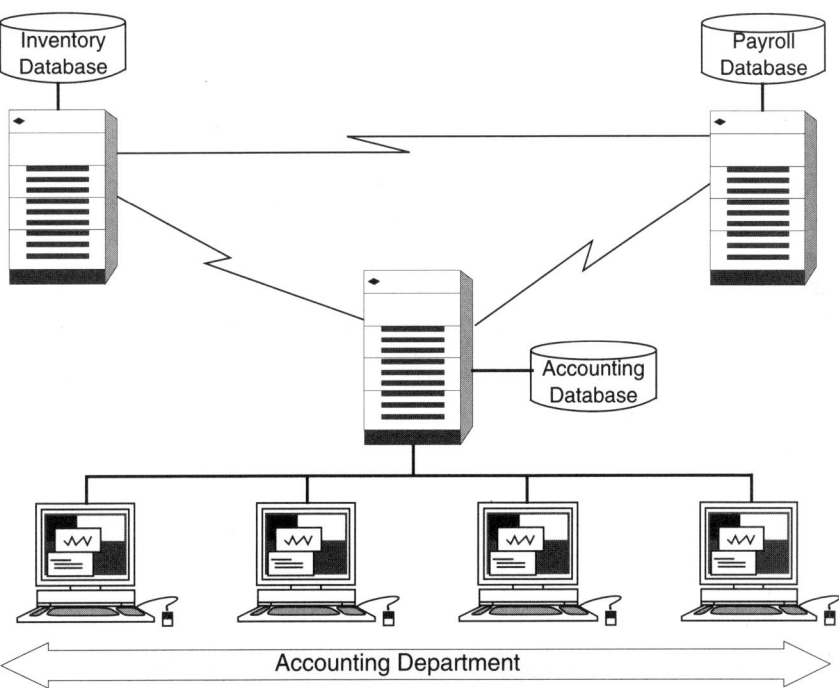

Figure 2-9   Distributed Databases Locate Independent Databases at Different Sites

Distributed database technology solves the access and response problems that occur on centralized machines when numerous users contend for access to the central data resource. This bottleneck is resolved by dividing larger databases into discrete components. By means of using client-server technology, these components can be positioned on servers local to the specific users who need access to them. Distribution reduces WAN traffic so that users are served faster. Processing power can be scaled to match each workgroup's needs.

Database Replication

Database replication technology makes copies of data available wherever it is used. Companies have performed data replication manually for as long as computers have been in use by sending tapes of copied data to distributed sites. Recently, the major client-server database vendors have announced support for replicated technology to automatically distribute copies of data to remote sites. Many vendors are finding that replication is the first practical distributed database option.

There are two ways to manage replicated databases: *synchronous replication* and *asynchronous replication.*

Synchronous replication is used to ensure that the replicated databases update all copies of the database at the same time; for example, a banking database needs to process a check and clear several accounts at the same time. Figure 2-10 illustrates this concept.

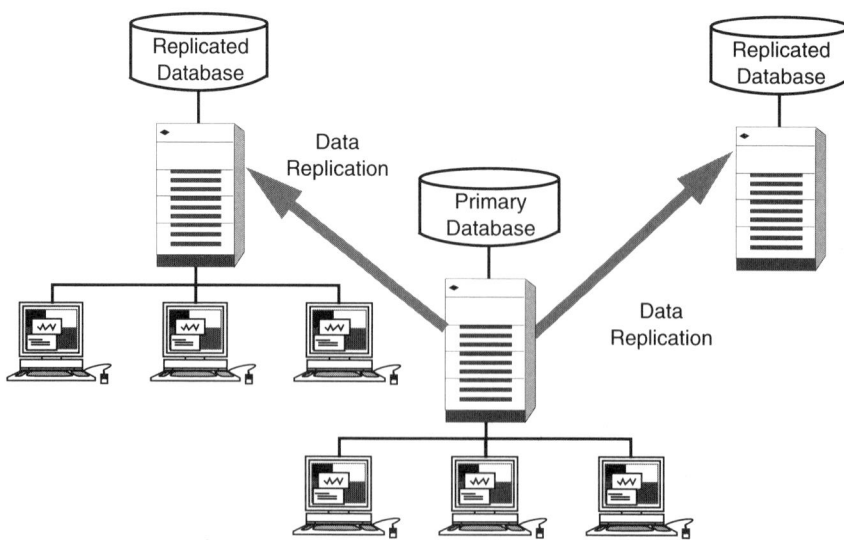

Figure 2-10 Copies of Data Are Kept Remotely

Asynchronous replication can be used when the business will allow some copies of the database to contain different data for a short period of time. In this case, although it is important for all sites to ultimately receive all changes, a small delay in the update process is not a critical problem. For example, in the retail business, each outlet might store transactions in a replicated database and then transfer them to the headquarters database for processing.

Database replication technology can also be considered as a strategy for disaster recovery. In some cases, companies use the replicated sites as a "hot spare" (or recovery site) for critical data in the event of a disaster. Since the same data is on-line and up-to-date, the information can be remotely accessed or quickly replicated back to the downed site with far less disruption than a manual reload. These alternatives, when compared to the monthly costs of disaster recovery services, provide another cost-effective option for companies to consider.

Legacy Database Access Technology

Although relational DBMSs are easy to access, most companies still have a large investment in non-relational technologies (such as IMS, VSAM, and RMS). With most rightsizing projects this "legacy" data needs to be accessed and merged with other data for decision-makers.

One example of this technology, database gateways, provides access from relational systems to legacy DBMSs. These gateways take the SQL database calls and translate them into the native calls required by the legacy database management system. For example, an Oracle*SQL call would be translated by the gateway into an IMS database call for the host to process.

Gateway technologies are usually built for specific DBMSs, communicating over specified network protocols; for example, Oracle's SQL*Connect gateway for IMS and the Sybase® CICS Open Server. Figure 2-11 illustrates how gateways provide remote access to data.

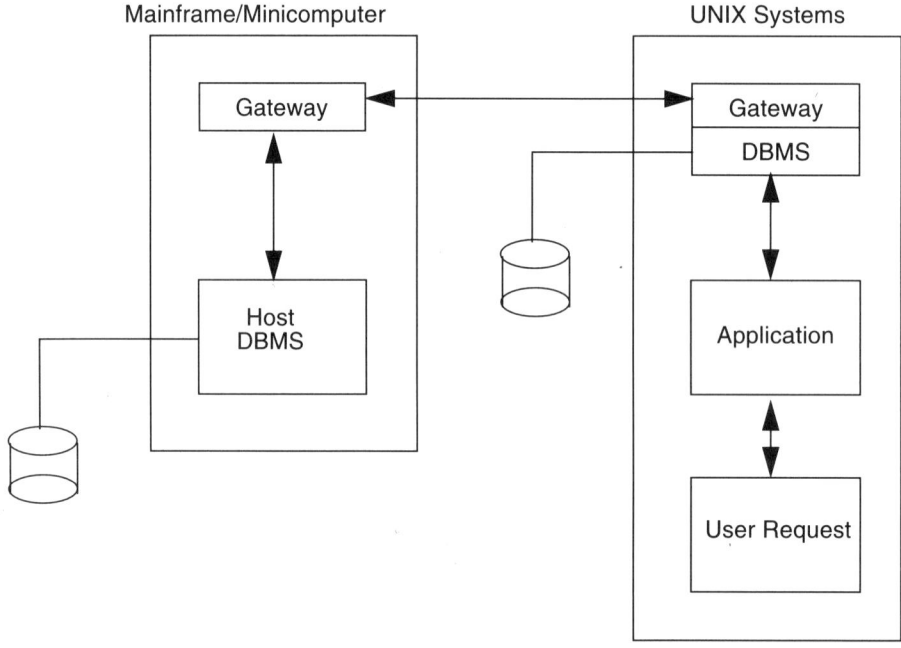

Figure 2-11   DBMS Gateways Provide Remote Access to Legacy Data

Another example of data access technology occurs in a set of products loosely defined as "middleware." Residing between the client and the server, middleware facilitates communication between application components by transparently resolving various networking protocols. Middleware products use an application programming interface (API) to support a broad range of connectivity solutions, acting as the "go-between" for data repositories and end-user tools or applications. With these products, network-independent applications can be developed in less time with more portability. Examples of middleware include Information Builders' EDA/SQL, Covia Technologies' Communications Integrator, and Teknekron's TIB.

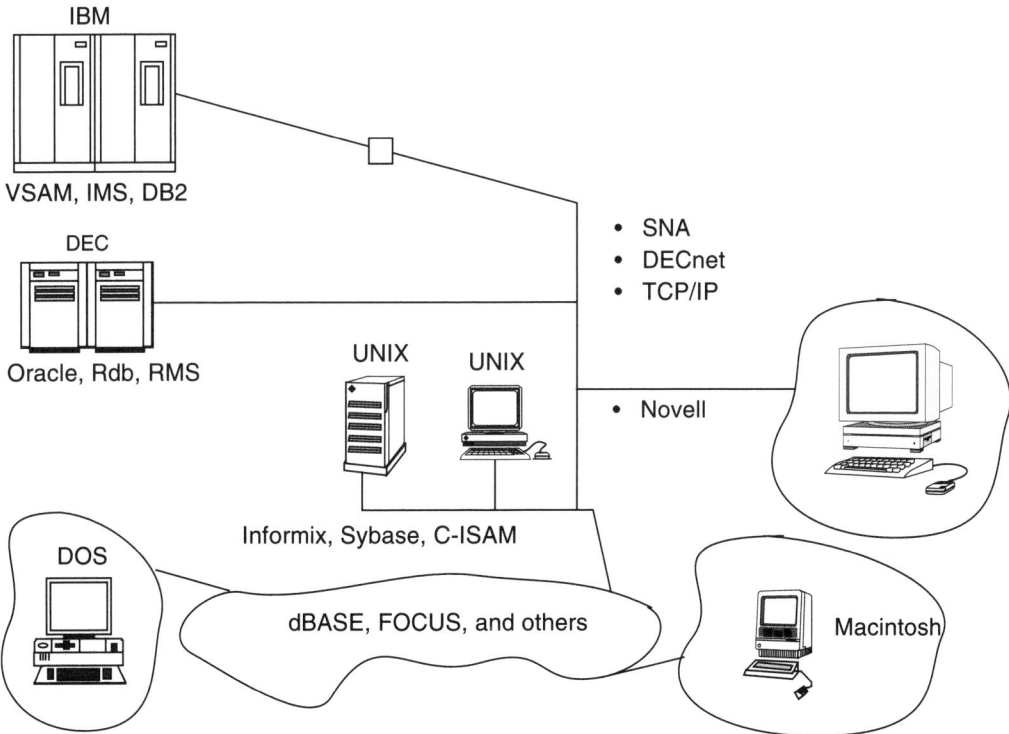

Figure 2-12 Middleware Technologies Enable Access to Existing Systems and Data Models

Enterprise Networking

As companies examine ways to rightsize systems, a predominant requirement is connectivity between new client-server systems and existing legacy systems. Most companies are trying to create a single, integrated network that supports a range of heterogeneous computers, including mainframes, minicomputers, UNIX servers and workstations, PCs, and Macintosh systems. At the same time, they are trying to allow users to access information that may be distributed across the network from any point in the network.

Figure 2-13 illustrates some data center connectivity requirements.

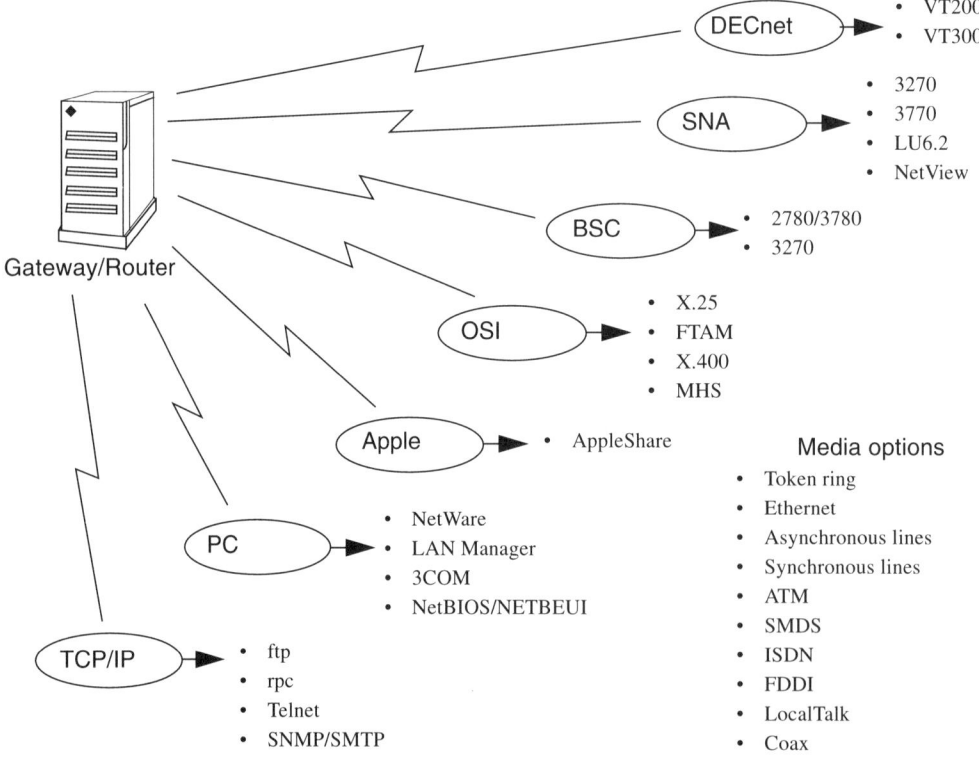

Figure 2-13 Networking Capacities of UNIX Systems

Many companies are introducing UNIX servers as a middle layer in their computing architectures to connect their data center systems with their desktop systems and introducing standard protocols such as TCP/IP as the backbone of their network.

The UNIX servers enable these companies to connect their legacy systems together. Many solutions exist to allow users of UNIX servers to share files, printers, and applications with users in an IBM SNA, BSC, or AS/400 environment; or with users in DEC®, HP®, Unisys®, Bull, and other environments. Furthermore, solutions exist to connect UNIX servers to DOS, OS/2®, and Macintosh desktops using NetWare®, LAN Manager®, 3Com®, and AppleShare® networks. Connectivity can occur over Ethernet, token ring, ASYNC, or SYNC over emerging technologies such as FDDI and ATM networks. (See Appendix G, "Recommended Reading," for more information about these technologies.)

TCP/IP is being widely used as a network backbone because it is supported by numerous platforms today. Using TCP/IP, companies can standardize on a single network protocol and connect all of their heterogeneous systems together. By standardizing on one protocol, they are greatly simplifying their network and system management operations.

The creation of enterprise networks is enabling companies to increase the power of their computing resources by distributing many functions. Examples include:

- Remote information access
  Allows users to access remote databases over the network to get information that they previously were not able to obtain in a timely manner and allows new client-server applications to access data in legacy applications.

- Inter-process communication
  Allows database, application, and user interface processing to be distributed over multiple machines. Inter-process communication is also being used to partition application processing and distribute it over multiple machines.

- Network backup support
  Allows an entire network of information to be backed up from a single node on the network or a remote location to be backed up from a central location.

The importance of these and many other functions in a client-server environment has led many companies to state that properly defining and designing an enterprise network architecture is the most important technology decision to be made in a rightsizing effort.

Enterprise Management

Enterprise management encompasses the overall operation and management of a system, including software, hardware, and network components. Enterprise management is not a new technology for most IS organizations. New, however, is the management of distributed, heterogeneous environments. It is not uncommon for IS organizations involved in rightsizing efforts to be concerned with how they are going to perform distributed enterprise management. Companies that have undertaken a rightsizing program realize that computers in a client-server environment should be managed with many of the same principles used in a centralized environment.

Components of Enterprise Management

With one exception, network management, the components of enterprise management are the same in both centralized and distributed environments. Figure 2-14 on page 45 illustrates the following components of distributed enterprise management:

- Storage Management
  Ensures the availability and integrity of data. Key aspects include backup/recovery, data archival, hierarchical storage management (HSM), and volume management.

- Performance Management
  Monitors the performance of all systems. Key aspects include capacity planning, performance monitoring, and resource accounting and chargeback. In the client-server environment, high availability is also included, since most UNIX or PC systems are not inherently highly available as for mainframe systems. High availability usually must be added as an option to most UNIX or PC systems.

- Security
  Ensures the security and integrity of the resources in the environment. Key aspects include audits, policy assessment, and management and control.

- Production/Operations Management
  Ensures a reliable and efficient data processing operation. Key aspects include batch scheduling and management, console management, report distribution, help desk, and software distribution.

- Network Management
  Manages network traffic, performance, and availability. Network management tools use Simple Network Management Protocols (SNMP) to collect statistics and monitor events. They work to diagnose and correct network problems across a heterogeneous enterprise network, triggering alarms when pre-defined events occur. These tools also cover advanced networking devices such as bridges and routers. Today, network management tools are being linked with other enterprise management tools, including trouble ticketing and console management.

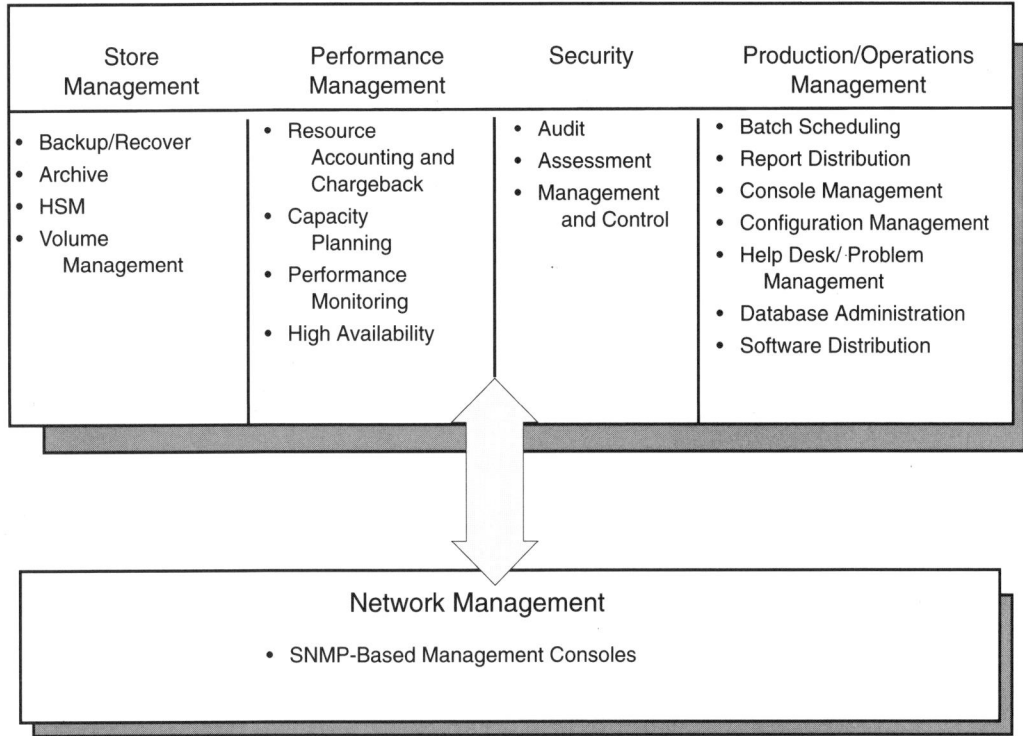

Figure 2-14 Components of Distributed Enterprise Management

Comparing Centralized and Distributed Environments

Despite the similarities in enterprise management components between centralized and distributed environments, there are key differences between the two environments. Traditionally, centralized environments have had the following characteristics:

- "Simple" application architectures consisting of large, monolithic applications running on one machine and displaying output to terminals

- High user-to-system ratios, meaning that fewer machines have to be managed to support more users

- One network protocol, such as SNA or DECnet, from one supplier

- Centralized data that is managed in one place

- Mostly homogeneous hardware architectures

In contrast, distributed environments have the following characteristics:

- "Complex" application architectures consisting of distributed applications where components can reside on multiple machines

- Large numbers of users but a low user-to-system ratio, meaning that more machines have to be managed to support the same number of users

- Numerous network protocols; the network backbone is no longer just SNA or DECnet® but rather SNA *and* DECnet *and* Novell *and* LAN Manager *and* TCP/IP

- Large amounts of decentralized data that must be managed across the network

- Heterogeneous hardware architectures

While the basic functions of enterprise management (such as storage management and security) are similar, the complexity of the environment and the difficulty of managing it has increased. The impact of these changes is that the traditional systems management tools could not simply be ported to distributed environments. Instead, these tools have needed more functionality to handle the distributed architecture.

Distributed Enterprise Management Tools

Contrary to the perception of many IS managers, a large number of tools are available today for managing distributed environments, particularly on UNIX platforms. Furthermore, this number is growing rapidly. These solutions are coming from two directions:

1. Many of the mainframe vendors who have been very successful in the traditional, centralized environment are re-architecting their tools to manage distributed environments. These vendors provide the functions and the disciplines that many data centers use today. Examples include Computer Associates, Candle, 4th Dimension, Legent, Storage Tech, IBM (Adstar), and BGS.

2. There have also emerged a new set of enterprise management vendors that have specifically designed tools for managing distributed environments. These tools provide advanced capabilities like load balancing across heterogeneous systems, distributed storage management, and network security. Examples of these vendors include Tivoli®, Compuware (EcoTools), OpenVision, and AIM Technology.

While managing distributed systems *is* more challenging, these solutions have enabled many large companies to move ahead with their distributed management strategies. For those needs that are not being met today, the rapid expansion of this market will continue to produce a broadening number of solutions in the near term. One Fortune 500 company noted: "Doing good systems management in a distributed world is still 90 percent procedures and 10percent tools."

This statement re-iterates that enterprise management principles do not change from the mainframe world to the client-server world. Continuing to implement these principles is the key to successful management of distributed systems.

For a more detailed discussion on solutions available for enterprise management and their capabilities, refer to Appendix G, "Recommended Reading." (Recommendations include *Rightsizing the New Enterprise* by Harris Kern and Randy Johnson, and *Rightsizing Guide: Tools and Services.*)

2

Application Development

To achieve competitive advantage, companies are asking IS to create new applications in ever-shortening time periods. Today, with traditional development techniques, many applications are obsolete before they are ever deployed because the business requirements change during the development period. Once the application is deployed, continually changing business conditions can necessitate rapid modification of the application to remain competitive.

To respond to these demands, companies need application development technologies that shorten development time and ensure that applications reflect current business processes. As a result, many companies are moving their development environment to more productive platforms that enable the use of new development approaches that change the way software is developed.

Typically, the new development platform is a client-server-based environment consisting of PCs and/or UNIX workstations and servers. The reasons for moving to these platforms for development include:

- Graphical interfaces enable the use of graphical diagrams and browsers to more quickly develop and understand applications.

- Multi-tasking and multi-windowing allow developers to analyze multiple views of an application simultaneously or to perform multiple operations at once (such as modifying one source module while compiling another).

- Dedicated, desktop processing power improves productivity by significantly reducing wait time.

Development Approaches

Beyond achieving platform benefits, companies are using client-server development platforms to make use of more productive development approaches. Today, companies are using a wide range of approaches to speed the development of new applications or modifications to existing ones. It is not unusual for one company to utilize several different development approaches or tools—the best solution depends on the needs of the particular project, the team size and skill sets, and the business requirements. Table 2-3 contains an overview of development approaches frequently used today for rightsizing projects. (For more information on specific tools available in each area, see Appendix G, "Recommended Reading.")

Table 2-3   Software Development Approaches

Approach	Description
Traditional CASE	These environments use front-end analysis and design tools and back-end construction tools to develop applications in third-generation languages (3GLs) such as COBOL or C.
Integrated CASE (I-CASE)	These full-life-cycle environments employ structured methodologies to analyze, design, and specify applications. The information is stored in a data repository and then used to automatically generate the application logic and data definition language.
4GL	These environments employ high-level languages to rapidly develop all components of an application (including user interfaces, reports, logic, and database access).
Object Oriented	These environments support building applications from reusable components (objects) with languages such as C++, Smalltalk, or Objective C.

With 4GLs, developers are able to perform Rapid Application Development (RAD) to quickly develop an application, gain feedback from end users, and respond to changes. These toolsets have advanced graphical tools to assist developers in quickly and accurately trapping end users' needs (examples include Powersoft's PowerBuilder and Oracle SQL*Forms).

Traditional CASE environments allow developers to choose a front-end structured analysis and design tool (such as IDE's Software through Pictures or KnowledgeWare's ADW) to define and design the specifications for the application. A back-end construction tool (such as Centerline's CodeCenter or Micro Focus COBOL) is used to construct the actual 3GL code of the application. The front-end tools may not be fully integrated with the back-end tools. Developers prefer this approach when they want full life-cycle support for development but do not want to be locked into a tool or rigid methodology (such as Information Engineering).

I-CASE environments (such as TI's IEF or IPSYS's ToolBuilder) are often used with larger applications to speed development by automatically generating up to 100 percent of the 3GL code from analysis and design diagrams. Typically used in larger organizations, these environments often require significant up-front investment but can deliver substantial payback. Based upon a data repository, these tools can not only reduce the time to develop applications but also the time to change applications. In many cases, developers can change applications by simply modifying elements in the repository and then regenerating the code.

Object-oriented languages and environments enable developers to reuse code rather than having to develop code from scratch. In addition, object-orientation usually results in programs that are easier to maintain.

An *object* is a software component that combines a collection of *methods* (or procedures) and data. The data is generally encapsulated by the methods, meaning that the data is only accessible by invoking a method. Each method has a well-defined interface that is used to separate the user of the method from the implementation of the method. Encapsulating data improves maintainability (if the data structure or the method changes, it only needs to be changed in one place) and reusability (the implementation is separated from the interface, enabling more general-purpose software to be created).

Perhaps the most important concept in achieving reuse with object-oriented programming is *inheritance*. Each object can inherit the properties of one or more other objects, so methods and data can be reused from one object to another. At the same time, the inheriting object can be customized to support requirements specific to the application in which it will be used. Using inheritance, it is easier to design and reuse units of code.

Today, many vendors are developing environments that will use objects to reduce the complexities of developing distributed applications, such as managing network interfaces, accessing remote data, and partitioning applications. In these environments, object-request brokers (ORBs) are used to enable objects distributed across different machines to communicate. Table 2-4 describes some of the benefits of using object technology.

Table 2-4   Benefits of Objects

Benefit	Description
Greater Functionality	By separating interfaces from implementation, more reusable objects can be created, enabling application developers to rely on larger inventories of objects to create greater functionality.
Portability	By hiding platform-specific differences, objects can be used to create portable applications quickly.
Maintainability	Using data encapsulation and well-defined interfaces, object applications can be structured so that data and logic are defined in one place, enabling changes to be made more easily and with fewer errors.
Reduced Development Cost	Assembling new applications out of an inventory of existing or purchased objects greatly reduces the time and hence the cost of new development. Moreover, once an object is developed and tested, it never needs to be tested again.

Table 2-4   Benefits of Objects (Continued)

Benefit	Description
Network-Transparent	Distributed objects can be designed to hide the complexities of the network, including remote data access and inter-process communication. Using these objects, developers can write distributed applications focusing only on the functionality of the application.
Language Independence	Using the OMG's Interface Definition Language (IDL), an object can be designed to inter-operate with any other object, regardless of the language in which it is implemented.
Higher Quality	When developing with objects, developers only need to write and test application-specific code. Code in reused objects already has been tested and need not be tested again.

Legacy System Development and Maintenance

Many companies that are implementing client-server still rely heavily on mainframes. To increase productivity during the maintenance of legacy applications, many companies are off-loading maintenance of these applications by using cross-development tools.

A productive cross-development environment requires a compatible language and the ability to test applications on the development platform. For example, since most 4GLs offer portability across platforms, mainframe applications developed in 4GLs can now be maintained on client-server platforms (examples include Software AG's Natural and Information Builders' FOCUS). Cross-development options also exist for 3GL applications; for example, Micro Focus COBOL enables developers to maintain IBM COBOL applications on PCs or UNIX workstations.

Electronic Imaging

Electronic imaging is a mix of computer hardware and software that converts paper documents into electronic data—typically through a process called *scanning*—and then manages the electronic documents as data records. In essence, electronic imaging replaces paper documents with digital documents. These data records can be stored and managed in a database for fast, efficient retrieval. They can also be copied, transmitted, analyzed, modified, and printed across the enterprise as well as be electronically faxed.

Imaging technology delivers competitive advantages to companies involved in re-engineering business processes that have been hampered by the use or exchange of paper documents (such as loan agreements, checks, plane tickets, and design drawings).

Using imaging technology, companies can now automate the business processes that revolve around these manual documents—which can result in saving money and time as well as improving the quality of goods and services.

As the cost of manual processes, file space, and record retention increases and the cost of imaging technology declines, the payback time for imaging projects is shortening. For example, advanced recognition systems today can recognize hand-printed, bar-coded, or machine-printed information and load this information in digital form. These types of solutions have many practical applications, including claims processing, customer correspondence, and human resources.

Solutions also exist that are specifically designed for controlling and distributing engineering documents in aerospace and manufacturing companies, greatly reducing the time currently spent by technical professionals to route manual specifications, drawings, and other design documents.

For example, a financial services company used to manually sort, batch, and mail its customers' checks back to its customers each month. Today, the company scans the checks and stores their images on optical disk drives connected to a network. Once a month, the company prints the checks on a double-sided statement and mails the statement to the customer. By sorting the checks electronically, instead of manually, the company was able to reduce monthly processing time by 50 percent and check processing time by more than 30 percent. The images are stored online and in a customer service application, allowing agents to view check images graphically while assisting customers on the phone. If a customer wants a copy of a check, the copy can be faxed. The results of these process improvements include reduced handling costs, shorter cycle time, and improved customer services.

Some of the benefits of imaging include:

- Improved document management
  The time required to file and retrieve digital documents can be decreased from hours to seconds. The time and effort necessary to route and deliver documents can also be significantly reduced.

- Greatly enhanced document access
  Digital data can be networked and telecommunicated. The instant availability of this data can mean broad usage—many people in distributed locations can review the data at the same time. Office procedures previously done in a sequential manner can now be managed in parallel. Since the cost of copying and distributing digital documents is decreased, using multiple copies of documents becomes much more practical.

- Reduced document storage
  Electronic documents take up less space than paper documents. In this context, imaging can help to free up expensive office space and, in many cases, reduce document storage requirements by 50–80 percent.

Summary

This chapter provided a brief introduction to the key technologies companies are using in their rightsizing efforts. The intent of this overview was to provide you with a basic understanding of the technologies and why they are important to rightsizing. This basic understanding will be useful throughout the remainder of the book. For example, Chapter 3, "Rightsizing Opportunities," discusses specific examples in which companies have used the technologies discussed in this chapter to achieve their rightsizing goals.

☰ *2*

Rightsizing for Corporate Survival

Rightsizing Opportunities 3≡

Once you understand the reasons why companies are rightsizing and the technologies that are important to rightsizing ventures, your next questions are probably *"Where do I start?"* and *"What are good applications or opportunities to initially rightsize?"* This chapter identifies several good areas where your company can begin its rightsizing efforts.

Dividing an Enterprise by Application Type

Most businesses today consists of two primary types of systems: *operational* and *management*, as illustrated in Figure 3-1.

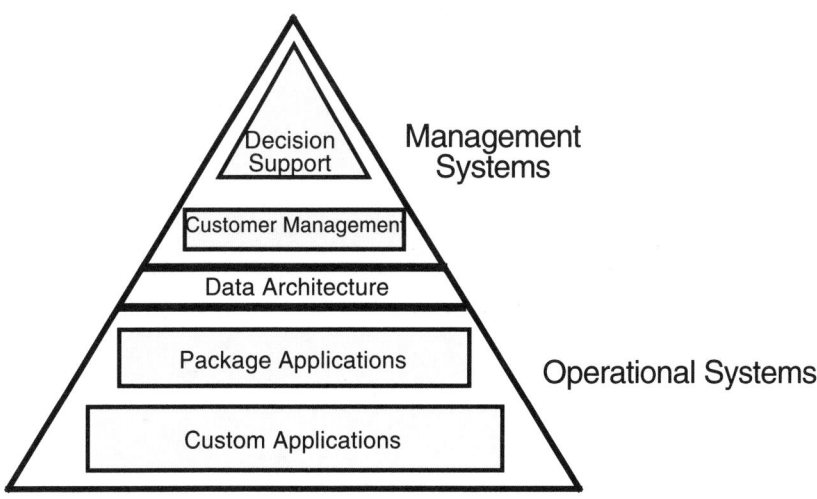

Figure 3-1   Enterprise Divided by Application Type

Operational systems are the traditional, transaction-based systems such as order processing, distribution, and accounting. Operational systems can be subdivided into *custom-developed applications* (such as applications written using COBOL/CICS on an IBM mainframe) and *package applications* (such as applications bought off-the-shelf from an independent software vendor, or ISV). Operational systems have been good for quickly processing data and bringing information into the data architecture of the business; however, they have not been good for allowing people to make use of the information—especially to make decisions which are often critical to the business—in a timely manner.

During the late '80s and early '90s, many companies have focused on creating management systems that allow people to make more effective use of information. Management systems can be subdivided into *decision support applications* and *customer management applications*. Decision support applications (such as inventory management, scheduling, and general ledger) enable users to access information to make key decisions for running the business. Customer management applications are applications that use information to improve the interface between a business and its customers; for example, a customer service application that is used by service representatives who are responding to customer problems or inquiries.

Although many people believe that most businesses today begin their rightsizing efforts with custom operational systems, in reality most businesses begin with one of the following areas:

- Decision support applications
- Customer management applications
- Package applications

Once the company has gained rightsizing experience with one of these applications, it can proceed to rightsize other applications, including custom operational systems.

This chapter discusses each of these rightsizing opportunities in more detail. For each application, both the business and the technology issues that make the application a good opportunity for rightsizing are discussed, and a typical rightsizing solution and the benefits associated with it are presented. Each opportunity is followed by a case study of an actual company that rightsized this type of application.

Decision Support

One of the best applications with which to begin a rightsizing effort is a decision support application. Rightsizing these applications generally involves lower risk to your business because decision-support applications, unlike operational systems, are usually not mission-critical.

Rightsizing in this area can also result in a large return-on-investment. By providing better access to information, these projects enable better decision-making—which can result in huge paybacks for your business. At the same time, the investment required to move these applications is typically small, especially when compared to custom operational systems.

Business Issues

In most businesses today, decision-makers are making key decisions every day that often affect the bottom line of the business. Making these decisions requires access to information—but in many cases, decision-makers are unable to get complete data in a timely manner. Information architectures today are usually designed to optimize the operational systems, not the decision-making systems. As a result, critical business decisions are often either delayed or made without complete information. Decision support systems can be found in every industry, including:

- The retail industry
  In this industry, a typical operational system is an order-processing system, and a typical decision-support application is an inventory-management application. A frequent problem is that the Inventory Manager cannot make optimal decisions about how much inventory to purchase to fulfill orders. Critical information needed to make these decisions often is stored in the order-processing system and is not accessible during peak times because the system is overloaded and cannot handle compute-intensive queries. As a result, the Inventory Manager must wait until non-peak times to obtain the information needed, or purchase inventory with incomplete information. The result can be either excess inventory or stock outages, either of which adversely affects operating costs.

- The insurance industry
  In this industry, a typical operational system is an insurance-application-processing system while a typical decision support system is an application- approval system. A frequent problem is that the Application Analyst cannot make optimal decisions about whether or not to approve an insurance application. To make these decisions, analysts need to assess risk, based on an applicant's past history. This information is usually located in many different sources, which can make getting complete information difficult and expensive. Application approvals made without complete information can result in a high-risk applicant being insured at a low-risk premium.

- The transportation industry
  In this industry, a typical operational systems is a reservation system, and a typical decision-support system is a scheduling system, such as those used by airline or trucking companies. A frequent problem is that the Scheduler must design a schedule for airplanes or trucks and the personnel to staff them that optimizes the business's resources. However, because this task is a compute-intensive process, it often fails to get the necessary compute cycles. The result can be a business that operates at less than optimal efficiency.

Technology Issues

A number of technology issues have made it difficult for businesses to provide timely access to information. In most mainframe environments today, operational and decision support systems run on the same machine, as illustrated in Figure 3-2.

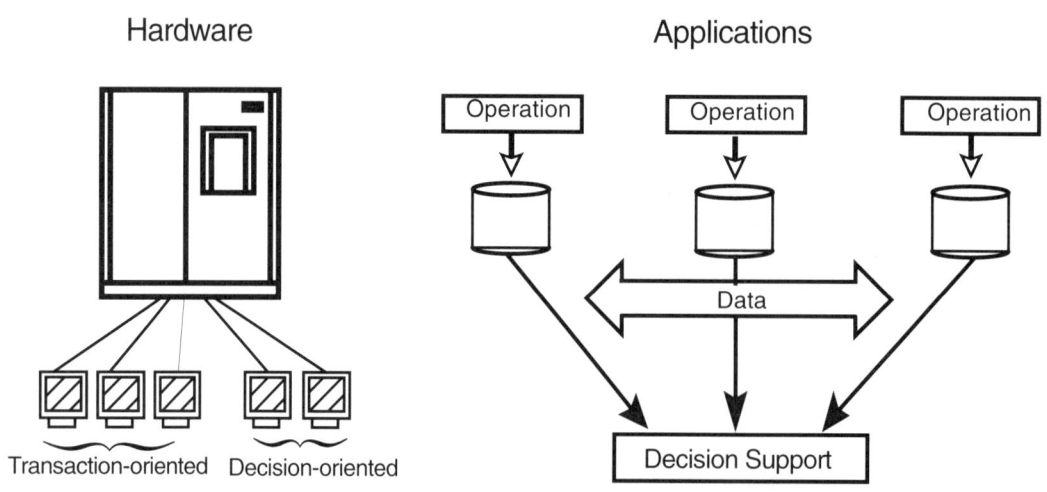

Figure 3-2   Typical Decision Support Environment

In this environment, the data architecture was typically designed around the operational systems. Each operational system accesses one or more databases that have been designed for that system. Usually hierarchical or networked, these databases are designed to process transactions very quickly. In contrast, decision-making systems usually need to access data across a number of databases and perform compute-intensive, cross-functional queries that hierarchical or networked databases are not designed to perform easily. As a result, most decision-makers experience significant *data latency time,* the time between when the data is required and when the data is actually received by the person requesting the data.

These problems often occur because both operational and decision-making applications run on the same overloaded mainframe. When a shortage of CPU cycles occurs, operational systems typically receive first priority, whereas decision-support systems usually receive last priority. This prioritization does not mean that businesses view decision support systems as unimportant. However, if running compute-intensive reports during normal business hours bring operational systems to a halt, these reports will be run in batch overnight. As a result, a minimum 24-hour delay cycle is often introduced into many requests for information.

When a requestor does receive the information, it is often in a fixed-format report. Viewing the information in a different format requires a custom report. With hierarchical or networked databases, custom reports are difficult to write and expensive to execute because these databases were not designed for easily extracting information in multiple ways. Consequently, IS usually has to create custom reports. Since most IS organizations are overwhelmed by application maintenance requests, many companies are experiencing lead times for custom reports that are weeks in length, causing many users to not even ask for such reports.

If a decision-maker does have on-line rather than batch access to data, it is usually through a terminal. Because terminals do not support graphical analysis, many companies have resorted to rekeying data into PCs. However, the time and cost to re-key the data can often offset the benefits achieved from the graphical analysis.

Figure 3-3 highlights these technology problems.

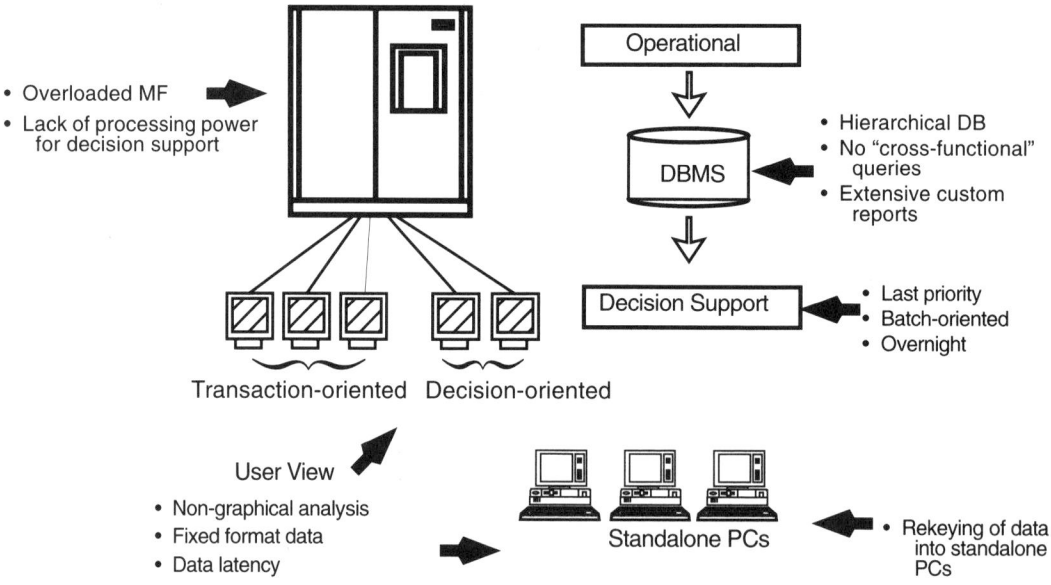

• Overloaded MF
• Lack of processing power
  for decision support

Operational

DBMS

• Hierarchical DB
• No "cross-functional"
  queries
• Extensive custom
  reports

Transaction-oriented   Decision-oriented

Decision Support

• Last priority
• Batch-oriented
• Overnight

User View

• Non-graphical analysis
• Fixed format data
• Data latency

Standalone PCs

• Rekeying of data
  into standalone
  PCs

Figure 3-3   Typical Technology Problems for Decision Support

Typical Rightsizing Solution

There are many rightsizing solutions to the decision support problems; a typical hardware/software solution is illustrated in Figure 3-4.

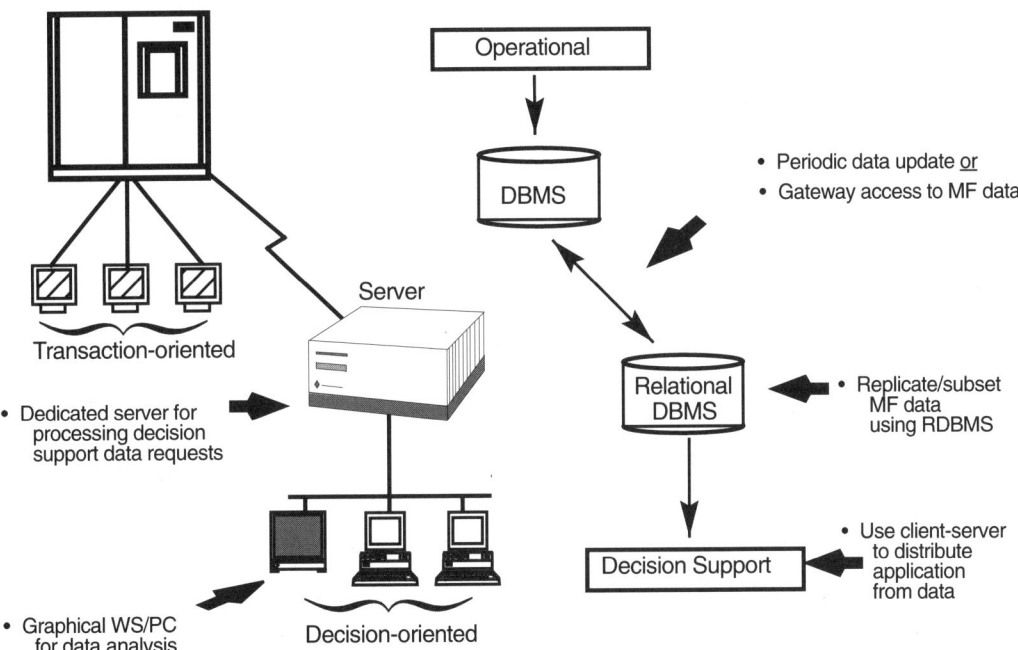

Figure 3-4   A Rightsizing Solution for Decision Support

The mainframe, the operational system, and the hierarchical or networked database remain intact. However, a UNIX server running an RDBMS is introduced and connected to the mainframe. A subset of the mainframe data is replicated in the relational database on the UNIX server. This data is periodically updated, the frequency of which can vary dramatically, depending upon the business problem. In some cases, a gateway is used to connect to the mainframe database; in other cases, a custom transfer utility is created.

Attached to the server are desktop clients (typically PCs or UNIX workstations, although terminals attached to an application server are also used). The clients are used to run the decision-support application, which has been moved from the mainframe to the clients either through migration, replacement, or by rewriting it.

Benefits of the Rightsized Environment

The primary benefits of the rightsized environment result from the creation of a new, dedicated data source for use by the decision-makers. Instead of waiting overnight for a batch report, users can now immediately access online the information they need. There still is some delay time needed to update the relational database from the mainframe database; however, this delay time is typically much less than the time delay in the previous environment.

Custom or ad hoc queries are much easier to perform, enabling users to perform their own queries without IS involvement. Users can perform as many queries as they require—and use graphical analysis to view the data in many different ways—instead of relying on a single, fixed-format report.

The net result is faster, more-informed decision-making. As discussed previously, having more complete and timely access to information can impact the profitability of a business in numerous ways.

High payback, low investment, and low risk make this opportunity an excellent starting point for rightsizing in many businesses.

Case Study: Decision Support

Banc One

Banc One (headquartered in Columbus, Ohio) is the twelfth largest bank holding company in the United States and the second most profitable bank holding company in the world. Banc One provides a wide variety of services, including branch banking, mortgages, loans, and credit cards.

The Risk Management Department of Bank One Columbus, a subsidiary of Banc One, is responsible for all strategic and tactical decisions regarding risk or profitability of credit card accounts. Relying on information that enters through various sources, the department supports the main decisions for the following functions:

- Approving or declining credit card accounts
- Increasing or decreasing lines of credit
- Reissuing existing credit cards
- Creating feasibility studies of the bank's future credit card activities
- Forming the bank's credit card policies within each state

Environment Prior to Rightsizing

The bank's previous computing environment consisted of three IBM mainframes running CICS applications accessing flat-files on MVS (as illustrated in Figure 3-5).

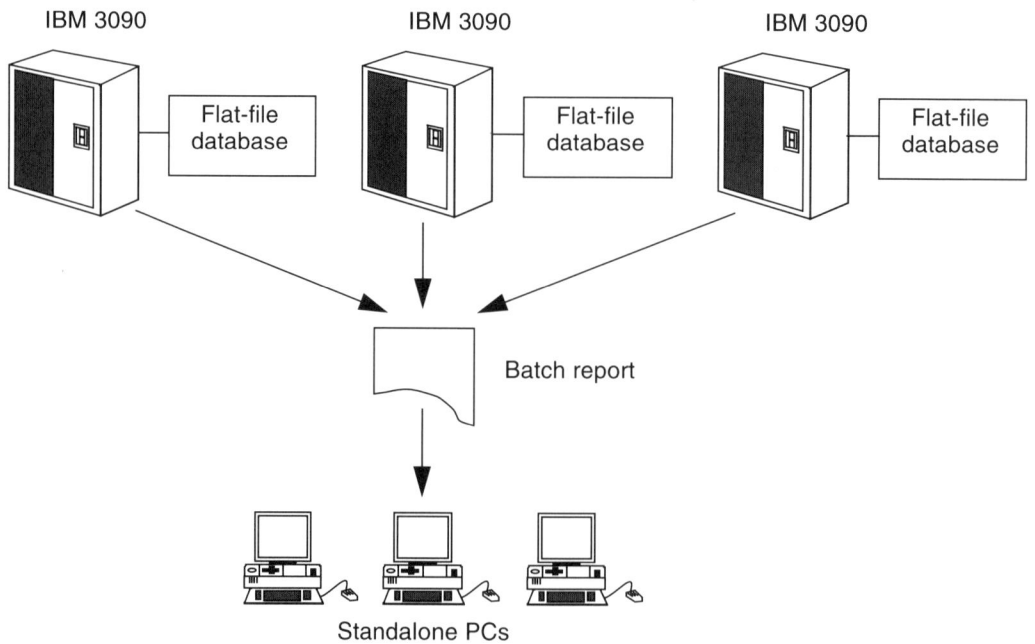

Figure 3-5   Environment Prior to Rightsizing

To perform risk management, the department relied solely on reports produced by batch processing on the mainframe, using data extraction and analysis tools from the SAS Institute. The department ran 60 normal production reports and produced ad hoc reports as needed. Most of these batch processes were run at night because the mainframe batch processing could not handle the load effectively. The overloaded mainframes caused the department to experience the problems described in Table 3-1.

Table 3-1   Problems Experienced by Bank One Columbus

Problem Experienced	Affect on Business
Inability to effectively analyze data	The batch job from each mainframe produced a paper report of unsummarized information. To manipulate data into the management information reports needed to make credit decisions, 15 temporary employees were needed to enter this data into non-networked PCs. Analysts were limited in their ability to view and assess the information they needed to make decisions because of the difficult process to extract data into a format in which it could be manipulated.
Lack of timely access to information	The batch reporting system required two days to create production reports: one day to produce the report and one day to enter the information into the PCs. Ad hoc reports required one to six weeks, depending on the type of report, with an average of two weeks. The department often needed to either make important risk management decisions without complete information or significantly delay decisions.
Excessive computing costs	Standard production reports were charged back at $.05 per page, which meant the average cost of a report was $300. Ad hoc reports, because of custom programming and special jobs, cost an average of $2000. As a result, the department spent more than $2 million in mainframe chargebacks each year to run its operations.

Faced with these problems, the department decided to improve its operations by:

- Significantly speeding up risk management decisions by improving access to information

- Reducing the computing costs required to run the department each year

The Rightsizing Solution

To address these requirements, Bank One Columbus introduced a Sun client-server configuration into its production environment. This configuration (illustrated in Figure 3-6) consists of a SPARCserver™ 670MP, 3 SPARCserver 2s, and 30 SPARCstation™ systems. A dedicated database server, the 670MP runs Informix RDBMS and is connected to the mainframe by SunLink® SNA 3270. The SPARCserver 2 application servers run SAS, Informix Wingz®, Frame Technology's FrameMaker®, and reports written in Informix®-4GL.

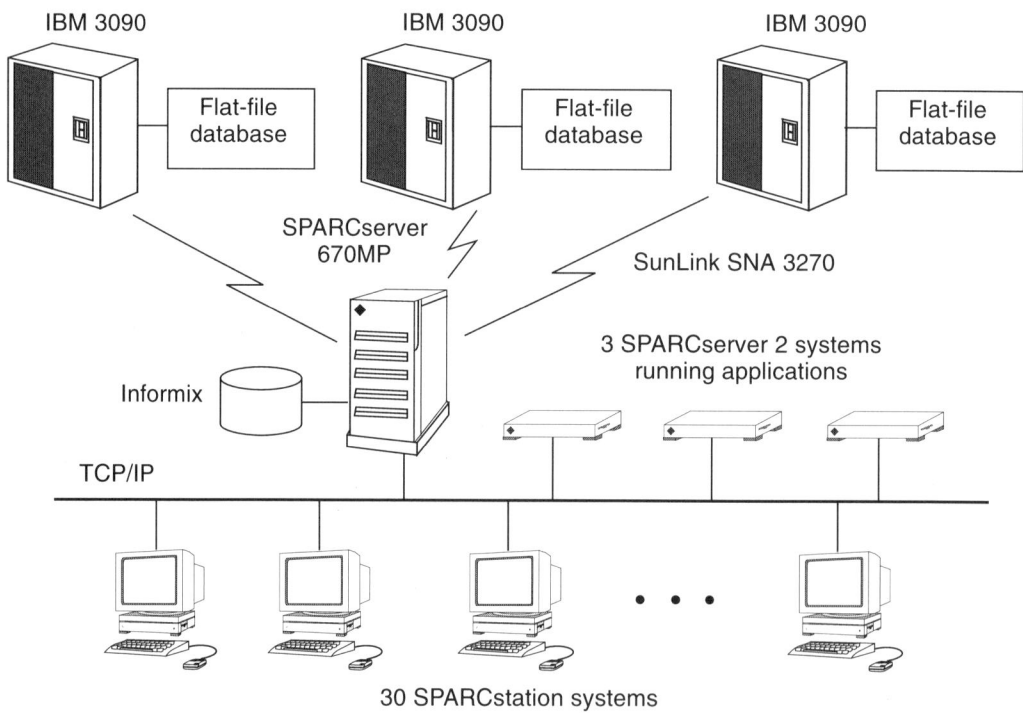

Figure 3-6   Rightsizing Solution

Using the Informix database on the 670MP, the department built a complete historical profile of each customer by replicating data stored on the IBM mainframes. Once a month, the department updates the Informix database by extracting three million customer records from the mainframes. Once a day, the previous day's financial data (such as purchases, cash advances, payments, and delinquencies) is downloaded from the mainframes to the Informix database.

The existing SAS applications on the mainframes were easily moved from the mainframe to the Sun platform and still run the normal batch production reports. The department uses SAS and Informix-4GL to perform the ad hoc reports and all production reports. Analysts use SAS and Wingz to study and manipulate the data from these reports.

Results of Rightsizing

With its client-server solution, the bank achieved the results and solutions to its business problems depicted in Table 3-2.

Table 3-2 Results Achieved by Bank One Columbus

Result	Solution
Lower computing costs	The total cost of the new system was $600, 000. Because the department is currently saving $2 million a year in mainframe chargebacks, the new system paid for itself in four months.
Faster, more timely access to information	The department now runs, and has available, 90 to 100 production reports each day, rather than having to wait 48 hours for information. The information is online in summarized format and does not require data to be re-entered. In addition to the normal production reports, the department now executes 30 to 40 ad hoc SAS programs and 100 to 150 Informix queries daily. The average time for ad hoc reports has decreased from two weeks to overnight. The department can produce the reports more quickly and produce more of them, enabling analysts to look at data in different ways.
Improved decision-making and responsiveness	The superior access to and analysis of data enables Bank One Columbus to make better, faster, more-informed risk management decisions. It is also now able to react to regulatory and economic changes within hours rather than weeks. The bank estimates that it saved more than $6 million last year as a result. In addition, it projects a savings of $4 million a year by reducing delinquency and write-off losses that previously occurred because relevant information was not available.

The Rightsizing Process

When the Risk Management department announced its plan to use a client-server solution, it encountered tremendous resistance within the company because the solution represented a major change in the company's computing architecture. To overcome this resistance, the department demonstrated that the bank was spending an additional $5000 to $10,000 a day by *not* introducing the system. These statistics persuaded upper management to grant approval to proceed with the project.

The department began a four-month pilot project, based on a SPARCserver as the database server and a mix of six SPARCstation systems as clients. To provide UNIX expertise, the company hired both an administrator and a developer with UNIX knowledge. After successfully completing the pilot, the department finished and deployed the system within another month.

Leveraging the Rightsizing Investment for Future Growth

The Risk Management department is currently increasing the number of analysts using the client-server system from 30 to 45. It is also developing applications to move more reporting off the mainframe. The success of this project has also led the department to evaluate moving on-line transaction processing systems (such as processing credit card applications and customer service) to client-server architectures.

Summary

The department observed that it did not need data that was accurate to the second to make the decisions necessary to run its operations. A customer account history that was updated every 30 days and financial activity from the previous day were accurate enough to make risk management decisions. However, the department did need the ability to access the data directly (without having to wait for a batch report) to easily perform ad hoc queries and reduce the cost of obtaining information.

Making these business observations enabled the department to restructure the way information flowed throughout the business. Rather than having one source of data on the mainframe, the Risk Management department created a dedicated database server for the department, dramatically reducing information access time for both scheduled and ad hoc reports. In addition, by employing a relational database, graphical workstations, and tools such as SAS, Wingz, and Informix-4GL, users are able to analyze data in multiple ways and view data more intuitively.

Off-loading the decision-making from the mainframe not only reduced the computing costs of the department but also increased the mainframes' value. They are now more efficient, providing more CPU cycles for other applications, and more effective, serving as an enterprise data repository.

Customer Management

Customer management is broadly defined to be any interactive process a business has with its customers. Usually, it involves the integration of computers and voice services to improve information flow between a business and its customers. The most common customer-management application is customer service, but customer management also includes a wide range of customer-driven processes across all industries (such as directory assistance in telecommunications, brokerage applications in financial services, and diagnostic systems in health care). In some cases, the focus of these applications is to solve customer problems; in others, it is to answer customer inquiries for information.

Business Issues

As discussed in Chapter 1, "Rightsizing: The Corporate Solution," many business today are re-engineering their business processes. Applications involving customer management are one of the most common starting points for re-engineering because of the following statistics:

- On average, it costs six times as much to sell to a new customer as it does to an existing customer. [1]

- A customer who has had a problem and has received a good response to that problem is more likely to repurchase from the company than is any other customer, including one whohas *never* had a problem with the company or its products. [1]

In a terminal-based environment, many companies have not been able to provide world-class customer service. As a result, retaining existing customers and attracting new ones has been difficult. Recognizing the importance of customer service for repeat business, two-thirds of all businesses with terminal-based customer service applications are planning to replace the applications within the next two years. [1]

Today, most service centers are viewed as cost centers because most service contracts are paid in advance and allow unlimited usage. Each time a customer calls the service center with a problem or an inquiry, the time a service agent spends on the phone with the customer is a cost to the business. Most businesses are trying to reduce the time required and, hence, the cost of servicing these calls.

---

1. Sentry Market Research.

Although most service centers are viewed as cost centers today, many businesses are trying to turn these cost centers into profit centers. Regardless of why a customer calls—whether the customer is upset and has a problem or is calling only for information—a situation exists where a customer is talking to a business. After the customer's problem or request has been handled, many business opportunities exist:

- Cross-Selling
  Suggestively selling another product or service or identifying customers that should receive follow-up.

- Identification of Product Deficiencies
  Gathering information on problems with existing products, especially new products, and quickly feeding this information back to the development team.

- Market Research
  Asking questions about new products or services desired and quickly feeding this information to marketing.

By making full use of the customer call, businesses are using customer-management applications to increase sales or to reduce the cost of obtaining valuable product or market information.

Technology Issues

Today, most customer service centers are run in a mainframe environment. Customer Service Representatives (CSRs) use terminals to access mainframe databases to respond to customer problems and inquiries. An Automatic Call Distributor (ACD) routes incoming calls to available CSRs.

Another important statistic related to customer service is that 80 percent of all the problems in this world have already been experienced by someone else. One of the keys to providing good service is to record the solution to the problem the first time and then to be able to find the recorded solution quickly if the problem arises again.

When solving a problem initially, most customer service processes require access to data stored in multiple databases, as shown in Figure 3-7 on page 71. In a terminal-based environment, access is accomplished by logging in to one application, obtaining information, manually writing the information on a piece of paper, and logging out of the application. This process is repeated until the problem is solved. The information written on paper is usually the key to the solution, but it is rarely recorded electronically.

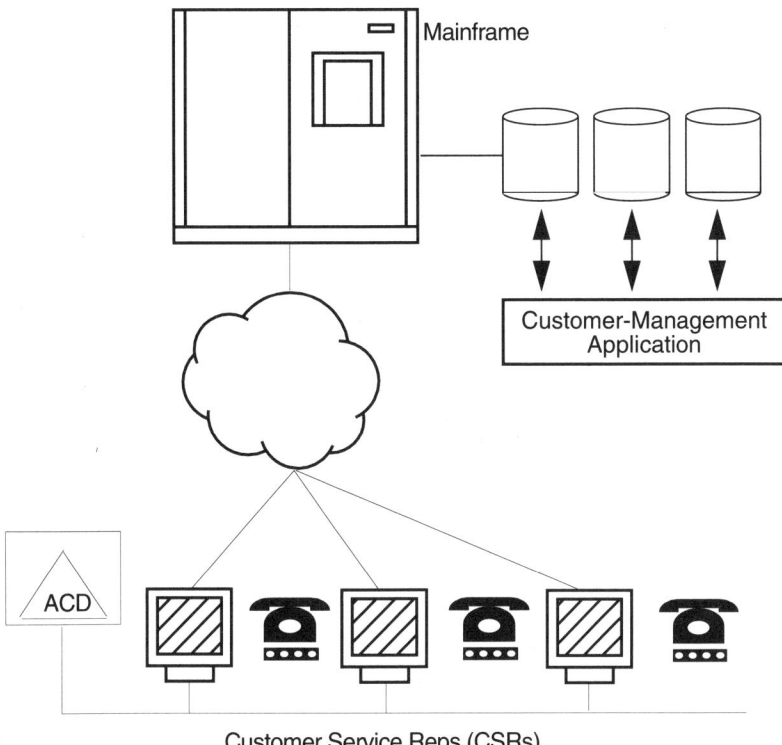

Figure 3-7   Typical Customer-Management Technology Problems

When the solution is recorded electronically, hierarchical databases make it difficult to find information again. To add to the problem, historical data is often moved to tape because it is very expensive to keep data online in mainframe environments. Once the data is moved to tape, it is difficult to access again.

From a user-interface perspective, terminal-based applications tend to be form-driven rather than customer-driven. In other words, the serial order of the forms in the user interface drives the interaction with the customer. Also, terminals limit the types of information that can be viewed or stored and preclude the use of graphical images as part of the process.

Rightsizing Solution

With customer management applications, numerous variations to the rightsizing solution exist. Servers can be used for databases, applications, communications, or call management. Voice response units are often installed to handle some calls without human intervention. In situations where cross-selling or information gathering is desired, expert systems are used to assess customer profiles and prompt CSRs. Almost always, however, the rightsizing solution will involve a client-server configuration where the mainframe is still used as a data source, as illustrated in Figure 3-8.

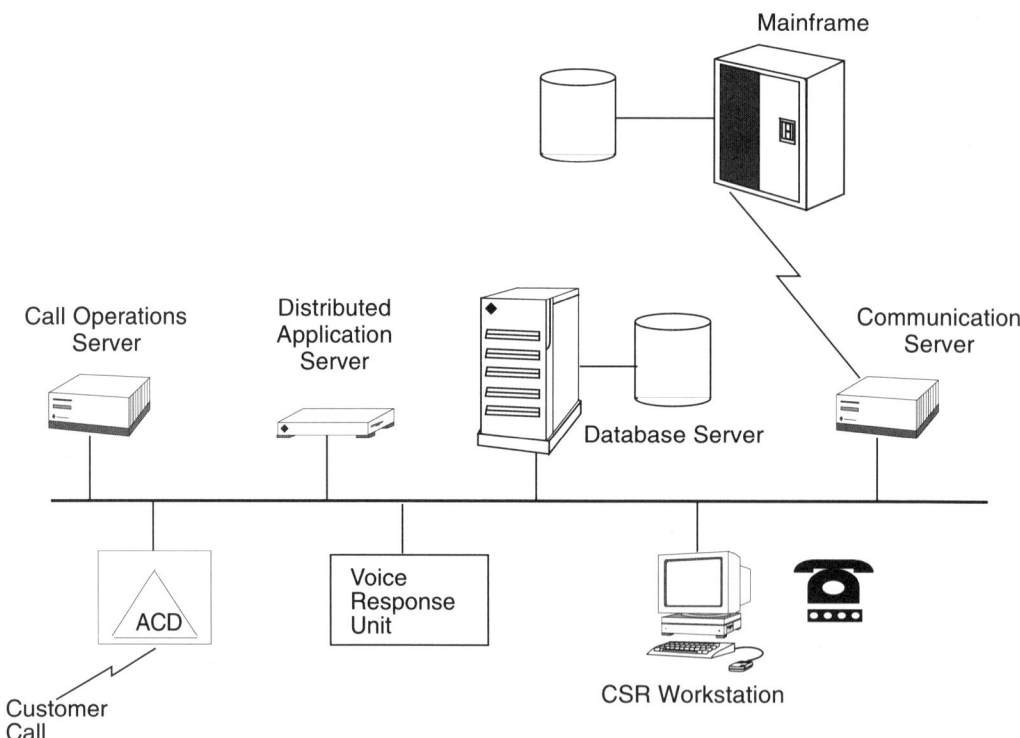

Figure 3-8   A Rightsizing Solution for Customer Management

Probably the most important change in the architecture is the installation of workstations on the desktop to support the CSR. Because of the high degree of multi-tasking and the large number of concurrent applications that need to be run, UNIX workstations are often used instead of PCs for this type of system. As shown in Figure 3-9, the process of interacting with the customer is usually dramatically re-engineered.

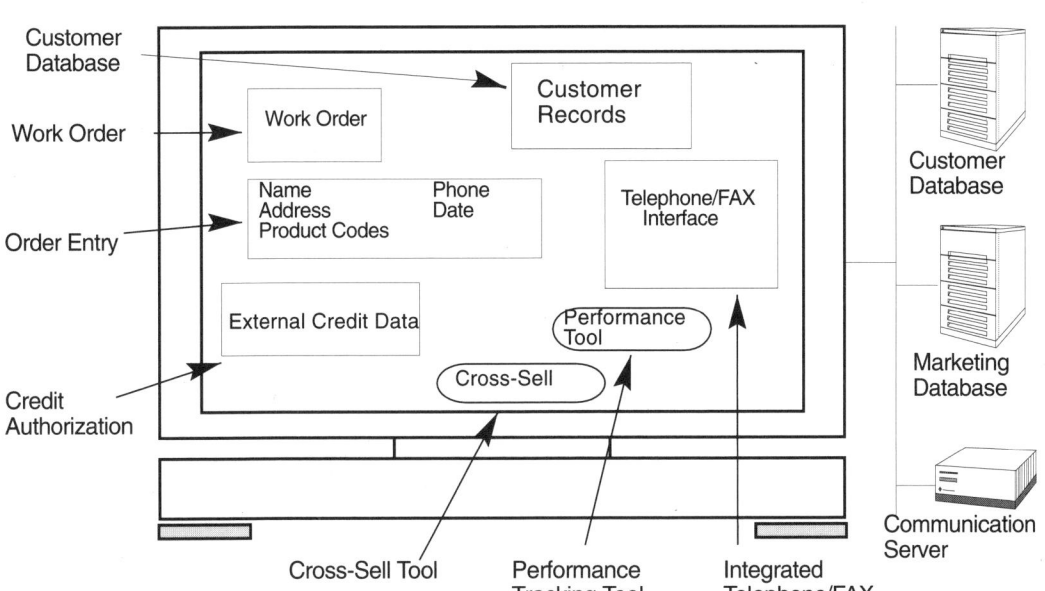

Customer Database

Work Order

Order Entry

Credit Authorization

Figure 3-9   Example of Re-engineered Customer Management Interface

An example new CSR environment might consist of the following applications:

• When the customer calls, a profile of the customer and a record of past interaction is brought up in a window.

• A work order application runs in another window to handle the customer problem or request.

• In the background, an expert system analyzes the customer profile and current problem and prompts the CSR to cross-sell or cross-question the customer.

• Order entry and credit authorization are used to handle any customer orders.

• Computer interfaces to telephones and FAX services are available.

The scenario in Figure 3-9 represents a significant re-engineering of a customer-management environment. Not all customer management rightsizing projects will be this complex. Many companies are simply using better access to information to respond faster to customer inquiries and problems. Others are using graphical interfaces to place images rather than characters in front of CSRs. For example, displaying an image of a part (rather than a part number) the customer is ordering in an order entry application can reduceads ordering errors. Regardless of the amount of re-engineering, many companies have reported significant business benefits from rightsizing customer management applications.

Case Study: Customer Management

New Zealand IRD

New Zealand Inland Revenue Department (IRD), the nation's central tax collection agency (comparable to the U.S. Internal Revenue Service), is responsible for collecting NZ$27 billion (US$15 billion) each year from 3.5 million people. IRD is responsible for collecting a broad range of taxes including income, fringe benefits, goods and services, estate, and gaming (gambling).

Headquartered in Wellington, the IRD operates 26 district offices and 3 regional processing service centers throughout the country. It has 5500 employees who process 6.5 million tax returns and respond to over 4 million taxpayer inquiries annually.

In 1987, the IRD produced its first major Information System Plan (ISP), which has completely re-engineered the way that the IRD runs its business. As a result of this ISP, the IRD began revamping its computer systems in 1990 to become more service-oriented and efficient.

Environment Prior to Rightsizing

Each district office used anNCR® Tower mini-computer to record tax returns in a flat-file database. IRD personnel performed much of the tax-return processing manually, using typewriters and other outdated equipment to collect payments and process refund checks.

After a tax return was processed by the district office, the return information was sent to the central office in Wellington. A Unisys™ A16 mainframe collected the information and built a historical profile on each taxpayer in a centralized flat-file database. However, only the district offices had complete information about taxpayers—the centralized database contained little more than names, addresses, and a record of the most recent transactions. The central office also contained an IBM 3090 to run financial and accounting applications. Figure 3-10 shows this environment.

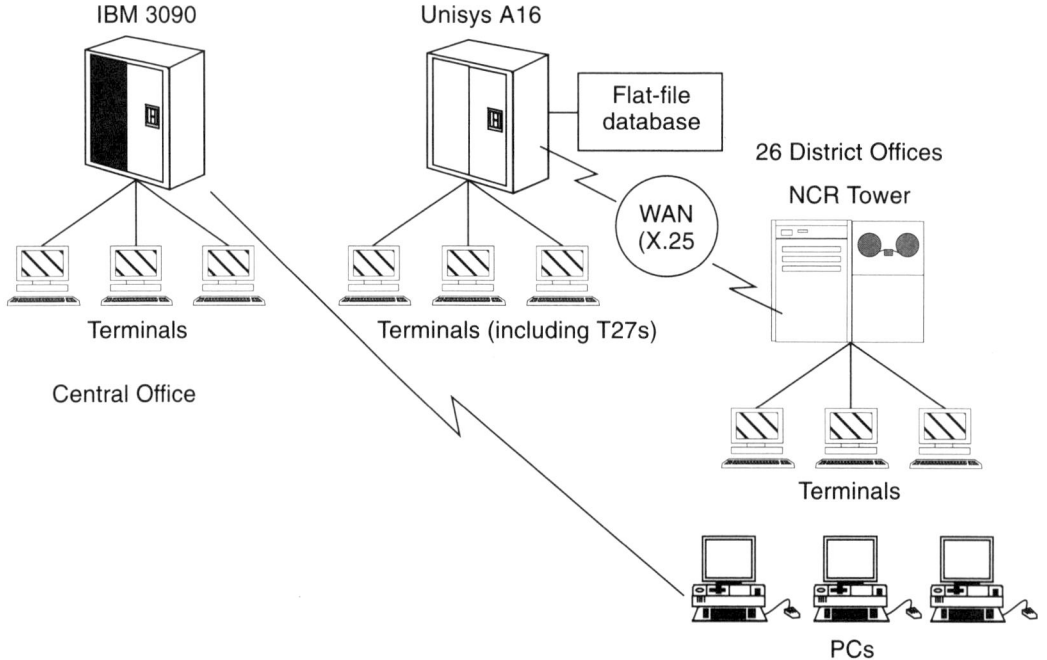

Figure 3-10   Environment Prior to Rightsizing

New Zealand citizens were demanding higher-quality customer service from the IRD and complaining about long processing times for returns and delayed responses to inquiries. With this computing environment, the IRD experienced the problems described in Table 3-3.

Table 3-3   Problems Experienced by New Zealand IRD

Problem Experienced	Affect on Business
Tax return backlogs	The district offices were overwhelmed by the volume of tax returns. Long backlogs were resulting from the overloaded minicomputers and the manual process of handling tax returns. In addition, because most information was stored locally, district offices lacked access to information held by other district offices. Many problems arose if a taxpayer sent a payment to the wrong district office or moved to another area. On average, most returns took three to four months to process.
Slow response to taxpayer inquiries	District offices could only answer inquiries for taxpayers from information maintained on their computer system or in paper files. Tracking down the needed information was difficult because of the volume of records kept, a constant backlog of filing, and misplaced or warehoused records. A response that required a staff person to access the database and obtain a printed report could easily take four to six weeks. The IRD needed to respond instantly to on-the-spot inquiries and to provide answers to written inquiries within three weeks.
Unautomated office tasks	IRD personnel were frustrated by the lack of modern office equipment, such as up-to-date word processing, spreadsheet, and electronic mail systems. An office staff person might have to place several phone calls or even mail hardcopy memos to get information or to communicate within the department. The inability to automate basic office tasks made cost-efficient operation impossible.

The Rightsizing Solution

To solve these business issues, the IRD decided to re-architect its computing environment by introducing the following technologies:

- A centralized database coupled with networking, allowing any IRD personnel at any office to answer any taxpayer inquiry

- Distributed computing, enabling much of the tax-return collection, report generation, and inquiry responses to be accomplished at the district level

- Open systems, preserving existing hardware investments and supporting a heterogeneous computing environment

Using these technologies, the IRD moved from a mainframe-based terminal network to a client-server network of 2 mainframes, 18 SPARCserver 490s, 128 SPARCserver 1s, 65 SPARCserver 2s, a SPARCserver 10 system, 570 PCs, and 4000 WYSE 60™ terminals. Figure 3-11 illustrates this new environment.

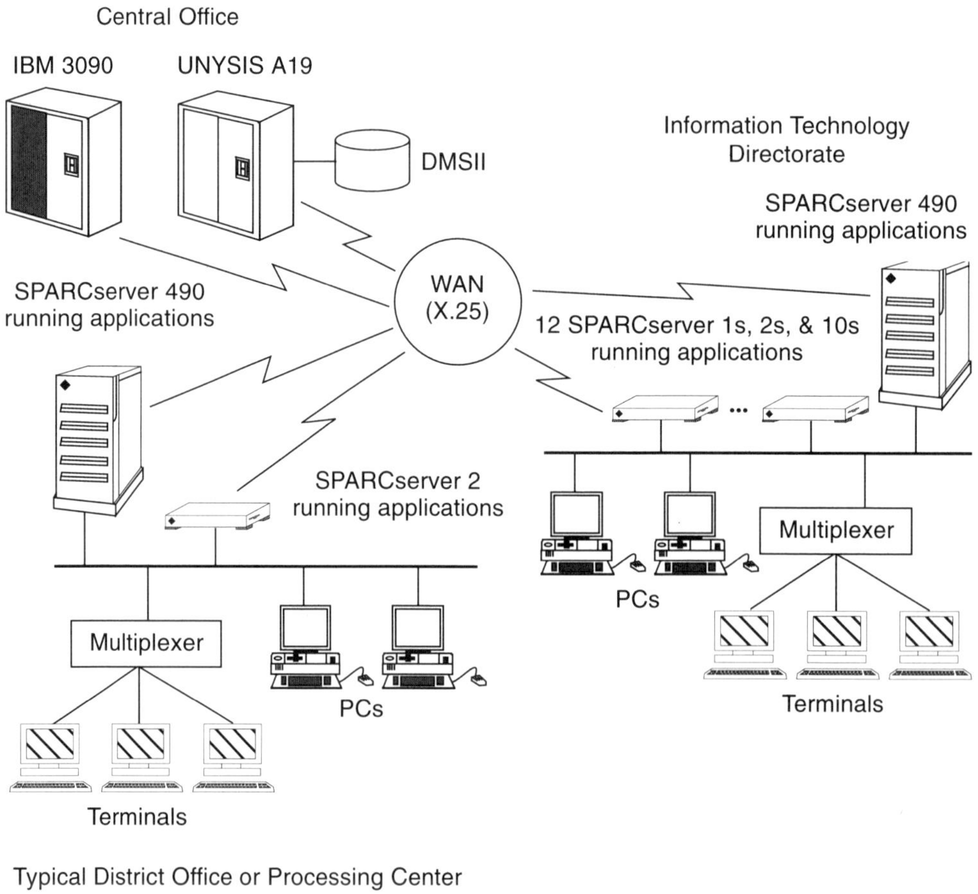

Central Office

IBM 3090   UNYSIS A19

DMSII

Information Technology
Directorate

SPARCserver 490
running applications

SPARCserver 490
running applications

WAN
(X.25)

12 SPARCserver 1s, 2s, & 10s
running applications

SPARCserver 2
running applications

Multiplexer

Multiplexer

PCs

PCs

Terminals

Terminals

Typical District Office or Processing Center

Figure 3-11   Rightsizing Solution

In the central office, the IRD upgraded its Unisys mainframe from an A16 to an A19 and moved the tax-processing applications to it. Using a Unisys DMSII database on the A19, the IRD created a central taxpayer database. To support the system, it created an Information Technology Directorate (ITD). The Directorate contains a mix of SPARCserver systems, running applications that select taxpayer audit cases (accessing an Oracle database), provide fault tracking (accessing an Informix database), perform payroll tasks, and enable electronic filing of tax returns. The IBM mainframe continues to run financial and accounting applications.

To supplement its 26 district offices, the IRD established 3 regional processing centers. In each processing center, SPARCserver 490, 1, and 2 systems run an automated data entry application that captures tax-return information. The data from the returns is transmitted to the A19 for processing. Once processed, the record is sent back over the network to the original processing center and then on to the district office.

At each district office, SPARCserver 490, 1, and 2 systems run several applications, including data entry, file transfer, on-line access security, and office automation. ICL's OfficePower automates a wide variety of office tasks, including email and word processing. Additionally, it integrates the PCs into an OfficePower LAN, allowing the DOS-based PCs to access the applications running on the SPARCserver systems. The SPARCserver systems, PCs, and video terminals are connected by Ethernet and the PC-NFS® distributed service.

The UNIX networking capabilities are the key to this large-scale, distributed computing network, enabling personnel at any IRD location to access the central taxpayer database from a desktop. The entire system is connected by a WAN, running over X.25, that IRD personnel developed using TCP/IP and Optimation Software's Co-Connect.

Results of Rightsizing

Today, nearly all 5500 employees at the IRD use the new solution. With this system architecture, the IRD is achieving the results described in Table 3-4.

Table 3-4   Results Achieved by New Zealand IRD

Result	Description
Faster processing of tax returns	Using the automated system, with distributed processing but centralized data, the IRD reduced processing time for tax returns from three to four months to between four to six weeks. Taxpayers now mail returns to the three processing centers instead of to the district offices, eliminating confusion if returns are mailed to the wrong office. An additional benefit is that the networked Sun system allows taxpayers to file their tax returns electronically.
Quick response to inquiries	With the new system's centralized database and networking capabilities, IRD personnel in each district office have on-line access to information and can resolve on-the-spot inquiries immediately. If they need a report, they can generate it locally and usually mail it the next day. Response time to inquiry letters dropped from four to six weeks to three weeks. The IRD's new goal is to respond to inquiry letters in less than one week.
Automation of office activities	Largely replacing phones and letters, email has greatly improved interoffice communication. IRD personnel no longer have to place phone calls and mail hardcopy memos to obtain information.
Cost-efficient operation	These benefits have saved the IRD money. During the project's first year, for example, the agency saved enough to meet its goal of covering 90 percent of that year's implementation costs for the project. Since then, the project has been completely self-funded, paying for itself every year. The total project cost is about NZ$300 million (US$165 million) spread over five years.

The Rightsizing Process

The project consists of two five-year plans overlapping during seven years. After a nine-month pilot study, the IRD installed the initial system and the network in five months. During the next year, the entire system was installed. Migration of all existing applications took about two and a half years to complete. IRD has used a systems integrator, Andersen Consulting, to perform much of the work.

Also included in the five-year plans are periods for employees to adjust to the structural changes caused by the use of the new computer system and the organization's re-orientation to customer service. Andersen Consulting and the IRD have conducted three-month training sessions for all IRD personnel as they became affected by the new systems.

Leveraging the Rightsizing Investment for Future Growth

The IRD has completed the rewrite and migration of the tax-collection applications from the old architecture to the new architecture. Currently, the agency is building new applications, such as those to expand electronic filing of tax returns. In addition, the IRD is looking at ways to further distribute applications to take full advantage of the new client-server architecture.

Summary

IRD realized that it was not providing good service to its customers, the citizens of New Zealand, with its old computing architecture. Many of its processes were either still manual or had been automated by use of a computing model that was no longer effective. To solve these problems, the agency used client-server and networking technology to re-engineer its two primary business tasks: processing tax returns and resolving inquiries.

In the old system, each district office performed tax return processing, relying on an NCR Tower minicomputer. Much of the process was not automated and information that needed to be available centrally was held locally, impeding tax-return processing in each office. The Unisys mainframe was not used effectively to store information or process returns. As a result, each office was overwhelmed with the volume of returns, and long backlogs ensued.

In the new system, nearly all of the data has been centralized in one data store on the mainframe. While data has been consolidated onto one machine, processing has not. Part of the processing occurs on the mainframe and part occurs on UNIX servers in either the regional processing centers or the ITD. In effect, the IRD has surrounded the central mainframe with UNIX servers and distributed the workload throughout the network. By consolidating data but distributing processing, the time required to process a return has been reduced from three to four months to two weeks and customer satisfaction has been improved.

In the old system, the process for resolving customer inquiries was ineffective because each office could use only information that was available in its own computer systems and paper files. In the new system, a network backbone allows any desktop in the system to access the central database on the mainframe. As a result, each district office has immediate access to all data in the system, enabling quick and efficient resolution of customer inquiries.

Package Replacement

Although decision support and customer management applications are both excellent starting points for rightsizing, not all businesses initially rightsize a management system. Many companies are beginning their rightsizing efforts with operational systems, most commonly using package applications. By replacing existing custom applications with package applications, applications can be moved to client-server system much faster than if they were to be rewritten. Companies are also replacing existing mainframe packages with new client-server packages, either because the old package is obsolete or because it does not provide the benefits and functionality of the newer client-server packages.

Business Issues

Some of the most common functions to replace with packages are accounting, human resources, and selected manufacturing applications. Many businesses today are concluding that using custom applications for these functions does not provide any payback in terms of competitive advantage for the business but does result in a large application maintenance cost. The traditional environment for running these applications is a mainframe attached to terminals, as illustrated in Figure 3-12.

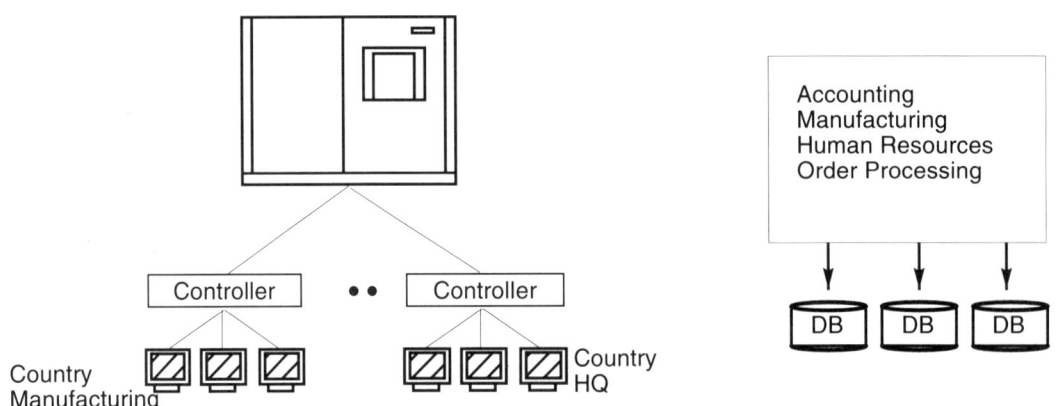

Figure 3-12 Typical Package Application Environment

Often developed 5–20 years ago, these applications are typically monolithic and access one or more databases. Since the time the applications were developed, many business conditions have changed significantly. Acceptable cycle times for business processes (such as materials costing and planning, or revenue accounting) have decreased dramatically. Growth in international business has demanded support for multi-country requirements and international currencies. New business information has emerged and must be tracked. Most IS departments have had a difficult time maintaining existing systems and keeping pace with these changes. In fact, some applications are so regimented that to implement these changes would require rewriting the entire system.

Many business issues result when any of these applications are shared among multiple departments or divisions, a common scenario in many businesses today. If one department wants to make a change to the application (for example, implementing a new chart of accounts in an accounting application), the other department must approve the change. If one department is experiencing trouble completing a business process (for example, month-end for accounting), the other department is usually impacted as well. As a result, departments do not have control over their own information or processes and their results can be impacted through no fault of their own.

Technology Issues

In a typical order processing/manufacturing/accounting cycle, each application interacts with its own database, as illustrated in Figure 3-13.

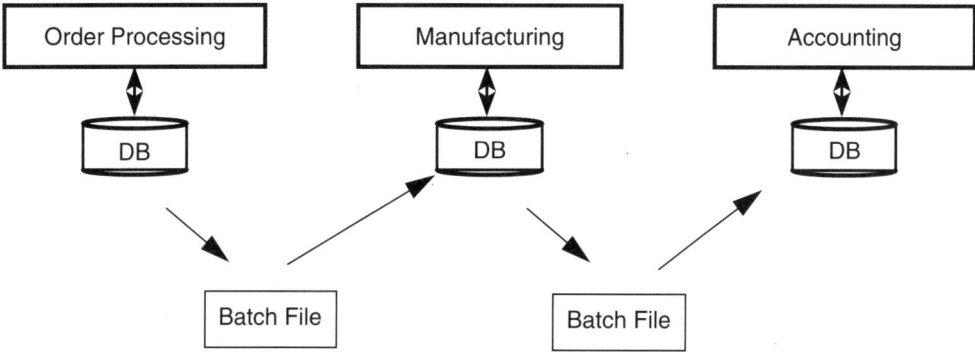

Figure 3-13 Typical Order Processing / Manufacturing / Accounting Cycle

Each application uses its own copy of the data, resulting in duplicate and frequently inconsistent data. Communication between systems is typically done through batch files. For example, at the close of the business day, orders are extracted from the order processing system into a batch file, which is then sent to manufacturing and loaded into the MRP system. Transfer times between systems can vary from hours to days, but there is almost always a delay time that increases cycle time for business processes. Different representations of data between systems often also makes it difficult for systems to communicate.

Accounting, human resources, and manufacturing systems typically contain decision-support applications in addition to the operational applications. Users of these decision-support applications experience the same problems (such as inability to produce customer reports and data latency) discussed previously. For example, the general ledger application in an accounting system typically queues up entries until the end of the month when a batch job processes all the transactions for the month. Any decision-maker who wants to analyze general ledger information mid-month must wait until the end of the month before the data is available. In addition, terminal-based user interfaces limit the type of information that can be displayed and the analysis that can be performed on it. (See the section "Decision Support" on page 57 for more information on technology issues related to decision making.)

Rightsizing Solution

Many variations to the rightsizing solution for package application replacement exist but a typical configuration is illustrated in Figure 3-14.

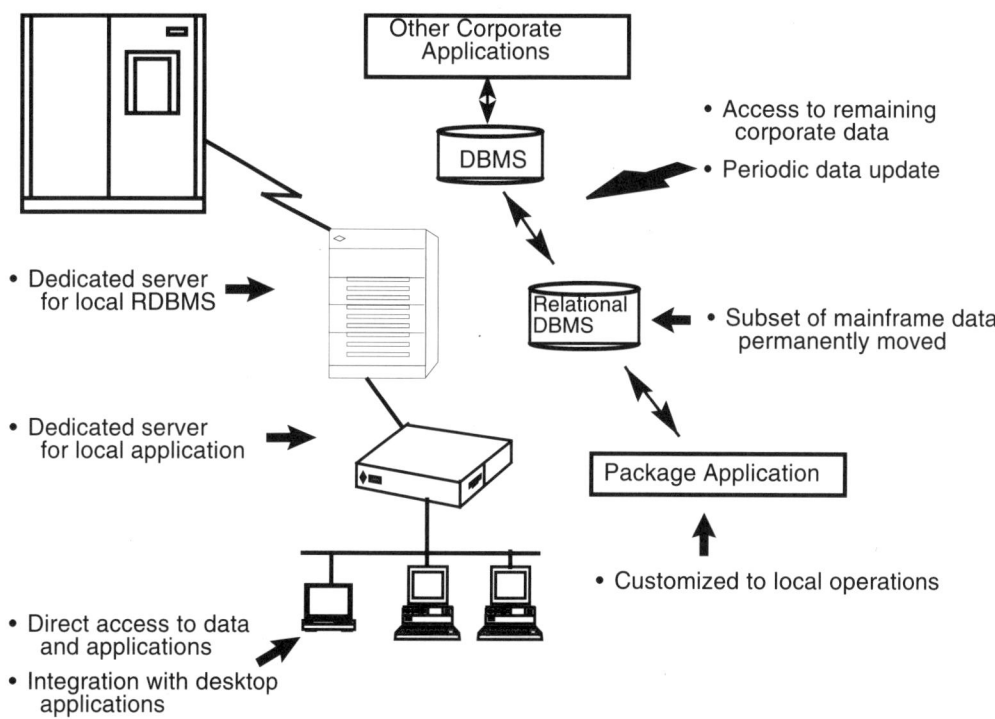

Figure 3-14   Typical Package Application Rightsizing Solution

A UNIX server running an RDBMS is introduced and connected to the mainframe. A subset of the data is usually *permanently* moved from the mainframe to the UNIX server (unlike decision-support application rightsizing, where this database is usually used to replicate data). Updates still occur, but in the reverse direction—from the UNIX server to the mainframe—to communicate information to other organizations in the company or to corporate headquarters.

The mainframe application is replaced by a package application that runs on either a dedicated application server or on desktop clients, usually either PCs or workstations. The package application is customized to support operations and requirements specific to the business.

Some businesses continue to use the mainframe to run other corporate applications just as they did before rightsizing; others have a long-term strategy to completely eliminate the mainframe and will eventually move all remaining applications to the client-server architecture.

Benefits of Package Replacement

The primary benefits of the rightsizing solution result from the new package application and from gaining control over the data. Client-server package applications typically contain more functionality, are easier and quicker to implement, and enable rapid response to changes in business conditions. Many of these applications eliminate batch processes and provide on-line access to data. For example, some of the accounting packages contain general ledger applications that process transactions throughout the month. As a result, decision-makers can immediately access month-to-date information at any time, and month-end close times are significantly reduced.

By gaining control over the data, many departments report that they are able to better map their information architecture to their business. For example, some departments finally have the freedom to update their chart of accounts that are years out-of-date.

Some businesses are also using client-servers to implement a more advanced, message-based model of workflow between applications. In this model, each functional application, such as order processing or manufacturing, is moved to a separate server. In the mainframe model, transactions were queued until the end of the day and batch files were used to communicate between applications. In the client-server, message-based model, a message is immediately sent to post the transaction to the next system in the business process when a system completes a transaction. Using this new workflow model, many companies are able to reduce the cycle time for numerous business processes.

Case Study: Package Replacement

WorldCorp

WorldCorp is a $400-million air transportation and transaction processing enterprise based in Herndon, Virginia. It consists of three companies, including World Airways, a leading provider of air transportation for commercial and government customers, and US Order, a developer of patented automated ordering services.

In early 1991, WorldCorp began re-evaluating its mainframe-based financial system to solve several business problems, such as inflexible applications that prevented MIS from being able to respond to end-user requirements.

Environment Prior to Rightsizing

WorldCorp's financial computer system consisted of a leased IBM 4381 mainframe running McCormack and Dodge financial applications software and an HP 3000 to run a separate aircraft parts inventory and reliability application. The communications network was an SNA SDLC terminal-to-host configuration, which included three Novell NetWare LANs supporting local workgroups. Figure 3-15 depicts this environment.

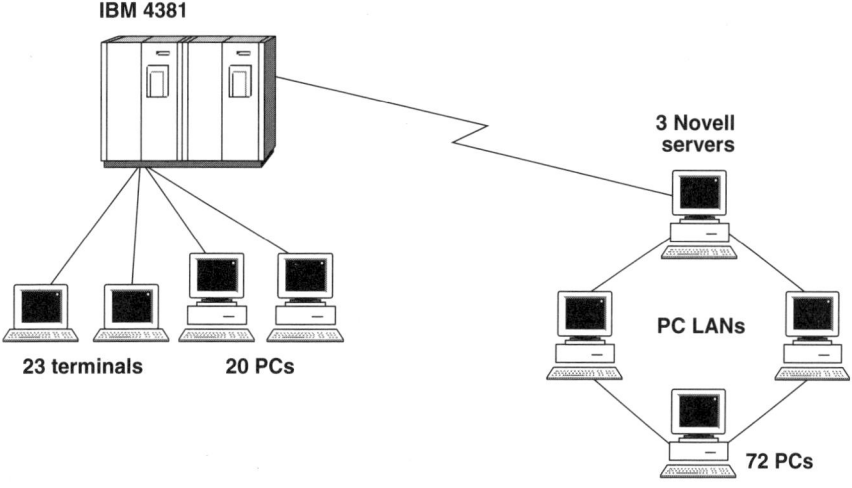

Figure 3-15   Environment Prior to Rightsizing

WorldCorp's accounting requirements had resulted in a complex set of COBOL applications that were difficult to operate, maintain, and enhance. Specific business problems resulting from this system are described in Table 3-5.

Table 3-5   Problems Experienced by WorldCorp

Problem Experienced	Business Impact
Lack of reporting flexibility and timeliness	Obtaining even basic reports had become a time-consuming process requiring a lengthy setup the night before, a process that sometimes had to be repeated for a single report.
Limited access to application functions	To process payroll for one of the six companies, the payroll application for the other five had to be frozen. When accounts payable and the general ledger were processed, those applications also had to be frozen.
Inadequate turnaround time	Management decisions increasingly required faster turn-around time than would ever be possible with the existing system.
High maintenance costs	The complexity of the existing financial system had resulted in a very expensive standard maintenance agreement.

The Rightsizing Solution

To address these problems, WorldCorp decided to rightsize its financial system by replacing the mainframe with a client-server environment based on UNIX technology. To meet the current and anticipated future processing demands of its financial applications and to provide an open computing environment, WorldCorp selected Sun as the platform vendor for its new client-server system.

The new system configuration included one SPARCserver 490, two SPARCserver 2 systems, and one SPARCserver 1 connected by Ethernet to PCs and X-terminals, as depicted in Figure 3-16. The client-server network supported 151 local users and 26 remote ones.

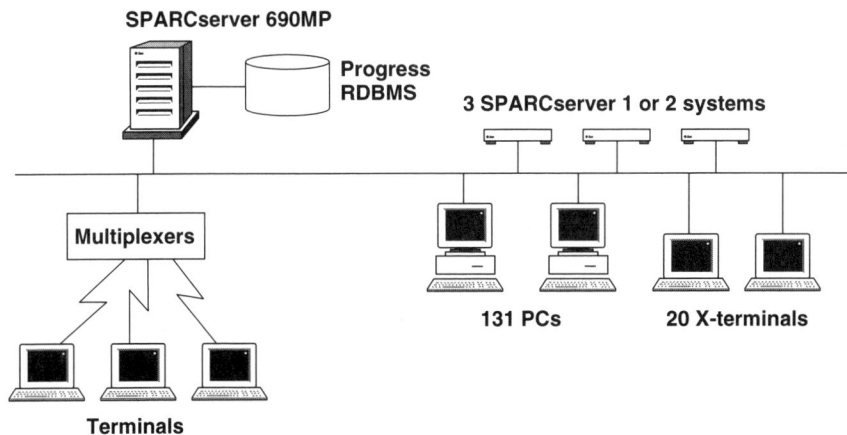

Figure 3-16   Rightsizing Solution

After reviewing several 4GLs, WorldCorp selected the Progress environment because of its robustness, ease of use, and interface-creation capabilities. The company also based its decision on recommendations from other users.

For financial accounting software, WorldCorp chose Financial Dynamics from Dynamic Business Systems (DBS)—a Progress value-added reseller (VAR). WorldCorp decided that working with a VAR would be the most effective way to get the financial application up and running quickly while getting the WorldCorp COBOL programming staff retrained in the Progress software environment.

Results from Rightsizing

WorldCorp has realized several business benefits from rightsizing to the client-server solution, including:

*   Separate WorldCorp companies can run their payrolls and financial reports at the same time, regardless of what the other companies are doing, overcoming the old system's biggest operational roadblock.

*   Downtime for the company's financial systems has decreased by 90 percent.

*   The Progress software's ease of use has helped shorten, from days to hours, the learning curve of moving to the new financial system.

*   Faster ad hoc report generation has improved decision-making.

*   Programmer productivity is up by an estimated 300 percent.

*   Per-year costs for the new system are approximately $500,000 less per year than the per-year mainframe costs over five years.

In addition, rightsizing has given WorldCorp the flexibility to respond to information needs its IS department did not even know existed previously because of users' reluctance to approach IS. This flexibility means IS is getting closer to the system's users and, as a result, WorldCorp is getting closer to its customers.

The Rightsizing Process

By deciding to rightsize, WorldCorp faced transition challenges. For example, the internal technical staff had no prior experience with UNIX systems or client-server technology. By exploiting the VAR's expertise to customize the financial software to its needs and handle the data conversion and loading, WorldCorp completed the initial phase of the project within six months. The VAR also played an important role in training the IS programming staff in the Progress 4GL.

Leveraging the Rightsizing Investment for Future Growth

WorldCorp is currently moving additional applications to its new system. They are complex, processor-intensive applications that previously ran on the mainframe. In addition, the company is planning to move its aircraft inventory application from an HP3000 to the Sun environment.

Summary

WorldCorp realized that its existing accounting package was no longer meeting its business requirements or its operating cost objectives. As a result, the company decided to replace its mainframe accounting package with a new accounting package from a VAR. By doing this, it also enabled the replacement of the mainframe with a lower-cost, client-server environment based on UNIX servers and PC clients. This environment reduced operating costs by approximately $500,000 on average per year.

By moving to the new system, each WorldCorp division gained control over running its own accounting system, eliminating division inter-dependencies that arose from shared computing resources. Furthermore, the new package improved decision-making through improved information access, reduced end-user training time through graphical interfaces, and reduced development time through the use of a 4GL.

≡ *3*

Rightsizing for Corporate Survival

Economics of Rightsizing 4

In Chapter 3, "Rightsizing Opportunities," we discussed rightsizing starting points. The next issue is how to economically justify your rightsizing project to obtain both approval and funding. Because IS is often being asked to do more projects with less funding, economic justification of any project is critical. In this chapter, we will analyze the factors that affect the cost and benefits of rightsizing to help you build a business case for rightsizing.

Why Economic Analysis?

Developments over the past few years have put tremendous cost pressures on business computing environments. As global competition increases, more than half of businesses worldwide are trying to reduce or flatten information system budgets.

Overall computing costs continue to be expensive, however. The price of hardware, software, maintenance, system administration, application development, and even floor space and utilities continues to strain budgets. At the same time, end-users continue to approach IS organizations, asking for better access to information, new features and applications, and the latest technologies that will give them a competitive advantage. Figure 4-1 on page 94 illustrates the crisis IS organizations face today.

Faced with these challenges, UNIX systems, which typically cost much less than mainframe or minicomputer systems, look increasingly appealing. Nevertheless, concerns still linger about the true cost of ownership of distributed systems: *What are the costs of a transition to a client-server environment, and will these costs outweigh the benefits of moving to the new environment?* Because distribution of data and applications complicates critical data center operations such as system management, a common belief is that distributed UNIX environments cost more to operate than centralized mainframe environments. Companies' results from moving to client-server computing can differ, but numerous companies have benefited financially by replacing or off-loading their mainframe or mini-computer environments.

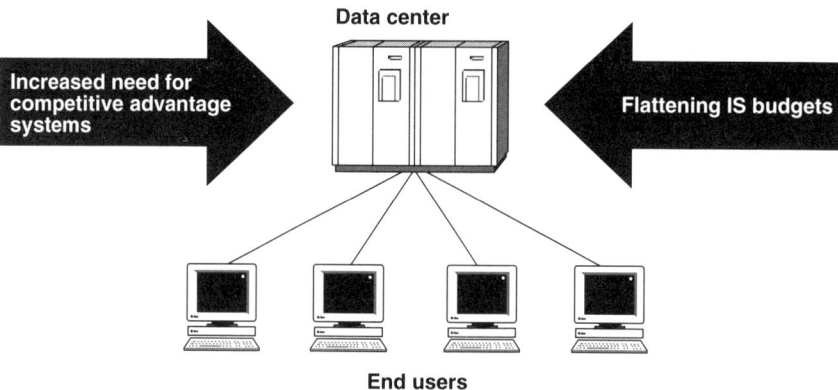

Figure 4-1 The IS Challenge

Economic Objectives

Before beginning any rightsizing project, you should first identify your economic objectives for the project. Economic objectives for a rightsizing project vary from business to business, but typically consist of one or more of the following: *cost reduction, cost avoidance,* and *profit improvement*. Deciding which of these objectives apply to your company's situation is important because the objective impacts the way the rightsizing project is justified.

Cost Reduction

Cost reduction typically involves decreasing operating costs by replacing or downsizing systems. To replace a system, you would move all current applications to another system with lower costs.

> The *U.S. Department of Defense, Office of the Director of Program Analysis and Evaluation*, saved an average of more than $3 million annually in operating costs by moving its applications from a mainframe to a client-server environment. The agency expects its total savings over six years to be nearly $19 million.

If an organization owns several mainframes, replacing a system may involve consolidating applications as well as off-loading them. For example, if an organization has three mainframes, it can off-load easily movable applications from all three mainframes to a UNIX server and consolidate non-portable applications on two of the mainframes. This strategy eliminates one mainframe and replaces it with a UNIX server.

The meaning of cost reduction can vary, depending on whether an end-user department or a data center is attempting to save money.

In departments, cost reduction typically means reducing data center chargebacks rather than replacing systems. To reduce chargebacks, many end-user departments have begun purchasing and managing their own systems based on UNIX technology, dramatically reducing their chargeback costs. In many cases, these departmental systems are used for functions such as decision support, which previously dissatisfied end-users because of limited ability to access information on the central mainframe.

Traditionally, executives have viewed departmental cost reductions skeptically, because chargeback reductions in one department typically increase chargebacks in others. Today the trend in business is toward decentralization, and many top-level executives are driving profit-and-loss responsibility down to the department/division level and eliminating cost centers. The philosophy is that if each department/division is profitable, the entire company will be profitable, as illustrated in Figure 4-2.

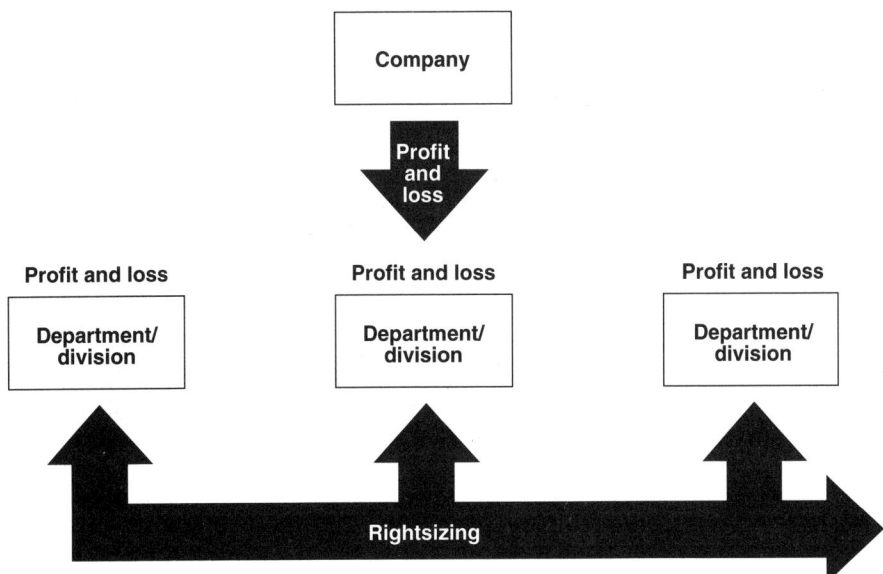

Figure 4-2   Company Versus Departmental Cost Reductions

Data centers have typically resisted departmental attempts to reduce chargebacks by moving off mainframes. However, many IS managers are helping departments do just that. Each department that moves frees mainframe cycles that can be used elsewhere, potentially making mainframe upgrades unnecessary. During the transition, chargeback costs have gone up for departments still using the mainframe, but, in the end, the companies reduced overall computing costs.

Cost Avoidance

Cost avoidance refers to purchasing a new, lower-cost computer and off-loading applications to it, in lieu of buying a new system or a system upgrade. Many companies are using this strategy today to keep computing costs from exceeding their budgets.

➤ *Gulf Canada Resources Ltd. of Calgary, Alberta, Canada* redirected the deployment of three new applications—originally targeted for the mainframe—to a UNIX server. The action avoided $1.2 million in mainframe upgrades over three years and saved an estimated $1 million per year in additional data center costs.

Profit Improvement

Profit improvement refers to investing in new systems to run new, competitive-advantage applications that either change the way you do business or better align your systems with your business processes.

➤ *Northwest Airlines of Minneapolis, Minnesota* is saving millions of dollars annually by changing its process of auditing passenger revenues. Their system uses image technology to scan sales receipts and flight coupons and to electronically match them for accuracy.

Pursuing profit improvement objectives may increase IS costs because it involves the purchase of new systems, but these costs are offset by the increased business profits the new applications allow. Performing an economic analysis will enable your company to understand, and minimize, the size of this increase.

Major Economic Factors

When performing an economic analysis, you should assess the following factors that contribute to the total cost/benefit of the system:

- Hardware/software ownership
  Cost of owning both the hardware and the software, including purchase or lease costs and annual support or maintenance costs

- Application development and maintenance
  Cost of developing applications and maintaining them

- Business benefits
  Increased business profits resulting from the changes in computing architecture or applications

- System operation and management
  Cost of operating, administering, and managing a system

You can save costs or achieve benefits in any of the areas just listed; initially, however, you will probably undergo a transition period in which costs increase. Transition costs represent one-time expenses, such as application migration/redevelopment costs and retraining costs associated with moving to the new environment. (For a detailed discussion about transition costs, see the section "Transition Costs" on page 104.)

Hardware/Software Ownership

Hardware/software ownership costs consist of purchase or lease costs and annual support and maintenance expenses. Nearly all companies that have moved off mainframes or minicomputers save in these areas.

In most mainframe environments, if the hardware and software are purchased, they are typically depreciated over a period of years, so the annual cost is typically some fraction of the overall purchase price. If the business leases, it pays an annual fee to the hardware and software vendors.

In either case, processing power, RAM, and disk space cost more in mainframe environments than in UNIX environments, as discussed in Chapter 1, "Rightsizing: The Corporate Solution." Furthermore, the licensing costs for software such as operating systems, databases, transaction-processing monitors, and applications are typically higher for mainframes. Although mainframe vendors are working aggressively to tighten the price gap and purchase costs are decreasing rapidly in the mainframe environment, maintenance costs are not decreasing as rapidly.

➤ *The Naval Air Warfare Center of Patuxent, Maryland* saved more than $900,000 annually in hardware/software ownership costs by replacing two mainframes with SPARCserver systems even though the existing hardware/software environment was fully paid for. Both mainframes were old and expensive to maintain, costing almost $1 million annually. The hardware/software maintenance cost in the UNIX environment was approximately $60,000 annually.

Application Development and Maintenance

By moving application development and maintenance from terminal-based environments to client-server environments, you can reduce the time required to develop and maintain applications. Reductions have resulted not only from using client-server environments with multi-tasking, multi-window interfaces but also from using more productive development tools, such as I-CASE and 4GLs.

Furthermore, you can employ techniques such as rapid application development to quickly develop applications, get feedback from end-users, and revise applications until they meet the users' requirements. As a result, you can save costs by reducing the time and the number of people required to develop applications. Perhaps more importantly, you can also enable your company to be more responsive to changing business conditions, as illustrated in Figure 4-3.

➤ *WorldCorp of Herndon, Virginia* replaced its traditional development environment with one based on Progress Software's Progress and realized a 300 percent programmer productivity improvement.

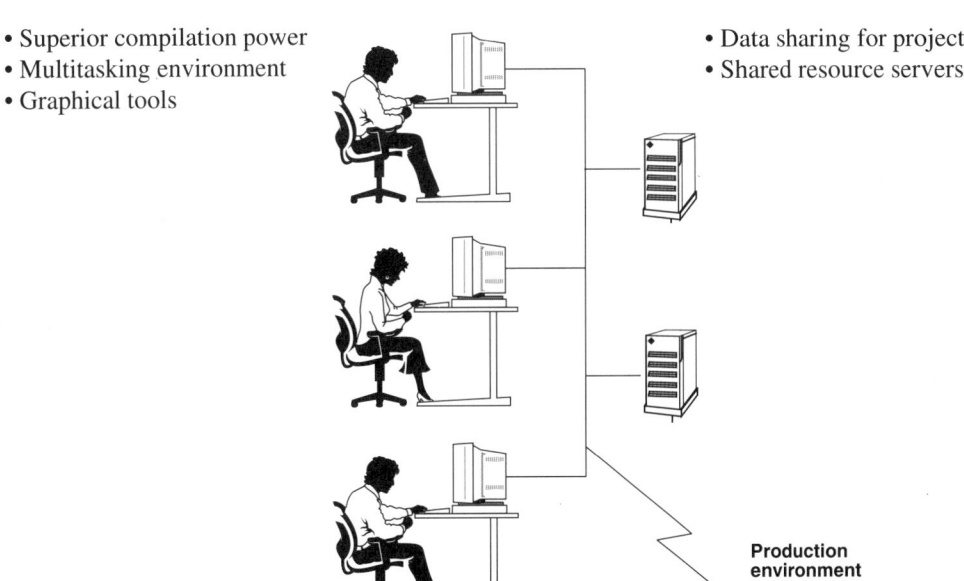

- Superior compilation power
- Multitasking environment
- Graphical tools

- Data sharing for project teams
- Shared resource servers

Production environment

Figure 4-3 Application Development and Maintenance

Business Benefits

Many of companies have justified rightsizing projects based solely on the resulting business benefits, even though in some cases the combined costs of acquiring, moving to, and managing the new environment were greater than staying with the current environment.

Technologies such as client-server computing, graphical user interfaces, multimedia, and imaging are enabling companies to fundamentally change, or re-engineer, the way they do business. The business benefits produced by these changes can be substantial, including better, more timely access to information and better alignment of systems with business processes, as discussed in Chapter 1, "Rightsizing: The Corporate Solution."

Although centralized environments have many advantages, they typically consist of one source of data and processing power that many users must share. Consequently, many users have to wait to access information or rely on batch processing cycles. Critical business decisions are often delayed or are based on incomplete information. Client-server environments provide faster access to information, enabling businesses to make better, more-informed decisions, as illustrated in Figure 4-4.

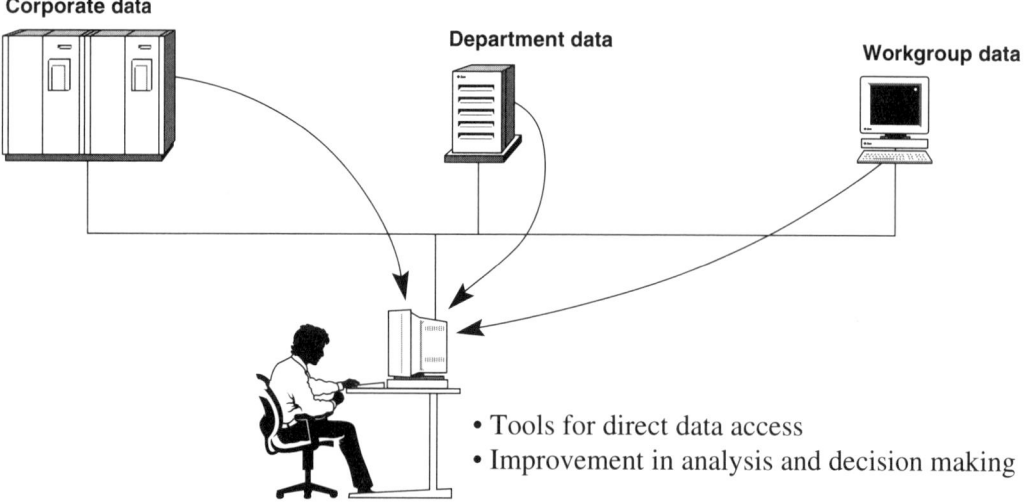

Figure 4-4   Enabling Better, More-informed Decisions

In addition, many business processes do not meet current business needs because they are based on manual procedures or outdated technologies or because business conditions have changed. By re-engineering business processes and applications to take advantage of new technologies and address current needs, businesses have gained competitive advantage, resulting in increased profits.

➤ *Kodak Imaging Services (a wholly owned subsidiary of Eastman Kodak Company) of Rochester, New York* provides a broad range of image and output services. The company revamped its billing statement processes with a SPARCserver-based system and saves $2 million annually. Its invoicing and mailing operations are now integrated and ensure that invoicing occurs no more than 24 hours after an order is received.

System Operation and Management

Managing Centralized Systems

Many companies have established architectures in which a mainframe or a minicomputer is replaced by servers that are still used in a centralized manner. These companies move data and applications to a central server that users access from desktop computers. In such environments, you typically reduce system operation and management costs. Although most mainframe and minicomputer environments are expensive to manage—requiring a large team of operators, system programmers, and support staff—you may be able to manage UNIX systems with less effort for the following reasons:

- Many applications, when moved off a mainframe, are converted from batch to on-line systems, resulting in less batch job management and less printer management because the target device of these new systems is often the display rather than the printer.

- Because disk space on UNIX systems is cheaper, less data has to be moved to tape, resulting in less tape library management.

Many mainframe system management tools are available on UNIX systems, providing traditional data center levels of storage, performance, security, and production or operations management. Furthermore, several tools of this kind have been augmented on UNIX systems to perform these operations more effectively, making it easier for one console operator to manage multiple systems from a single console, for example.

➤ The *Naval Air Warfare Center* saved an average of $709,000 annually in system and operation management costs by replacing its two mainframes with SPARCserver systems.

Managing Distributed Systems

In a distributed environment, many companies are concerned that the cost of system management will increase significantly. However, you will find that the degree to which you plan for a distributed environment and architecture can greatly affect the cost of managing that environment.

For example, many companies today have numerous PCs connected to mainframes. To take full advantage of their PCs, these companies have begun to move both data and applications to them, as illustrated in Figure 4-5.

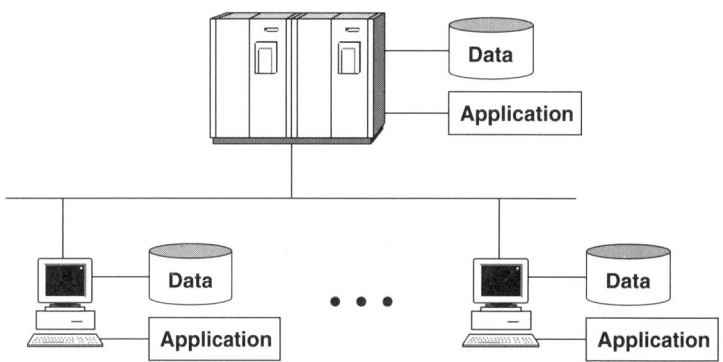

Figure 4-5   Mainframe/PC Architecture

However, doing so creates an architecture that is difficult and expensive to manage. Moving applications to the desktop has enabled users to obtain the benefits of distributed processing—but whenever the applications need to be updated, thousands of nodes, rather than just the mainframe, need to be updated. Moving data to the desktop has improved information access—but whenever data needs to be backed up, backups must occur across hundreds or thousands of nodes. In addition, the security and integrity of data become difficult to manage.

To deal with these issues but to still obtain the benefits of a distributed environment, you can implement an architecture containing UNIX servers. In this architecture, a layer of servers between the mainframe and the desktop allows your company to set up environments consisting of distributed processing with semi-centralized data, as illustrated in Figure 4-6.

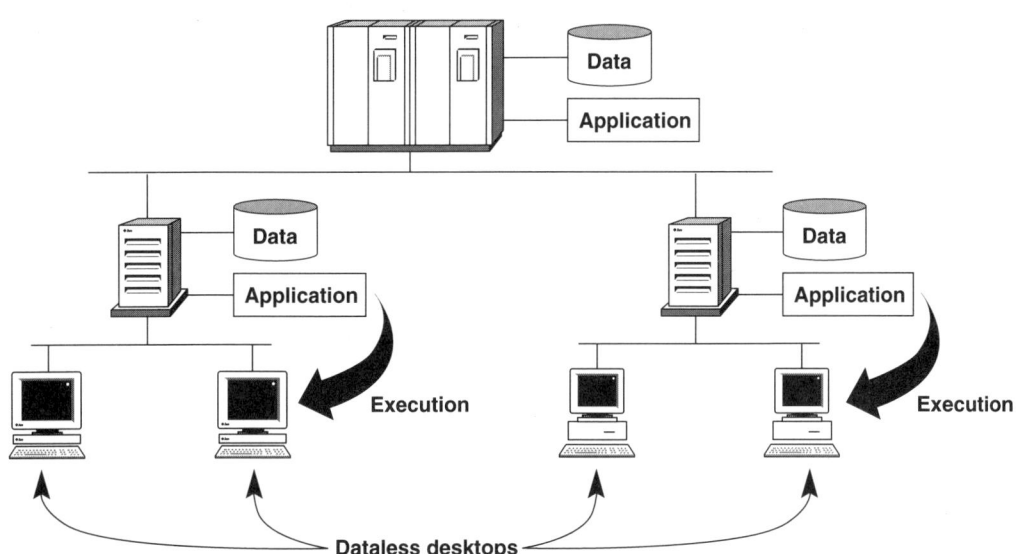

Figure 4-6   UNIX Server Architecture with Dataless Desktops

In this architecture, mainframe data is either replicated or permanently moved to database servers. Connected to these servers are "dataless" desktop systems that contain disk space (often used for swap space) that does not store data. The dedicated database servers enable users to access information without having to compete for limited mainframe cycles. At the same time, the cost of managing and securing the data does not increase significantly because the data, although no longer in just one location, is still centralized on a limited number of servers, thereby simplifying such functions as backup.

Applications in this architecture are typically executed at the desktop level to take full advantage of the processing power on the desktop. However, the application binaries are stored at the server level, thereby reducing the number of update points when a new version of the application becomes available. Many studies on the total cost of ownership of client-server environments attribute a large cost to the time end-users spend managing their systems. In this architecture, system management is performed at the server-level by administrators, not at the desktop level by end-users.

➤ *Sun Microsystems, Inc. of Mountain View, California* moved more than 100 applications from a centralized mainframe to a distributed network consisting of 222 SPARCserver systems and reduced data center management and operations staff from 65 to 37. The company's network now consists of more than 3,000 servers and 23,000 workstations at a total cost of ownership that ranges from $3500 to $6500 per seat.

When not properly designed, distributed environments can be difficult and expensive to maintain and manage. However, by planning for distributed environments and by effectively designing system architectures, you can manage the costs associated with running a distributed environment. In addition, numerous products are now available for distributed systems management, performing such functions as distributed backups, job scheduling, and security enforcement. Choosing the right products can also reduce the cost of managing a distributed environment. (See Appendix G, "Recommended Reading," for more information.)

Transition Costs

Because you need to achieve a net return either through cost savings or business benefits to justify a rightsizing project, your next questions may be:

- How much return can my company expect?
- How long does it take?
- What investment is required?

In other words, what is the cost/benefit curve over the duration of the project?

Initially, while the new system is being implemented or the old system is being moved or re-engineered, costs increase. An investment in the rightsizing project is required during this transition period. Once the new system is completed, costs begin to decrease and savings result. The time required to recoup the initial investment in the project is called the *payback period*. After this time, the resulting savings are the return for the project. Figure 4-7 shows the cost/benefit curve that companies have typically experienced in rightsizing projects.

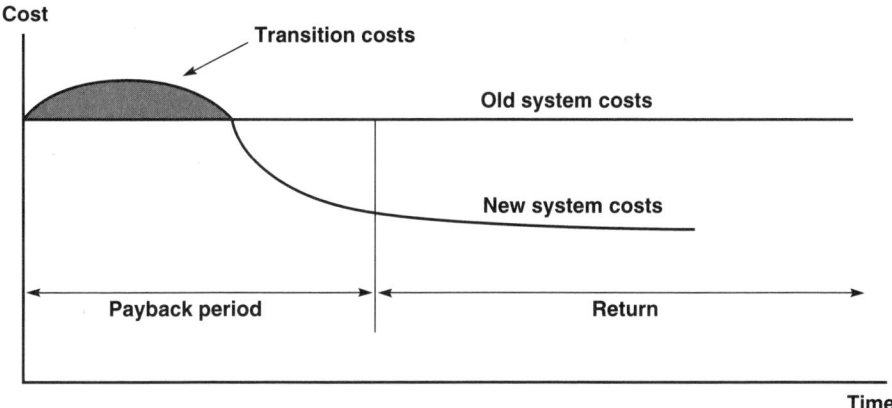

Figure 4-7   Typical Cost/Benefit Curve for a Rightsizing Project

The following is a list (shown graphically in Figure 4-8) of the major transition costs for which you need to plan and manage:

- New hardware/software acquisitions
- Removal/disposal of old equipment
- Application migration/redevelopment
- Skills training and user retraining
- Parallel operations

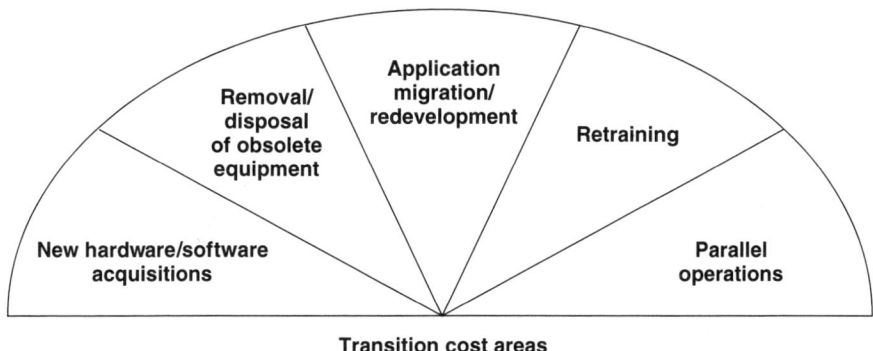

Figure 4-8   Transition Costs

Managing the size of the costs during the transition period is critical to achieving the desired return, especially for initial projects when you are still trying to gain internal acceptance for new technologies. One of the keys to effectively managing transition costs is to wisely select which applications will be rightsized and which system will be removed (in the case of system replacement).

When selecting an initial rightsizing project, you can use the payback period as one of the key criteria In other words, you usually want to select projects with shorter payback periods initially to demonstrate results quickly (in general, companies tend to select initial projects with a payback period of 6 to 18 months). Once the first project has proved successful, your company then may choose to undertake longer-term projects.

New Hardware/Software Acquisitions

This transition cost includes the expense of purchasing or leasing all the new hardware and software that would not have been required in the old environment. The new equipment either replaces existing systems, off-loads them, or runs new applications. The lease and purchase costs of hardware and software based on UNIX technology are significantly less than the cost of mainframe or minicomputer hardware and software. Although these costs may be sizable if a substantial amount of equipment is purchased, they are typically much less than the cost of comparable mainframe or minicomputers.

Furthermore, the scalability of UNIX systems also reduces costs. A pilot application can be implemented at little cost for a small system. The same application can then be deployed on a larger system without change. Then, as business conditions change, systems can be upgraded or downgraded, or systems can be added or removed, at small incremental costs.

Removal/Disposal of Old Equipment

System replacement involves the expense of removing the old equipment and disposing of it. This transition cost is incurred from either terminating a mainframe or mini-computer lease early or from the difference between the book value and market value for the equipment. In most cases, the book value exceeds the price a company can get by reselling the system on the open market, potentially resulting in a sizable net loss.

Good candidates for replacement are systems late in a lease cycle. Significant savings can result by replacing these leased systems. Because application migration or redevelopment can take 6 to 18 months, systems with a comparable amount of lease time remaining are the best candidates to avoid fees for early lease termination.

➤ *WorldCorp of Herndon, Virginia* replaced a leased IBM 4381 with purchased SPARCserver systems, reducing its annual hardware cost from $246,000–$270,000 to $42,000–$65,000 and its annual software cost from $126,000–$237,000 to $35,000–$87,000.

Other good replacement candidates are systems that were purchased and are either almost or fully depreciated. A fully depreciated system has no net loss between book value and market value. Whatever residual value the system has can help offset the cost of acquiring the new hardware and software. Replacing systems that have recently been purchased is typically not an attractive option because of the large remaining book value of the system.

Application Migration/Redevelopment

Another important transition cost is the expense of moving or redeveloping applications, a cost that can vary widely, depending on the size of the application and the effort required to move it.

The best applications for migration are those that require a minimal effort to move: in other words, applications that were written using portable technologies so that the amount of code that needs to be rewritten is minimized. Examples include package applications that run on both mainframe/minicomputer and UNIX platforms, as discussed in Chapter 3, "Rightsizing Opportunities." Other examples include in-house applications written with portable technologies such as relational databases, 4GLs, and even applications written with COBOL/CICS or RPG.

The best applications for redevelopment are those that no longer meet current business needs and would benefit from being re-engineered. In addition to reducing computing costs, application re-engineering typically produces increased business benefits that often far exceed the reduction in computing costs.

Applications that already meet business needs and will need to be rewritten just to move them to a lower-cost platform usually are *not* good candidates *unless* their redeployment is part of a larger project. For example, if six applications need to be moved from a mainframe to replace it and one or two of the applications need to be redeveloped to move them, this redevelopment might be cost-effective within the context of the overall project. Otherwise, the cost of redeveloping the application often offsets the savings that result from running it on a lower-cost platform.

Skills Training and User Retraining

This transition cost involves training programmers and operational staff to use new technologies and retraining end-users to use new applications. It can also include the costs of consultants used to assess current environments and plan for or design new environments. If not managed properly, these costs can also escalate in a rightsizing project. However, techniques for managing such costs have been identified.

A common technique is to start with an initial project in which a small team is retrained and then implements a rightsizing project. Once the initial project is completed, companies select other projects to follow. Members of the initial project team are dispersed and seeded into other teams to ensure the success of each following project. Some of the companies in our study believe it is also critical to hire outside experts in key technology areas, allowing inside staff to focus on the business issues. In such situations, it is important to allow time at the end of the project for transferring technology before the experts leave.

➤ *WorldCorp* paid a VAR $42,000 to perform the initial installation of and conversion to its client-server environment. Using the VAR's expertise, WorldCorp completed the initial phase of its rightsizing project within six months and achieved payback in just over a year.

Another technique is to initially move applications "as is" to lessen end-user retraining. Over time, the applications are re-engineered to take advantage of technologies such as graphical user interfaces. However, even as the applications are being changed, the new interfaces typically minimize retraining costs because the applications are now easier to use and learn, making it simpler to retrain current personnel and train new personnel in the future. (For additional ways to minimize retraining costs, see Chapter 5, "The Rightsizing Process.")

Parallel Operations

In an IS environment, any migration includes a period of final acceptance testing in which the new system runs in parallel with the old system. During this period, the hardware and software maintenance costs and the system management costs for the new system are an additional, transitional expense.

In general, parallel operation costs appear to be small relative to costs for a whole project. Operations usually run in parallel for a few months, at most. Furthermore, because the hardware and software maintenance costs for the new system are low, the incremental cost for maintaining a second system usually is also low.

Handling Transition Costs

In any rightsizing project, costs initially increase during the investment/transition period, and you should plan for this increase. Through careful application selection and project planning, however, these costs can be minimized and payback periods can be reduced.

Summary

This chapter has examined the major costs and benefits that need to be assessed in rightsizing projects. Economic analysis is useful not only for justifying a rightsizing strategy but also for selecting initial projects. To make this decision, most companies examine both payback period and return on investment. For the first project, consider weighting payback period higher to demonstrate results and gain buy-in quickly. If you want to perform an economic analysis of your own potential rightsizing projects, see Appendix C, "Cost/Benefit Model," for a cost/benefit model that you can use as a framework.

The rest of this chapter presents case studies that examine the total cost of ownership for three companies that have rightsized applications. These case studies are examples of the different economic objectives outlined in this chapter:

- Departmental Cost Reduction
  The Risk Management department of Bank One Columbus moved applications off the mainframe, thereby reducing its annual data center chargebacks.

- Data Center Cost Reduction
  WorldCorp replaced a mainframe, thereby reducing its total cost of computing.

- Profit Improvement
  ADCO re-engineered its information systems, thereby reducing its operating costs and increasing its profits.

Each case study compares the new system costs to the old system costs and identifies the major costs and benefits incurred in each year of the project. While the primary purpose of the first two case studies is to discuss how these companies have reduced computing costs, these companies have also achieved business benefits from rightsizing. Where applicable, these benefits are listed as well.

4

Case Study: Departmental Cost Reduction

Banc One

Banc One (headquartered in Columbus, Ohio) is the twelfth largest bank holding company in the United States and the second most profitable bank holding company in the world. Banc One provides a wide variety of services, including branch banking, mortgages, loans, and credit cards.

The Risk Management Department of Bank One Columbus (a subsidiary of Banc One) uses an Informix database to create a credit history of each credit card account from account origin to current status. Information from multiple corporate mainframes and outside sources is periodically transferred to the database. Dedicated to the department's needs, this newly created database contains the information necessary to assess account risk and report on profitability trends. This project marked the first time a system so critical to a department's operation was owned by, and operated within, that department. One of the biggest challenges the project team faced was overcoming management concerns about making such a dramatic and sudden change in the department's computing architecture.

Note – See Chapter 3, "Rightsizing Opportunities," for detailed information about the previous and rightsized environments of Bank One Columbus.

Cost Analysis

In early 1991, the Risk Management department was faced with rapidly escalating allocation costs commensurate with the rapid growth in the number of credit card accounts the department had to analyze. For example, from 1990 to 1991, the number of accounts grew from 2.2 million to 3 million. In 1991, the department's data processing budget of $2.17 million consisted of:

- $2 million in mainframe chargebacks to run reports

- $80,000 in chargebacks for programmers to write, set up, and run the reports

- $90,000 for temporary staff members to re-enter the data from the MIS-generated paper reports into the PC LAN system that electronically delivered information to analysts, statisticians, and management personnel in the department

The department expected the annual cost of supporting the basic reporting needs to grow to $3.27 million over the next five years. The volume of reports was expected to triple over this period, accounting for the growth in data entry and application programming costs. Table 4-1 summarizes the projected costs under the old system.

Table 4-1   Old System Costs

Old System Costs	$K				
	Year 1	Year 2	Year 3	Year 4	Year 5
MIS Chargebacks	2,000	2,200	2,400	2,600	2,800
Data Entry	90	135	180	215	250
Hardware & System Software	0	0	0	0	0
Hardware Maintenance	0	0	0	0	0
Application Software	80	120	160	190	220
Application Software Maintenance	0	0	0	0	0
End-User Training & Support	0	0	0	0	0
Operations & Systems Management	0	0	0	0	0
Outside Services	0	0	0	0	0
Staff Skills Training	0	0	0	0	0
Total	$2,170	$2,455	$2,740	$3,005	$3,270
Cumulative Total	$2,170	$4,625	$7,365	$10,370	$13,640

These data processing costs were placing an excessive burden on the department's operating budget and did not include any provision for the credit history database, a key element in enabling the risk assessment the department needed. Remaining with the status quo was not a financially feasible option.

Table 4-2 summarizes the costs associated with the new system.

Table 4-2   New System Costs

New System Costs	$K				
	Year 1	Year 2	Year 3	Year 4	Year 5
MIS Chargebacks	60	60	60	60	60
Data Entry	0	0	0	0	0
Hardware & System Software	192	457	60	470	250
Hardware Maintenance	0	60	49	62	65
Application Software	35	35	0	80	50
Application Software Maintenance	30	60	60	75	75
End-User Training & Support	0	0	0	0	0
Operations & Systems Management	0	0	0	0	0
Outside Services	10	10	10	10	10
Staff Skills Training	5	10	20	10	10
Total	$332	$692	$259	$767	$520
Cumulative Total	$332	$1,024	$1,283	$2,050	$2,570

Note: All purchases are fully expensed in the year in which they are incurred.

The hardware expenditures in the first and second years represent the UNIX workstations and servers that formed the basis of the new system. A major upgrade to the system was planned for the fourth year: adding a SPARCcenter 2000, a SPARCserver 10, eight SPARCclassic workstations, and 150 gigabytes of disk storage.

In addition to the hardware, the department acquired Informix-4GL, SAS, and Wingz. In the second, fourth, and fifth years, the licenses for these packages were expanded to accommodate growth in the number of users and applications.

The existing departmental staff developed the new database as well as the new reports without the creation of an IS support group. They also have provided all the ongoing application maintenance and system administration and support, so no additional staff had to be hired for this project.

The department spends an average of $11,000 per year on staff skills training. The amount of training required has been minimal because many staff members taught themselves how to use the new software tools. An outside consultant assisted in addressing technical issues during the transition and provides ongoing support backup. This service costs $10,000 a year.

The annual payments to the central MIS organization were reduced significantly, from $2 million to $60,000. The remaining $60,000 charge is for data extracts from the mainframe databases used to update the Informix database running on the SPARCserver 670MP system.

Table 4-3 summarizes the differences in costs between the old and new systems. Items with positive numbers reflect net cost savings in that category; numbers in parentheses show where costs increased as a result of the transition.

Table 4-3 Comparative Costs

Cost Saving with New System	$K				
	Year 1	Year 2	Year 3	Year 4	Year 5
MIS Chargebacks	1,940	2,140	2,340	2,540	2,740
Data Entry	90	135	180	215	250
Hardware & System Software	(192)	(457)	(60)	(470)	(250)
Hardware Maintenance	0	(60)	(49)	(62)	(65)
Application Software	45	85	160	110	170
Application Software Maintenance	(30)	(60)	(60)	(75)	(75)
End-User Training & Support	0	0	0	0	0
Operations & Systems Management	0	0	0	0	0
Outside Services	(10)	(10)	(10)	(10)	(10)
Staff Skills Training	(5)	(10)	(20)	(10)	(10)
Total Savings	$1,838	$1,763	$2,481	$2,238	$2,750
Cumulative Total Savings	$1,838	$3,601	$6,082	$8,320	$11,070

Summary

The new hardware and software investments have been more than offset by the dramatic reduction in mainframe chargebacks. On average, the Risk Management department is saving more than $2 million per year by moving to the new system. Over five years, the department will save more than $11 million in operating expenses by moving its reporting and analytical applications to the UNIX client-server system. In the process, the department also eliminated the need to hire temporary workers to perform data re-entry. Using the bank's internal discount rate of 6 percent, the net present value of the project's savings over five years is $9,214,000.

By choosing an initial application to off-load that was portable and inexpensive to move, the department achieved payback within a year.

Furthermore, the department successfully built a credit history database and is now performing the types of risk and profitability analysis on credit accounts that would have been impossible on the old system. Through better risk management, the company is saving more than $6 million annually, as discussed in Chapter 3, "Rightsizing Opportunities."

Case Study: Data Center Cost Reduction

WorldCorp

WorldCorp is a $400-million air transportation and transaction processing enterprise based in Herndon, Virginia. It consists of three companies, including World Airways, a leading provider of air transportation for commercial and government customers, and US Order, a developer of patented automated ordering services.

In early 1991, WorldCorp decided to rightsize its financial system by moving away from the mainframe to a client-server environment based on UNIX technology.

Note – See Chapter 3, "Rightsizing Opportunities," for detailed information about the previous and rightsized environments of WorldCorp.

Cost Analysis

In assessing whether to pursue rightsizing, WorldCorp first considered what it would cost to continue using the IBM 4381 system it had been leasing. WorldCorp built a cash flow model to evaluate these operating costs in detail over five years, which revealed the following costs for system requirements:

- Purchase price at the end of their lease, respectively, would be $147,000 for the mainframe and $9000 for the printer.

- Upgrading the network in the first year would cost $15,180 for hardware and $5200 for software.

- Upgrading from BTAM to VTAM would cost an additional $1500 per month.

- To accommodate planned growth, a second minicomputer would need to be purchased in the second year at a cost of $29,000, and an additional license for inventory-control software would cost $45,000.

Table 4-4 shows the impact of these transactions coupled with the ongoing costs of operating the existing system.

Table 4-4   Old System Costs

Old System Costs	$K				
	Year 1	Year 2	Year 3	Year 4	Year 5
Hardware	246	246	260	260	270
Hardware Maintenance	125	126	131	139	141
System Software & Tools	129	86	90	95	99
Application Software	108	109	107	40	27
Software Maintenance	166	174	183	192	202
End-User Training & Support	2	2	2	2	2
Communications & Networking	11	12	14	20	20
Operations & Systems Management	0	0	0	0	0
Outside Services	10	8	0	0	0
Staff Skills Training	9	11	13	15	15
Total	$806	$774	$800	$759	$776
Cumulative Total	$806	$1,580	$2,380	$3,139	$3,915

Note: This table is a summary of a more detailed set of tables used in the original analysis. Cost figures represent the net annualized expenditures in each category. All purchases have been depreciated over a five-year period.

WorldCorp also evaluated the acquisition costs of the new UNIX system and its ongoing operation and maintenance costs.

Table 4-5 depicts the acquisition and five-year ownership costs for the new UNIX system. Years 1 and 2 represent actual costs incurred, with the remaining years representing anticipated or projected costs.

Table 4-5   New System Costs

New System Costs	$K				
	Year 1	Year 2	Year 3	Year 4	Year 5
Hardware	42	61	65	65	65
Hardware Maintenance	21	41	36	37	39
System Software & Tools	1	1	7	8	9
Application Software	34	34	78	78	78
Software Maintenance	26	27	51	53	56
End-User Training & Support	6	2	2	2	2
Communications & Networking	12	12	14	16	16
Operations & Systems Management	8	19	12	13	14
Outside Services	52	6	0	0	0
Staff Skills Training	23	25	20	22	24
Total	$225	$219	$285	$294	$303
Cumulative Total	$225	$444	$729	$1,023	$1,326

Note: This table is a summary of a much more detailed set of tables used in the original analysis. Cost figures represent the net annualized expenditures in each category. All purchases have been depreciated over a five-year period.

A review of these comparative costs showed that significant savings in hardware and software would be realized, including:

- The low annual depreciation cost of the new hardware versus the high annual lease cost of the old system

- Lower cost of the application software

- Reduced annual hardware and software maintenance costs

These savings amounted to $650,000 in the first year. Table 4-6 shows the difference between the old system and the new system, illustrating the net effect on cash flow of moving to the UNIX solution. Items with positive numbers reflect net cost savings; numbers in parentheses show where costs increased because of the transition.

Table 4-6   Comparative Costs

Cost Saving with New System	$K				
	Year 1	Year 2	Year 3	Year 4	Year 5
Hardware	204	185	195	195	205
Hardware Maintenance	104	85	95	102	102
System Software & Tools	128	85	83	87	90
Application Software	74	75	29	(38)	(51)
Software Maintenance	140	147	132	139	146
End-User Training & Support	(4)	0	0	0	0
Communications & Networking	(1)	0	0	0	4
Operations & Systems Management	(8)	(10)	(12)	(13)	(14)
Outside Services	(42)	2	0	0	0
Staff Skills Training	(14)	(14)	(7)	(7)	(9)
Total Savings	$581	$555	$515	$465	$473
Cumulative Total Savings	$581	$1,136	$1,651	$2,116	$2,589

However, to achieve these savings, WorldCorp had to make incremental investments in training, support, outside services, and applications software.

For example, the company paid the VAR $42,000 to perform the initial installation and conversion. This project included making the necessary enhancement and changes to the Financial Dynamics product, converting all the WorldCorp files and historical data, downloading the converted files and data into the new system, and writing the custom software that would be used as the front-end to the WorldCorp payroll system. The project was accomplished within six months.

In addition, over the five-year span of the project, WorldCorp has allocated $51,000 to retrain the COBOL programming staff in the new Progress 4GL/RDBMS environment. Operations and system management requirements have grown slightly, averaging only an additional $12,000 per year. Application software costs are projected to increase in years 4 and 5, reflecting additional applications that would not have been included in the old system. In the first year, these transition costs amounted to $69,000, reducing the operating cost improvement in that year to $581,000.

Summary

WorldCorp replaced its leased IBM mainframe with a client-server network based on UNIX servers and PCs. Over the project's five-year life span, total savings are expected to amount to $2,589,000. As a result, WorldCorp is accomplishing one of its primary business objectives for the project: substantial savings in operating costs over the old system. Furthermore, as noted in Chapter 3, "Rightsizing Opportunities," WorldCorp achieved significant business benefits as well from rightsizing.

4

Case Study: Profit Improvement

ADCO

Headquartered in Dusseldorf, Germany, Attwoods Dixi Corporation (ADCO) is a subsidiary of Attwoods, one of the world's leading international waste management companies. With its portable sanitation business, ADCO serves more than 90 percent of the German population. ADCO also provides portable accommodation and waste management, which includes disposal of residential, commercial, and industrial waste.

ADCO's information systems were unable to keep up with the company's business requirements, which included automation of certain business processes, installation of a central network, decentralization of operations, and development of new applications. After determining that the existing computing environment would not solve its business problems, ADCO decided to re-engineer its information systems by moving to an open computing environment. In doing so, it would gain independence from hardware suppliers by having one common operating system running across multiple platforms.

Environment Prior to Rightsizing

ADCO's computing environment consisted of 2 IBM AS/400s in the corporate data center in Dusseldorf and 25 IBM System/36s in 21 local offices and 4 regional headquarters. Some 200 users accessed these systems through terminals. The System/36s were not networked to the AS/400s. In addition, ADCO had more than 140 standalone PCs. The data center supported numerous applications, including order processing, fixed assets, payroll, finance and accounting, stockkeeping, and CAD. Figure 4-9 illustrates this environment.

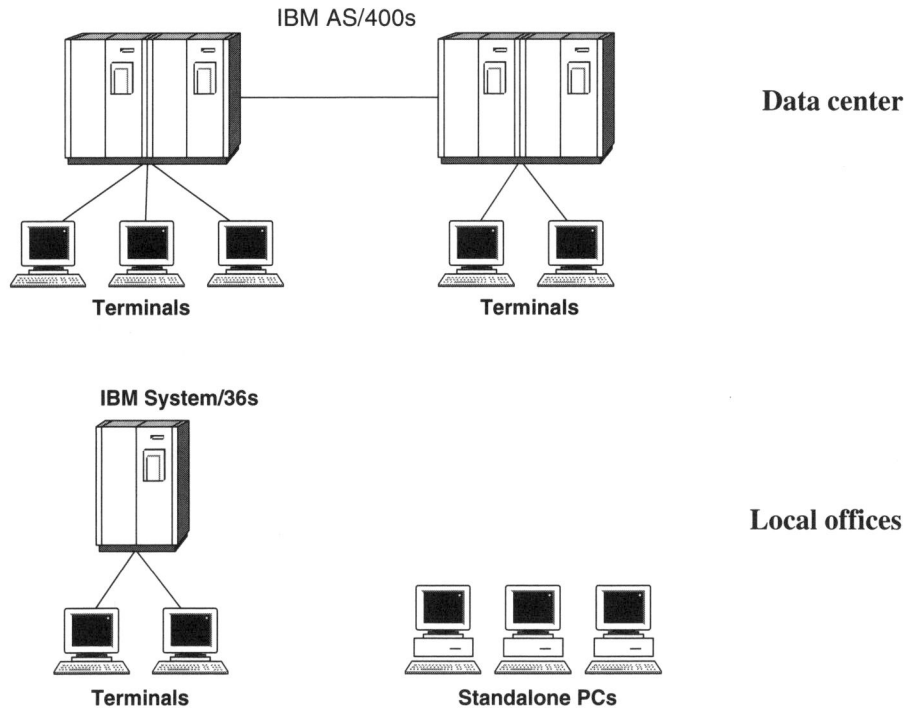

Figure 4-9   Environment Prior to Rightsizing

This system not only failed to meet ADCO's needs, but it also presented the company with the following challenges:

- Although ADCO was growing, the current system lacked the flexibility and scalability to grow with it.

- The company was attempting to decentralize its operations, yet it lacked a central network to communicate information effectively between corporate headquarters and the local offices. As a result, many business processes had to be performed manually.

- To make up for the absence of a network, the company would need to purchase courier services to transport diskettes from one location to another.

- The current applications, which were more than five years old, were not meeting the company's business requirements.

ADCO estimated the investment necessary to modify its current systems to address these problems and determined that it would be excessive. The application software investment would be substantial, and maintenance costs would be high. In light of the business problems its then-current system presented and considering the high cost and low payoff of modifying it, ADCO concluded that it had to replace its system and invest in a new one.

Rightsizing Solution

ADCO decided to rightsize by moving to a client-server environment. Its new data center contains two SPARCserver 1000 systems running Informix RDBMSs; each local office has a SPARCserver 10 Model 41 or a SPARCserver 20 Model 61. In the data center, two SPARCstation 10 systems are used for application development and system administration. The company plans to replace the existing AS/400s and System/36s with these Sun servers. The PCs will remain for desktop use and will be connected to the servers. Figure 4-10 illustrates the new environment.

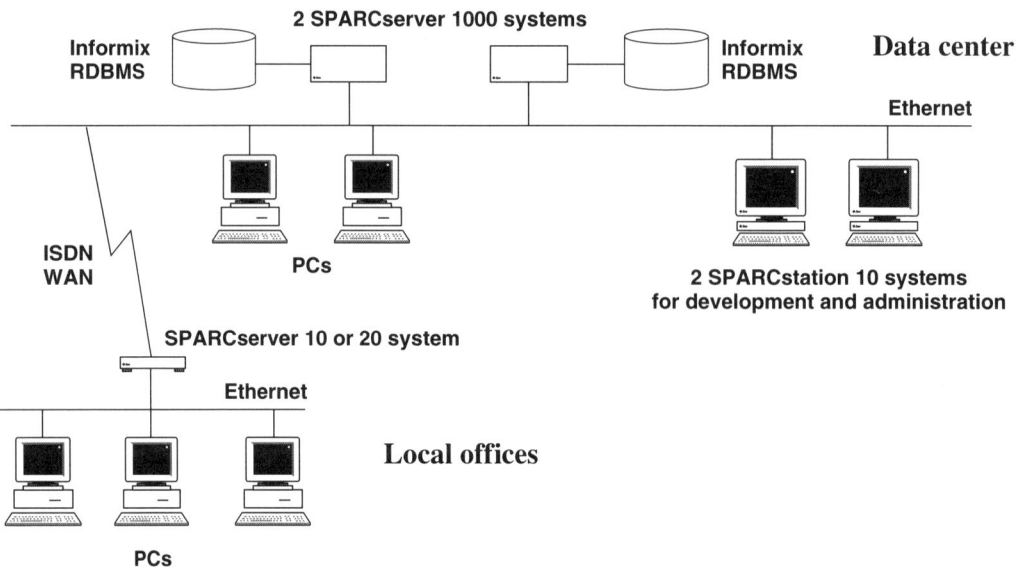

Figure 4-10   Rightsized Environment

ADCO is implementing its rightsizing project in three phases and expects that it will take two and a half years to complete. The first phase, lasting one year, will consist of the following milestones:

- Leasing the new SPARCserver and SPARCstation systems

- Building a wide-area network based on ISDN to connect the local offices to the data center and constructing local area networks based on Ethernet to connect the PCs to the Sun servers

- Installing the SunNet Manager™ software to manage the network

- Developing and installing a central database, using the Informix RDBMS

- Installing the corporate accounting system running against the Informix database

Ultimately, the new environment will run all of ADCO's business lines and integrate the company's applications into a comprehensive information system.

Cost Analysis

ADCO's ownership costs for its old system, presented in Table 4-7 on page 124, include:

- DM 292,000 per year in hardware ownership and maintenance costs, consisting of DM 232,000 in annual lease, depreciation, and maintenance expenses for the AS/400s and DM 60,000 in annual purchase expenses for other equipment

- DM 150,000 to 200,000 annually for software maintenance, covering support fees for package software and staff to maintain in-house applications

- DM 95,000 to 108,000 per year to operate and manage the system

- DM 40,000 each year, beginning in the second year, for end-user training on new releases of finance and accounting software

- DM 60,000 annually to purchase courier services to transport disks between locations

Table 4-7   Old System Costs

Old System Costs	DM in Thousands	
	Year 1	Year 2
Application Software	0	0
Software Maintenance	150	200
Networking & Database	0	0
Operations	95	108
End-User Training & Support	0	40
Staff Skills Training	0	0
Transportation	60	60
Installation & Project Management	0	0
Total Savings	DM 597	DM 700
Cumulative Total Savings	DM 597	DM 1,297

Table 4-7 covers only two years because staying with the AS/400s was not considered an option; the system would still contain many shortcomings even after substantial modifications. Although ADCO did not formally quantify the cost of modifying the AS/400s, the company estimated that these modifications would be three times as expensive as implementing the new UNIX system. Hence, it was clear to ADCO that the AS/400s needed to be replaced.

Table 4-8 on page 125 shows the costs of moving to and operating the new system. These costs include:

- Annual lease and maintenance fees of DM 80,000 to 228,000 for the new UNIX equipment

- DM 1.3 million over the life of the project to purchase package application software and to develop in-house applications. To handle the new set of skills needed for building the new system, ADCO hired five new staff members and an outside consultant to assist in the system implementation

- DM 85,000 over two years for staff training

- DM 323,000 for communications, networking, and database software

- One-time cost of DM 50,000 to retrain end users on the new applications and DM 30,000 to install the new system and project management

Table 4-8   New System Costs

New System Costs	DM in Thousands				
	Year 1	Year 2	Year 3	Year 4	Year 5
Hardware & Maintenance	175	228	130	80	80
Application Software	750	400	150	0	0
Software Maintenance	10	36	36	36	36
Networking & Database	223	70	0	0	0
Operations	10	10	10	10	10
End-User Training & Support	30	15	5	0	0
Staff Skills Training	48	37	0	0	0
WAN & ISDN	30	80	100	100	100
Installation & Project Management	30	0	0	0	0
Total	DM 1,306	DM 876	DM 431	DM 226	DM 226
Cumulative Total	DM 1,306	DM 2,182	DM 2,613	DM 2,839	DM 3,065

In addition to these costs, ADCO has to continue paying to operate the old system during the two-and-a-half-year transition period. During this time, ADCO will spend more each year than it did previously, even though system operation costs have dropped to DM 10,000 annually because the local offices can now be remotely managed from a central location.

Summary

ADCO justified its re-engineering project not on the basis of cost savings but, rather, on the basis of these considerations:

- The application advancements and business benefits it achieved would not have been possible with the old system.

- Modifying the old system would have cost much more than implementing the new one.

However, when the project is completed, ADCO's information systems will better match its business requirements but cost substantially less to operate, thereby improving ADCO's overall profitability.

≡ 4

Rightsizing for Corporate Survival

The Rightsizing Process 5 ≣

Once you have identified rightsizing opportunities and justified your rightsizing strategy, the next step is to begin your rightsizing project. An extensive study of rightsized information systems identifies many common processes and best practices.

During our studies, we also uncovered many lessons learned or "best practices" of rightsizing. Ranging from the general to the specific, these practices encompass strategies (such as involving people early in the process) to tactics (such as the targeted use of outside consultants). Throughout the chapter, we have included many of these practices, highlighted in the following manner:

╲╲

Best practices are noted in this manner.

╲╲

Phases of Rightsizing

Table 5-1 on page 128 summarizes a six-phase process followed by many companies while rightsizing, delineated in Table 5-2 on page 129. Each phase is discussed in detail throughout this chapter. This process is intended to be generally applicable to most rightsizing projects. However, you will need to adapt and modify it to meet the unique requirements of your specific project.

Table 5-1   *Six Phases of Rightsizing*

Phase	Description
I—Establishing a Rightsizing Vision	The company identifies the project's objectives, scope, responsibilities, and resources. An informal team drawn from management, IS, and end users creates a rightsizing project plan and communicates it throughout the IS department and to end users. The plan contains major tasks, target dates, and primary deliverables.
II—Assessing Current Applications or Processes	The company assembles a project team and then evaluates scaling and business process re-engineering options. If the project involves scaling, the team assesses current applications to determine portability. If the objective is to re-engineer the business process, the team documents and analyzes current methods. In all cases, the team gathers data through interviews, current documentation reviews, and resource measurements.
III—Defining a New IS Model or Process	The project team develops alternatives for the application systems or business processes. Brainstorming sessions generate ideas, which are then analyzed. The team examines viable alternatives, develops prototypes, and performs cost/benefit analyses. At the end of this phase, the team has identified, evaluated, and modeled the new application environment or business process and eliminated alternatives.
IV—Establishing a Migration Plan	The project team prepares a migration plan, which covers all issues related to implementing the new IS model or business process. The plan considers parallel systems, quality assurance testing, resources, training, and milestones.
V—Implementing the New IS Model or Process	The new IS model or business process is brought on line. If an application is rightsized to reduce costs, the primary focus is on tuning performance and validating the results with the current systems. If a new business process is being implemented, the main focus is on conforming with the redesigned process specifications and achieving performance objectives.
VI—Evaluating and Assessing the New IS Model or Process	Once the new IS model or business process is implemented, the project team performs a broad-based review to identify new opportunities and lessons learned and to measure the achievement of objectives and end-user satisfaction.

Table 5-2   Six Phases of Rightsizing Diagram

Managing the Rightsizing Process

• Communication		• Documentation		• Ongoing Review Against Objectives	
I: Establish project vision	**II: Assess current applications**	**III: Define new IS model or process**	**IV: Establish migration plans**	**V: Implement new IS model or process**	**VI: Evaluate and assess**
• Vision statement - Business objectives - Project scope - Architecture objectives - Measures • Project team • Project plan - Resources - Responsibilities - Task plan Project practices	Scaling • Application Assessment - Architecture - Usage - Costs - Grading • Identify entry application Re-engineering • Business process assessment • Identify entry process • Identify entry application	• IS architecture - Application architecture - Server standards - Desktop standards - Network standards - Integration w/existing systems Re-engineering • New business process - Industry best practices • Prototype	• Migration plan - Milestones /time lines - Responsibilities - Budgets - Parallel systems plan - Dependencies - Success factors • QA strategy • Training plan • Mainframe role defined	Scaling • Bring on line • Tuning and performance • Validate results • User acceptance • System cutover Re-engineering - Bring on line - Conformance to specifications - Meet objectives "Tweak" process	• Post implementation preview - Achievement of objectives - Lessons learned - User satisfaction - Projected ROI • Opportunities for further rightsizing • Disband

5

Managing the Rightsizing Process

In any rightsizing project, you should devote considerable attention to managing the rightsizing process during each of the six major phases. The three key process-management elements are communication, documentation, and ongoing review against objectives.

Communication

Since rightsizing has a profound impact on any organization, it is important to maintain open and direct communication with your entire enterprise. Effective communications set expectations, diffuse potential problems, and permit potential problems to be raised and addressed in a timely manner.

> *"Implementing change requires extensive communication. The communications goal is to get the entire business to understand that you are changing the way you do business. And to prove to them that it will be better."*

The communications hierarchy should consist of four separate groups, as illustrated in Figure 5-1.

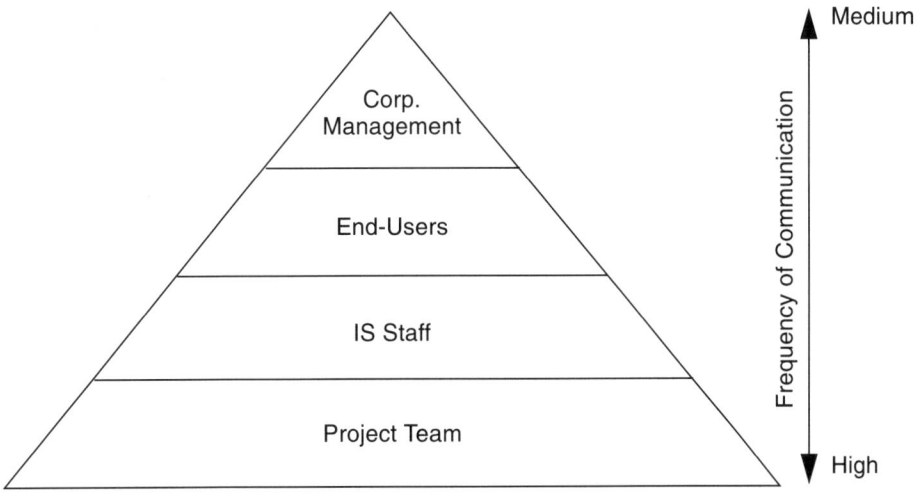

Figure 5-1   Communication Model

Corporate Management

Corporate management's support is critical to your rightsizing effort. Project teams need to keep senior management fully informed of the progress being made and issues encountered. Often, routine working sessions with senior management can be much more effective than status reports. A project sponsor, typically the CIO or VP/MIS, can provide valuable support to the team from top management's perspective.

In addition, corporate management needs to be kept informed about project costs and capital requirements. These requests are most effectively handled when senior management has been kept apprised of the various issues being raised.

Many companies stress the importance of education and its difference from training.

"We train the staff on the new technologies and processes, but we educate our executives so that they can understand how the business and its processes need to change."

End-Users

Typically, users are most directly affected by rightsizing projects. If your organization undertakes business process re-engineering, end-users will provide the detailed information required for the project and often identify significant shortcomings of current processes.

Get your users involved with the business and functional specifications early because they know the changing business requirements very well. One tactic is to teach users the processes IS uses to translate the business needs into technology requirements and functional specifications.

IS Staff

IS staff members can feel threatened by a rightsizing effort. Through consistent and clear communication, effective project teams can diminish that perceived threat in varying degrees. It is important to communicate with the *entire* IS staff early in the process.

> *"For us, gaining a 'united' IS management team was critical. Once we had that, we could address the concerns of executive or IS staff, with a united posture and commitment."*
>
> *"Allocate plenty of time up-front for communicating with the IS staff. Key concerns for them are understanding the business issues that are driving the need for change. They also need to understand the management's commitment to change."*
>
> *"Include the mainframe IS staff early in the decision making. They understand the mainframe processing environment and play a key role in translating those needs into a distributed environment."*

Project Team

Strong, open, and effective communication among all members of the project team is essential. Frequent status meetings can ensure that all team members feel fully involved and can participate in effective discussions about issues as they arise.

Documentation

You should establish formal procedures to collect, catalog, and make available the large volume of documentation that is gathered during the project. Many companies have found that is critical to keep documentation (including such obvious items as time lines, acceptance meetings, approvals and key assumptions, and architectures) to track their constant changes in approach and decision during the project life cycle.

Ongoing Review Against Objectives

An ongoing review process should feature open and honest appraisals of real progress made, the impact on milestones and deliverables, schedule slippages, technical problems, and the performance of team members, with corrective action taken when necessary. Share results with corporate management, end-users, and IS staff as appropriate.

Phase I: Establishing a Rightsizing Vision

A set of common questions faces all rightsizing companies at the start of each rightsizing project:

- Why rightsize: to reduce IS costs; to support a business process re-engineering strategy?

- Is the goal to rightsize a single application, all corporate information systems, or something in between?

- How important is an open systems strategy?

- How important is an adaptive systems strategy?

- Will the project entail new technical architectures? If so, can the standards that will support those architectures be established and enforced?

- How will the company establish and communicate its vision?

Establishing a well-defined business vision forces your company to drive its rightsizing initiatives and the expected outcome. Your company should have a vision before putting anything else, including the project team, in place. This vision should identify the project's objectives, scope, responsibilities, and resources. It is the basis for the project plan, which should contain major tasks, target dates, and primary deliverables.

The project plan is typically created by an informal team drawn from management, IS, and end-users, who then communicate the rightsizing plan throughout the IS and end-user communities. Creation of the vision—and project plan—is a methodical process with several key steps, as illustrated in Figure 5-2.

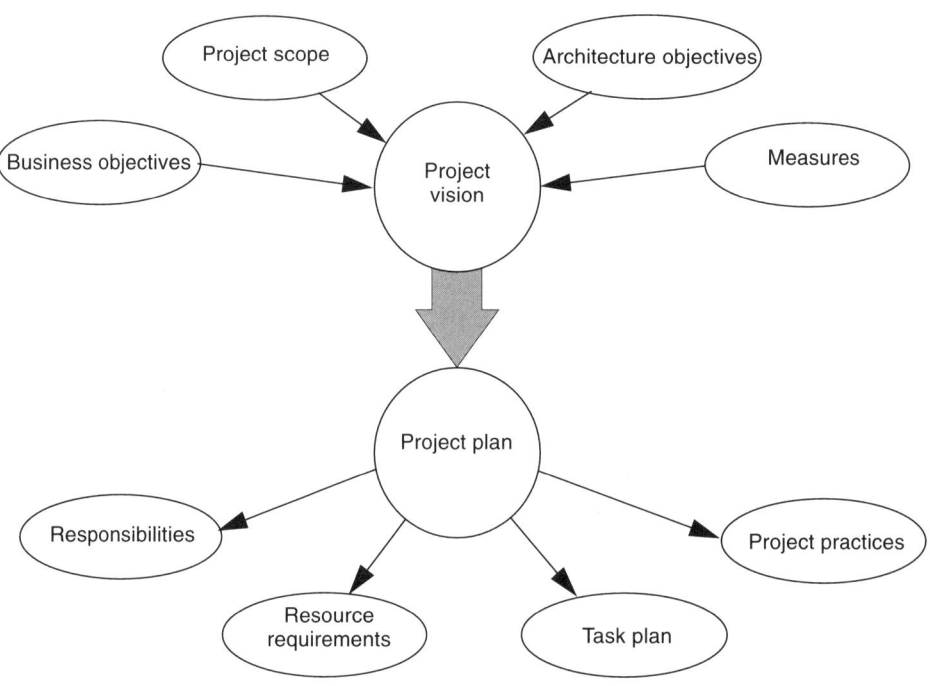

Figure 5-2   Initiating a Rightsizing Project

It is important to get senior management involved early—during the establishment of the vision. Many companies identify an "executive sponsor." The sponsor is educated about the technology and how it will address business needs. Successful executive sponsors participate in setting the vision. They establish initial directions and objectives, and they show commitment to change. Such active participation—letting the vision's *scope* flow initially from the visionary—validates commitment to change and risk taking.

"Get senior management involved early. Identify an 'executive sponsor.' Educate them on the technology and how the technology will address the business needs. Get their participation in the 'Vision Setting' meetings. They need to set the initial directions, objectives, and show commitment to change."

Establishing the Rightsizing Objectives

Make sure you start your rightsizing project with a clear, unambiguous vision and objectives tied to corporate business objectives. Successful rightsizing efforts are characterized by objectives that are directly tied to particular business objectives. Specific details are important: for example, defining an objective such as

a highly adaptive architecture

is not the same as making a statement such as

the corporation requires an adaptive architecture to facilitate the acquisition, integration, and divestiture of business units as required.

Objectives also need support from executive or line management as well as from end-users and IS staff. Support is an ongoing process because rightsizing objectives require constant reinforcement.

Scaling or Business Process Re-engineering?

One of the more difficult decisions to make during a rightsizing effort is whether to simply move existing applications to a less expensive processing environment (for example, from MVS to UNIX) or to completely re-engineer the environment. The fundamental question is: *Does the existing application system match the requirements of the business?*

- If the answer is *yes*, the rightsizing effort replicates current applications (to the extent possible) in a lower-cost environment. This approach is called *information systems "scaling"* because the objective is to scale down the processing cost.

- If the answer is *no*, the rightsizing effort becomes a BPR project. If BPR is new to your corporation, you need to introduce the process to top management as a way to define IS requirements.

  BPR efforts tend to embrace new technologies, such as imaging systems, which typically are absent from scaling or migration efforts because they usually are not found in the applications that are being moved. New technologies, when included in re-engineering efforts, often enable the cost-effective implementation of new processes.

Some companies' rightsizing projects feature a mix of scaling and BPR, but a single theme almost always dominates. Other rightsizing efforts begin with a scaling theme and then evolve to a BPR process. This often happens as the IS staff begins to understand the potential for client-server and network computing and then identifies opportunities to create leverage for the corporation. In these cases, the IS organization frequently becomes the catalyst for corporate-wide re-engineering.

5

Assessing High Payoff Versus High Impact

High-payoff applications are those with a very high return on investment. They are designed to recapture costs in as few as 6 to 12 months. UNIX servers' price/performance advantages over mainframes are the primary source of quick economic payback. High payoff often occurs with applications, such as decision support and querying, that simply were poorly suited for a mainframe implementation, as discussed in Chapter 3, "Rightsizing Opportunities." Payback often comes from the use of faster, lower-cost client-server development tools. Occasionally it comes more from moving applications to a relational database in a client-server implementation than from simple hardware price or performance.

High-impact applications have a strong, direct impact on the way an enterprise handles its business. A good example is revamping order processing to be more customer-driven. On occasion, rightsized applications have high payoff and high impact. Such dual benefits almost always result from business re-engineering efforts.

Achieving a Return on Investment

Return on investment (ROI) from IS scaling is tied to lower IS costs. ROI from business process re-engineering is tied to business profit improvement. Some re-engineering efforts actually result in higher IS costs but are cost effective because they increase business profits more dramatically than they raise IS costs.

Because many of the benefits are intangible, establishing ROI for rightsizing can be difficult. But most corporate executives require completion of an ROI analysis before they approve significant capital expenditures, as discussed in Chapter 4, "Economics of Rightsizing." A rigorous ROI analysis forces you to challenge your assumptions about hardware, software, network, development, and support costs. It provides target objectives that can only benefit later projects.

See Appendix C, "Cost/Benefit Model," for a cost/benefit model framework that can help you perform an in-depth analysis of the costs associated with your potential rightsizing projects.

Defining the Project Scope

A rightsizing project's vision needs to include a *scope*. Scope relates not only to what the vision entails but also to what it does *not* involve: for example, does moving a mainframe application off the mainframe indicate a long-term vision to abandon the mainframe?

Your project team should develop alternatives for the application systems or business processes. Use brainstorming sessions to generate ideas, then analyze them. Examine viable alternatives, develop prototypes, and perform cost/benefit analyses. At the end of this phase, your team should have identified, evaluated, and modeled the new application environment or business process and eliminated alternatives.

Determining and Setting Goals for Open, Adaptive Systems

If an "open" or "adaptive" system is one of your rightsizing objectives, you need to have clear definitions to avoid misinterpretation. The phrase *open systems* is subject to interpretation; that is, open systems can mean full compliance with OSI standards to one vendor; or a standard set of interfaces across all platforms to another vendor. Similarly, you need to define the phrase *adaptive system*, for example, by making such statements as:

> *We want to be able to add a new product line to the system within 24 hours.*

> *We must be able to open, close, and relocate offices without requiring any change to the application systems.*

Communicating the Vision and Gaining Support

Before announcing the vision to the entire enterprise, the project sponsor (typically the CIO or VP/MIS) should ensure broad-based satisfaction with the project scope and required resources. Issues are addressed and resolved before the vision's formal announcement. When fully developed, the vision statement becomes a primary catalyst for directing the IS organization and setting end-user expectations.

`\\\\\\\\\\\\\\\\\\\\\\\\\\\\\\\\\\\\\\\\\\\\\\\\\\\\\\`

> *"The executive sponsor should take an active role in the vision setting process. This validates commitment to change and taking risks. It also lets the vision scope be set initially from the visionary."*

> *"Issues and concerns that will be raised in the initial vision-setting meetings need to be addressed and openly discussed between management and the affected teams. Management needs to be prepared for 'healthy confrontations'."*

`\\\\\\\\\\\\\\\\\\\\\\\\\\\\\\\\\\\\\\\\\\\\\\\\\\\\\\`

The success of your rightsizing project will depend upon how well expectations are managed among corporate management, line management, end-users, and IS staff. Some people may believe that rightsizing will solve all underlying business issues, data integrity problems, and a myriad of other issues. However, experience shows that it will *not*. Other people may believe that rightsizing is not appropriate because of a lack of management tools, unproven platforms, misleading price/performance, staff training, and other objections. To manage expectations effectively, you need to clarify unrealistic assumptions and overcome objections.

An early and often-identified concern to manage is job security. In rightsizing projects, people immediately want to know the staffing strategy. They ask for position plans and responsibility guidelines.

> *"Once position plans are delivered, people can take interest in the new jobs and look positively toward the change. They need to see something written down. Perhaps this is just another illustration of commitment, but once a few people gain interest in the new positions, interest grows quickly."*

Defining Architecture Objectives

Your project vision needs to define specific architecture objectives; for example, developing a client-server environment, integrating a relational database or GUI, or outlining the network and operating system (OS) environments. You do not need to set the standards during Phase I; however, it is crucial that you recognize the required key enabling technologies. For example, you should decide whether to use relational technology, but you can choose an RDBMS vendor later in the process if you decide to do so. Figure 5-3 illustrates some architectural objectives.

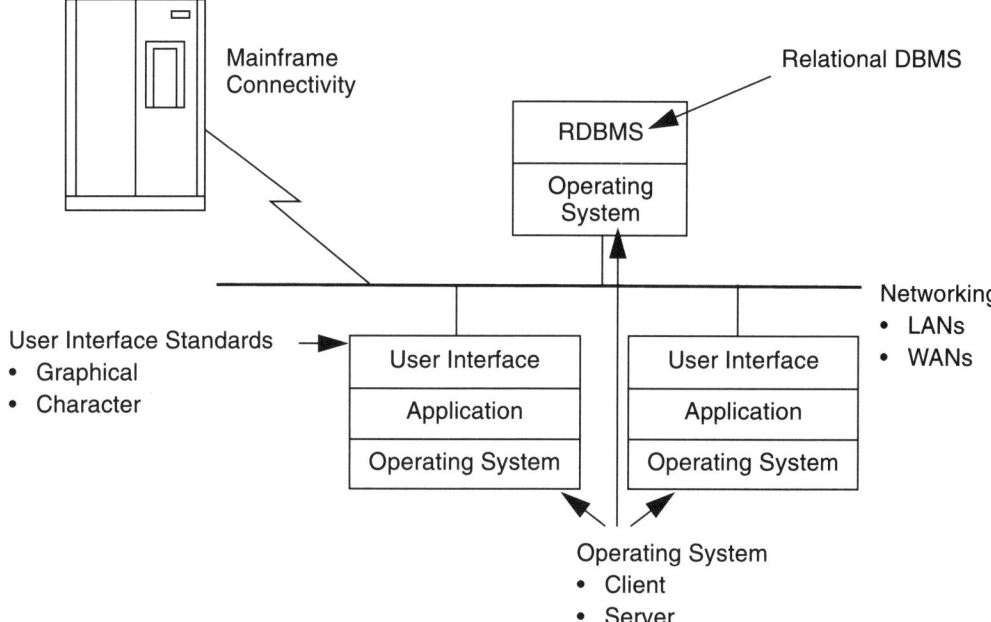

Figure 5-3   Key Architecture Decisions

In defining an architecture, a critical success factor is possession of a complete knowledge base of:

- Existing and planned applications, platforms, and networks
- Unmet and anticipated requirements
- A matrix of databases, applications, and user locations
- Network traffic and other usage data

Later, this knowledge base will be essential for creating the migration plan. It can also facilitate the selection of IS standards and entry applications. The knowledge base provides maximum benefits when stored in a database system.

\\

"Take the time to carefully link technologies with business needs. And educate people on the link between the two. All too often we've had people well-versed in only one of these areas, yet, for rightsizing to be successful, this gap needs to be bridged."

\\

Reorganizing IS for Rightsizing

A reorganization may seem premature at this point, but many companies have found it beneficial to start planning early for reorganization. Key organizational changes that some companies have identified include those listed in Table 5-3.

Table 5-3   Key Organizational Changes

Organizational Change	Description
Organizing around process	Companies rightsizing as a result of business process re-engineering are beginning to organize the IS staff in a way that is consistent with the major processes that IS supports. As a result of re-engineering, IS organizations embrace a broader array of technologies to support new processes. IS staffs need to evolve to manage "process infrastructure" rather than "computer systems."
Implementing a technical support function	Technical support is a critical element in every rightsizing effort. Although rightsizing often results in distributed and localized processing, organizations still want centralized technical support. For example, end-users want to have a single Help Desk number to call for handling all requests for assistance regardless of a problem's cause (application, LAN, server, WAN, host, or other).
Creating a CTO	Consider establishing a chief technical officer (CTO) position, or selecting someone from within IS to fulfill this role. Make this position pro-active and pragmatic to differentiate it from the traditional planning role. The CTO's specific charter often includes finding technology that can address current and future business problems and initiating its implementation. The CTO generally participates in all IS planning and standards activities but does not control either function.

Creating a Rightsizing Project Plan

After you define your vision, create a rightsizing project plan. The project plan should include:

- A vision statement that clearly identifies the project scope
- The project team's composition and structure
- The project's specific objectives
- Resources available to the project team
- The project team's responsibilities
- A task plan with milestones and deliverables
- Project practices

The Project Team

If you are scaling an existing application, your project team should be an equal mix of IS staff and end-users. IS staff members cover all areas of potential impact within IS, including operations, systems, and telecommunications.

If you are doing business process re-engineering, your team should be dominated by end-users and managers representative of all aspects of the process, with direct IS participation limited to one or two senior staff. Create a separate information systems re-engineering (ISR) team to support the BPR team's efforts.

Consider identifying at least one technical expert focused on implementing the project's new technologies. In some cases, you might share this person across multiple project teams or fold this responsibility into the chief technology officer's staff.

\\\

"We hired a system integrator to assist with the project. The integrator seeded the project team with experienced client-server UNIX people. We were careful to use the seeded people only as technical experts and use our own staff as the project leads."

\\\

Project Practices

Table 5-4 lists some typical project practices, or management methods, that should be included in your project plan.

Table 5-4   Project Practices

Practice	Description
Communicating status	Examines how status information is provided to team members and management; specifies the frequency and level of detail for status reporting.
Project documentation	Specifies what kind of documentation is maintained and how it will be captured, inventoried, and shared among project members.
Issue management and resolution	Resolves how issues are escalated to management and determines the frequency of management reviews.
Project communication	Determines how team members communicate with one another and establishes the frequency of project meetings and internal project reviews.

Phase II: Assessing Current Applications or Processes

In Phase II, your project team should evaluate the current environment. Gather and assimilate data through interviews, reviews of current documentation, and detailed analysis of existing systems, concentrating your analysis in three key areas:

1. People
   Use skills assessments to inventory end-user and staff skills. This assessment will help to define training requirements, hiring needs, and organizational decisions.

2. Technology
   In scaling projects, assess current technology to determine which application or application areas will be moved to more cost-effective environments.

3. Processes
   In re-engineering projects, document and analyze the current processes.

People Assessment

In any rightsizing initiative, you will need to make a significant investment in the human resources to develop the necessary skills in both the IS and end-user communities. To determine the types of training and development that will be required, first inventory the current skills of end-users and staff.

"There is a steep cost to reeducating the mainframe programmer/analysts. Do not underestimate it. While some of our best client-server people came from the mainframe side of the house, there were some that would never make the transition. For those people we gave them options to stay with the mainframe operations."

Look for specific skills based on the architecture objectives set forth in the project vision. Skill types typically fall into two categories: *technology knowledge* and *product skills*. Technology knowledge is a broad understanding of general technology concepts such as client-server computing, relational databases, networking, and distributed application architectures. Product skills encompass knowledge of the particular products to be implemented. The skills inventory leads to specific training programs as needed.

"You must have some people with UNIX experience, if UNIX is part of your rightsizing plan."

"Find the most open minds with the capacity for change and dealing with some unknowns."

"We used the mainframers to define and establish the rigors and controls necessary in the new environment."

"Look for individuals with a high degree of independence."

"Age is an imprecise indicator of who's willing to be trained. Those open to change are the easiest to train."

"Look for individuals that can work in teams and communicate well."

"Our company took the initial staff assigned to the project and had them build the first subsystem. Those that learned quickly and accepted the challenges became the programming supervisors and senior analysts for the other development teams."

Contrary to popular belief, layoffs are seldom associated with rightsizing projects. Most companies spent time setting their resource agenda and strategy, including how to retrain existing staff and the cost associated with doing so. Many companies found that retraining their staffs was much more cost-effective than re-hiring.

Technology Assessment

In scaling projects, information about the current application environment falls into three categories: *application characteristics*, *usage characteristics*, and *cost*. Your team should rate each application to determine the ease and estimated payback from moving to a rightsized environment. The goal of this assessment is to determine which application you will rightsize first.

Application Characteristics

Application characteristics determine the ease or difficulty of moving the application to a new environment. Some applications may be impossible to move because of the language or tool in which they were developed (for example, 360 assembler Mark IV, MODEL 204); other applications require significant retooling (for example, IMS applications). However, many mainframe-based applications are portable. Table 5-5 shows sample application characteristics.

Table 5-5   Application Characteristics

Characteristic	Examples
Programming language	COBOL, PL/1, Assembler
Tools	IBI Focus, Software AG Natural
Data format	IMS, DB2, ORACLE
Subsystems accessed	CICS, DEC Forms
Machine dependence	System calls
Inter-dependencies	HR system updates payroll system with wage and employee information

〟〟

"We have migrated our applications off the mainframe by business unit.We started with the smallest business unit, with the simplest application and the least amount of interdependencies. Then we've worked our way through the tougher applications in that same unit."

"To ensure an immediate and quick success, we looked for applications that had few interdependencies with other applications, preferably accessed only one database, and were read-only. The application chosen also had to be important to the business operations and could be prototyped in no more than 3 months."

〟〟

Applications typically well-suited for migration include:

- Applications developed with 4GLs that are portable to an open systems environment. Examples include Information Builder's Focus and Software AG's Natural.

- Applications with data stored in a DBMS or file system that is movable to an open systems environment. Examples include DB2, VSAM, ORACLE, and Cincom databases.

- General business applications that can be replaced with off-the-shelf solutions, such as general ledger, human resources, and manufacturing resource planning (MRP) applications.

- Applications developed where a migration or conversion tool exists. For example, migration tools are available to move COBOL/CICS or RPG applications.

Inter-dependencies among applications are important to assess. Applications with the simplest inter-dependencies become early targets for migration; for example, applications that are read-only or batch-file-oriented. (Applications that share read/write access with other application systems possess more complex inter-dependencies.) Figure 5-4 illustrates application inter-dependency.

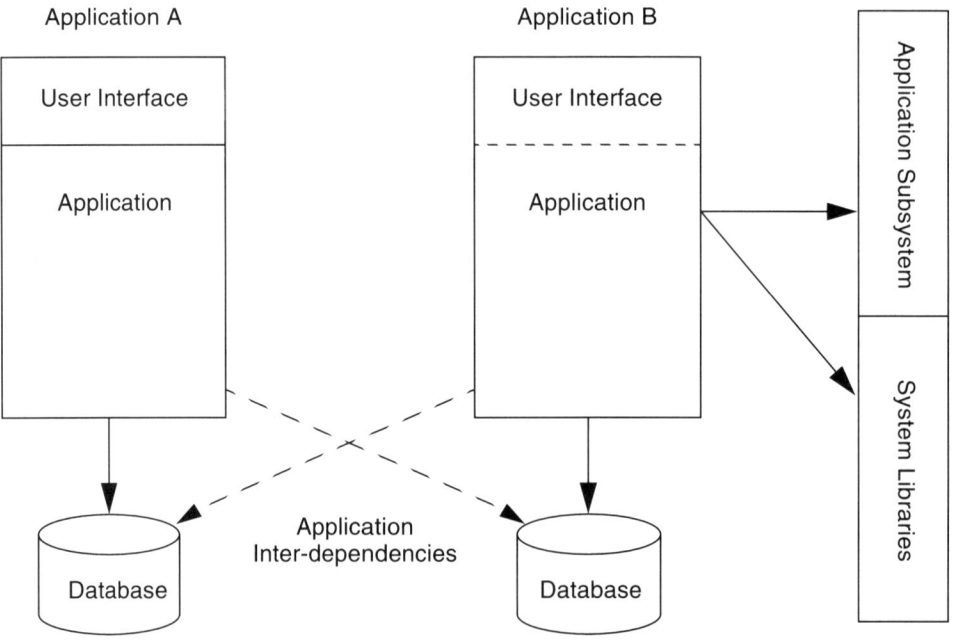

Figure 5-4   Application Architecture

Usage Characteristics

Application usage characteristics determine the new environment's size and influence the new technical architecture. Characteristics you should determine and evaluate include:

- CPU usage
- Data management (average and total working set size)
- DASD requirements
- End-user community (location, devices, network configuration)
- Transaction volume
- Number of read/write operations per transaction
- Number of users (total and concurrent)
- Peak usage characteristics

Cost Information

Application cost information is particularly important to assess if IS cost reduction is your overall goal. For a complete discussion on the type of cost information you will want to collect, see Chapter 4, "Economics of Rightsizing."

Once you have collected cost information, you can evaluate alternative, rightsized architectures. Use the model provided in Appendix C, "Cost/Benefit Model," to perform a cost/benefit analysis for each application and assess the business impact of rightsizing.

Scoring Applications

A critical, difficult Phase II decision is to identify the first application to rightsize. Scoring potential applications can be useful to determine which applications are the best candidates for migration to the new IS architecture. First, evaluate each application's architecture, usage, and costs. Table 5-6 identifies some application characteristics and scoring criteria (applications are rated from high 5 to low 1).

Table 5-6   Sample Application Scoring Criteria

Characteristic	Scoring Criteria
Interdependencies with other application systems	5 – Simple interdependencies (read-only, batch-file-oriented) with other applications. 1 – Complex interdependencies (read/write) with other application systems.
Percentage of mainframe CPU use	5 – Uses more than 12 percent of the mainframe CPU during prime shift. 1 – Uses less than 3 percent of the mainframe CPU during prime shift.
Payback period	5 – Payback period six months or less. 1 – Payback period more than two years.
Ease of migration	5 – Port to a UNIX environment requires few changes. 1 – Port to UNIX environment requires substantial rewriting of portions of the application.

Consider scoring applications by a committee to articulate different views and to ensure a consistent rating approach across applications. Applications with the highest point totals become the best candidates for further examination. Be wary, however, of applications with high point totals but low ratings (1) in any specific area.

5

Identifying Entry Applications

Scoring applications facilitates the sorting of candidates at a high level. It is not intended to be a single measure to determine the order of application migration. Besides rating, there are several entry application selection criteria, as described in Table 5-7.

Table 5-7   Application Selection Criteria

Characteristic	Description
Technical Architecture	The entry application uses the core technologies and platforms defined by the vision statement and matches the skill set of the project team.
High Visibility	The entry application has sufficient visibility; its success will increase management's commitment to the strategy and can increase resource availability.
High ROI/Impact	The entry application provides a strong ROI or has a major impact on the business.

"We migrated to the new environment by business unit: starting with the smallest unit, simplest manufacturing line, fewest technical dependencies. Then we worked our way (in the same business unit) into more complicated applications with higher degrees of interdependencies."

"We migrated the applications that were in development at the time. This was much easier to do since no one had been using these applications yet. So we short-circuited the delivery from mainframe to client-server. This avoided a lot of the operational disruptions."

"Our strategy for migration was to migrate the applications over in much the same way product flows through our stores: starting with purchasing and inventory control and moving through warehousing and distribution and then eventually into the 'in store' systems. By the time we get into any applications that directly affect customers, we'll be very experienced."

Entry applications typically occur at the start of the business cycle (such as order processing) or at the end of the business cycle (such as accounts receivable). Applications that are used primarily in reporting and decision support are also excellent candidates for early migration because they typically consume many resources and are frequently read-only, as discussed in Chapter 3, "Rightsizing Opportunities." The most common applications implemented are UNIX-based decision support/reporting systems. Figure 5-5 illustrates examples of good entry applications.

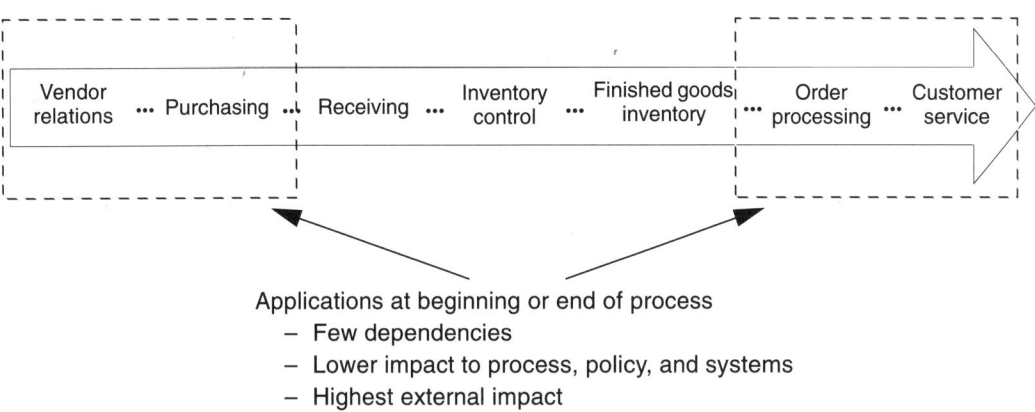

Figure 5-5   *Example of Choosing an Entry Application*

Process Assessment

"We spend much more time up-front understanding our business flows and processes than we did previously. Then we prototype the new processes as well as the new information system. This has greatly accelerated the delivery of more effective systems."

In business process re-engineering projects, you should confirm the critical business issues to ensure that everyone understands them. Then obtain and assess information about current business processes. Your result from this research, at a minimum, should be a detailed process flowchart and productivity/cost measurements for each task in the process. Table 5-8 describes the assessment process.

Table 5-8   Business Process Assessment

Category	Information to Obtain
Task description	Identify and describe: • Each discrete task in the process • All forms or electronic systems used within each task • Data elements used in each task • Documentation • Informal undocumented shortcuts
Task relationships	Identify and describe: • Relationship between each discrete task • Controls • All forms or electronic systems used between tasks • Documentation • Informal undocumented shortcuts
Task resource requirements	Identify and describe: • Time each task takes • Time between tasks • Jobs of people performing each task • Current productivity measures and any productivity history • Types of events that create delays in processing • Full-time equivalent (FTE) staff requirements • Costs associated with each task
Value added	Does the task add value? What new data is added during the task? How much of the task is associated with controls built into the process?
Duplicate/redundant effort	What data is entered onto a form or into a computer system more than once in the process? How many points of contact are established with customers/suppliers?
Processing time	How much time does the process take from beginning to end? How much time is spent performing each task? How much wait time exists between tasks? What is the estimated time spent performing value-added effort within each task and throughout the process?

After reviewing all business processes, choose the first process to re-engineer. The characteristics of the ideal first process are similar to those used to determine entry applications in scaling efforts (see Table 5-7 on page 148). Considerations for selecting the application include:

- Envision the entire business process and select applications with the fewest inter-dependencies with other application systems

- Where possible, focus on applications that are read-only

- Where possible, concentrate on applications with broad management visibility and representing a high payoff to the enterprise

- Focus on applications that gain leverage from the new IS architecture

Some of the most common entry applications in business process re-engineering include:

- Executive information systems that employ large UNIX servers, a powerful RDBMS, and GUI-based reporting and analysis tools

- Customer management systems that are re-engineered to be more customer-driven, providing better service or information to the customer

- Manual or electronic processes with data latency (wait time)

- Paper-based processes being moved to imaging technology

5

Phase III: Defining a New IS Model or Process

The primary Phase III objective is to define the new technical architecture for the rightsized application environment. Your new architecture should be consistent with your vision objectives and should define specific architectural components.

\\

"The first thing you must do is establish a technical architecture and then select the tools that will enable you to build and adhere to that architecture."

\\

If you are re-engineering, define the new process and its enabling technologies and develop a new business process. Document the new process flow, list modified and new tasks, identify changes in responsibility, specify new measures, design new forms, and assess resource requirements. This is an iterative process, with continual refinements. Once the business process is defined, develop the new IS technical architecture. Table 5-9 lists some primary outcomes of Phase III.

Table 5-9   Primary Outcomes of Phase III

Outcome	Description
Technical Architecture	Standards for servers, desktops, and networking are defined. The application architecture and how it will be integrated with existing legacy applications aredescribed.
New Business Process	Based on the process assessment made in Phase II, the new business process is redesigned, incorporating new technologies that improve efficiency.
Risk Assessment	When both the architecture and business process (if applicable) have been defined, an analyst evaluates the risk associated with the project.

Redesigning Business Processes

Most business process re-engineering is intended to improve productivity dramatically through "radical" change. Although each situation is unique, Table 5-10 describes several common goals.

Table 5-10 Common Re-engineering Goals

Goal	Description
Eliminate paper	Substitute electronic forms and imaging systems when possible.
Eliminate steps and tasks that do not add value	Move processes to electronic systems to allow controls to be built into applications, eliminating manual steps for logging forms and documents in and out.
Capture data once	Improve productivity while reducing inconsistent data and introduction of errors.
Implement workflow rules	Automatically push items (orders, policy applications, changes of status) through the process, making wait time a simple function of total volume. Workflow technology also distributes workloads and performs exception handling by routing items with certain specified characteristics to specialists and supervisors for review.
Reduce the number of contact points	Reduce contacts in two ways: 1. Reduce the number of people handling items. 2. Simplify customer and supplier interfaces; that is, provide a single account manager for all contact.
Use information systems to perform or assist routine tasks	Examples: expert systems to "approve" certain types of routine recurring invoices for payment; voice-response systems to screen customer order status inquiries; intelligent facsimile services to capture faxed customer orders.

New process flow models identify discrete tasks and their inter-relationships, forms, data elements, productivity objectives, and resource requirements. A model should be refined through multiple iterations. After identifying the best model, develop a prototype to ensure that it is workable and effective. If your model depends on new technologies, such as imaging or expert systems, make sure the new technologies are part of the prototype.

"Prototype, Prototype, Prototype! The investment in hardware, software, and networks necessary to deliver a client-server prototype is minimal. For less than $50K a prototype can be delivered. In our business, that's cheap! With the benefits of open systems and portable software we were able to deliver a variety of client-server prototypes for the users to choose from. Desktop options were PCs or UNIX workstations. Servers were UNIX or the mainframe. The users actually got to test and use both and make the decision with us."

Reducing IS Costs for Multiple Applications

If you are scaling multiple applications, you need to identify a standard architecture that supports the broadest set of applications at the lowest cost. This effort typically requires multiple iterations of matching the best rightsizing alternative for each application system with the best rightsized technical architecture for all applications. Once you select a target IS architecture, perform detailed cost/benefit analyses for each application as well as for overall IS costs. Use prototypes to evaluate and select specific architecture products. Prototypes enable proof of concept for the new technologies as well as provide benchmarks for technologies that have throughput requirements.

Defining the New IS Architecture

"Define your IS architecture early on. The transition to client-server is governed by the architectural plan. Spend time here."

Whether you are scaling or re-engineering, establish a corporate-wide IS technical architecture and clear standards. Wherever possible, standards should extend to specific hardware vendors and configurations; for example, the standard could be IBM 4/16 token ring cards with type 2 cabling. In addition, it is critical that you enforce the newly established standards. Typically, the IS architecture should include:

- Application architecture
  This architecture covers the application environment's technologies and characteristics.

- Server standards
  These standards cover platforms, operating systems, and RDBMSs.

- Desktop/workstation standards
  These standards cover platforms, operating systems, GUIs, development tools, and personal productivity software.

- Network standards
  These standards cover LAN topology, media, transport stacks, vendors, and network management, as well as WAN public versus private issues, transport stacks, vendors, and network management.

- Integration with existing systems
  This integration covers connectivity as well as application and DBMS integration.

\\

"We spent a fair amount of time defining a layered architecture before we started. The layering strategy required us to focus on standard interfaces between the architectural layers. This would allow us to isolate maintenance work or change a technology on one layer without affecting another layer."

\\

Figure 5-6 is an illustration of an IS architecture.

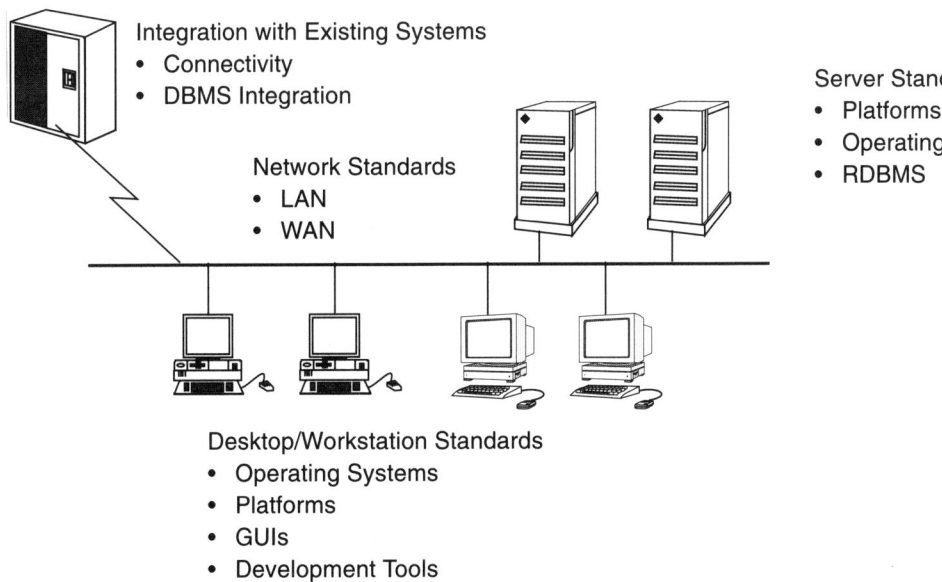

Figure 5-6   IS Architecture

Application Architecture

Decisions about the application architecture influence decisions about the other architectural components. Table 5-11 describes the components that you should consider when making these decisions.

Table 5-11 Application Architecture Components

Components	Description
Client-server computing	Determine whether a client-server implementation will be created. If so, define the application components that will run on the server machine and those that will run on the client machine. If an existing application is being moved from a proprietary environment, will the application remain a monolithic architecture in which all application components reside on a single system?
User interface	Establish whether a GUI will be used. The user-interface selection influences the desktop/workstation standards.
Distributed database	Decide whether a distributed database will be employed and the physical locations of the data.
Application interfaces	Determine how the new applications will interact with other applications; for example, will a batch file or a message-based interface be used to link applications?

Server Standards

Server standards consist of three primary product components: the *platform*, the *operating system*, and the *DBMS*. How these components are integrated and tuned for one another determines overall system throughput. Evaluate each of the different components both individually and collectively. Typical questions to ask when evaluating include:

♦ **Platform**
  ○ Does the product line offer the extensibility and scalability to support the long-term computing requirements?

  ○ Does the platform offer the transaction throughput that the environment requires?

  ○ Can upgrades be performed without box swaps and other disruptive procedures?

♦ **Operating System**
  ○ Is the operating system based on industry or de facto standards?

  ○ Does the operating system provide standard interfaces to ensure application portability?

  ○ Has the operating system been tuned for transaction processing?

  ○ Will the operating system scale to meet the organization's high-end computing needs?

♦ **DBMS**
  ○ Does the DBMS offer the features that the environment requires (for example, mainframe connectivity, distributed DBMS capabilities, stored procedures, or triggers)?

  ○ Has the DBMS been tuned for the target platform and operating system?

Desktop/Workstation Standards

The desktop standards define the end-user environment as well as the application development environment. Standards to examine include those for platform, operating system, GUI, and application development tools. Typical types of questions to ask when evaluating include:

♦ **Platform**

○ What are the system requirements of the new application architecture?

○ If the application processing runs on end-users' desktops, what type of system is needed to support it?

♦ **Operating System**

○ Does the application environment require multi-tasking?

○ Does the operating system support connectivity to the selected server environment?

♦ **GUI**

○ What GUIs are currently in use?

○ How much end-user training is necessary?

♦ **Application Development Tools**

○ Will the existing development tools be moved to the new architecture?

○ What tools are required for the application architecture?

"Once the architecture was defined, we spent time establishing specific standards for the desktop hardware and software. This allowed us to gain significant efficiencies in supporting a large number of end users. Having a set of standard desktop configurations helped us to set a monthly support charge based on user type (that is, programmer, end-user, engineer, and administrator) and hours of coverage."

Network Standards

The underlying network is the single most critical component of the IS architecture in a distributed computing environment. Successful network architecture implementations typically possess the characteristics described in Table 5-12.

Table 5-12 Characteristics of Successful Network Architecture Implementations

Characteristic	Description
Consistency	Has tightly enforced standards
Reliability	Has secure and error-free transmission
Availability	Runs 24 hours a day, 7 days a week
Extensibility	Takes advantage of new network technology
Adaptability	Can meet new business and application requirements
Security	Allows access only to authorized users and applications

To successfully rightsize, you should create an enterprise-wide network that appears to authorized end-users to be a single, integrated network. Any authorized end-user node connects directly to any other node as if they were on a virtual local area network.

In almost all cases, these highly layered networks include:

- Local area networks
- Intelligent hubs
- Multi-protocol routers
- High-speed WANs
- A network management console based on a simple network management protocol (SNMP)

Many companies emphasize the need to "get your media right," noting that cutting corners on media is simply not worth the trade-off in potential technical support problems. It is important to implement maximum available and potential local bandwidth; both support the highest possible throughput.

"We used unshielded twisted pair technology and installed Data Grade 5 because it can handle 100 mbps ("fast Ethernet" and CDDI). With a fiber network, we installed much higher capacity fiber than we projected (24-strand instead of 12-strand)."

UNIX-based network management consoles have emerged as the primary technology in the 1990s for managing enterprise-wide networks. Network management facilities include:

- Configuration management
  The capability to discover network elements and to inventory them, and to display topology maps

- Problem solving
  For identifying faults, handling alarm conditions, and tracking outstanding problems

- Capacity planning and management
  Including forecasting capabilities

- Resource accounting
  Encompassing system and network usage

- Security
  Permitting only authorized access and monitoring suspicious activity

Integration with Existing Systems

You should establish integration standards between rightsized applications and legacy systems as part of your overall IS structure. Table 5-13 describes some of the integration requirements that arise in connecting to legacy environments, as shown in Figure 5-7.

Table 5-13 Integration Requirements

Requirement	Description/Solution
Database integration and synchronization	Synchronizing databases between application environments can be very complex, but tools are available to simplify the process. For example, database gateways, such as Sybase's DB2 Gateway or Oracle's SQL*Connect for IMS, are available from RDBMS vendors. These products simplify the integration and synchronization issues associated with accessing legacy data.
File sharing	Providing access to mainframe files from other systems is a key requirement. One powerful solution to this problem is the NFS system/MVS, which is a VTAM subsystem permitting UNIX applications to access MVS files as if they were local to the UNIX system.

Table 5-13 Integration Requirements (Continued)

Requirement	Description/Solution
Connectivity	The most common connectivity issues are 3270 (LU2) terminal access, API access including LU6.2 and HLLAPI, and transport stack protocols. Connectivity products such as Sun's IBM SunLink gateway product offer 3270 terminal access as well as LU6.2 and HLLAPI connectivity. Products such as Communications Integrator from Covia Technologies provide transport stack normalization. Mainframe-based SNA-to-TCP gateways are available in either a channel-attached device or combination channel-attached device/mainframe software. Dozens of other technologies and products provide integration with mainframe-based legacy systems.

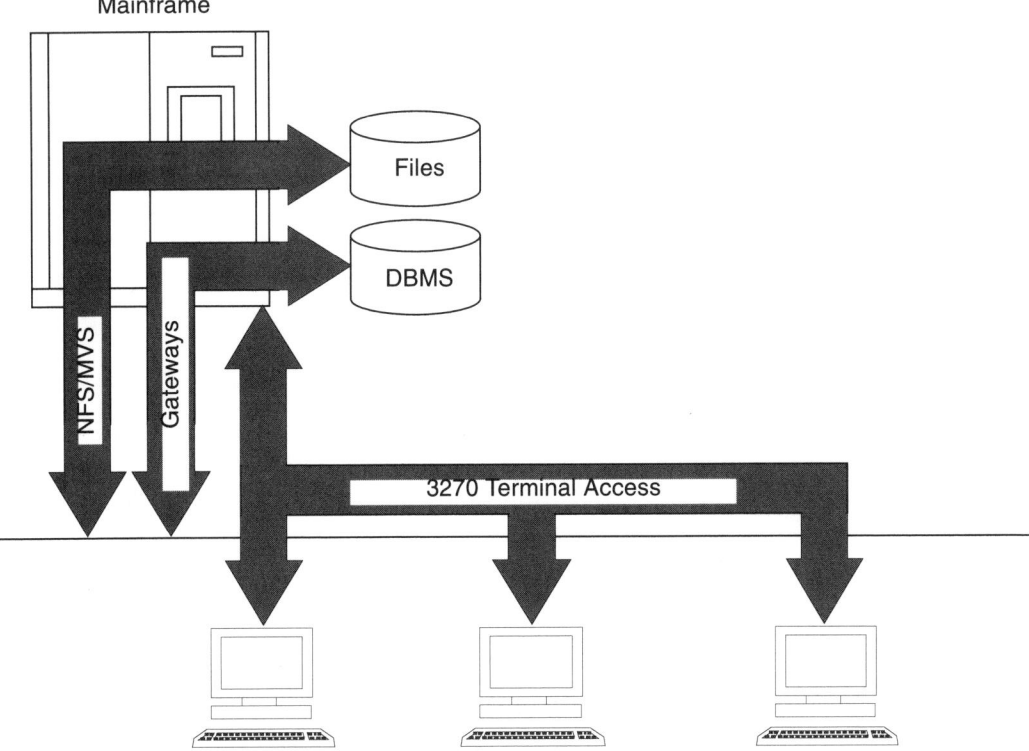

Figure 5-7   Integration with Existing Systems

Selecting Strategic Partners

After the technical architecture is defined, you then select each component's provider. These providers will become strategic partners in your rightsizing initiative. Your rightsizing success depends heavily on your ability to select partners that deliver and support their respective critical technology components. For vendor-selection criteria, see Appendix E, "Vendor-Selection Criteria."

Prototyping and the Showcase Concept

One of the most important and cost-effective investments you can make during a rightsizing project is to prototype the targeted application. The investment in hardware, software, and networks necessary to deliver a client-server prototype is minimal. Many prototypes are not thrown away; rather, they are refined and scaled into the full production environment.

Once the prototype is complete and approved, you can create a "showcase environment" that provides corporate management, end users, and IS staff with a prototype of the targeted future environment. The showcase communicates the vision, demonstrates the core enabling technologies, and generates support for the implementation strategy (and associated costs).

> *"Building and demonstrating a prototype was the single most important step in gaining acceptance from the nonbelievers."*

Risk Assessment

After the architecture's completion, you should perform a risk assessment to review the new IS model or business process. Determine the technical, financial, operational, and business impact of an implementation failure, the likelihood of such a failure, and the critical success factors that need to be achieved.

Phase IV: Establishing a Migration Plan

During Phase IV, you will need to prepare a comprehensive action plan to migrate from the current business process or IS architecture to the new business process and architecture. The plan should address all aspects of changing from the current to the new environment and minimize the negative impact of ongoing work. Careful development and implementation of the migration plan will ensure that:

- Re-engineering the network backbone is completed
- Application interdependencies are accounted for
- Technical staff have adequate training in the new technologies
- Parallel systems can be maintained until the new system's integrity is ensured

Creating the Plan

Migration plans are formal documents that communicate to the entire organization the strategy, component activities, responsibilities, milestones, and time lines for implementing the new system. The migration plan also communicates the impact to current operations during the migration period and the alternative strategies. It addresses all issues fully and sets expectations for people directly involved in the migration process as well as those who are affected by the changes.

"A key step in the migration strategy was to 'preserve the same rigors and disciplines used in the mainframe environment.' To do this, we developed a 'UNIX Acceptance Process,' which set controls and processes for placing UNIX applications into production status. We duplicated the mainframe acceptance processes. Over time, these processes were reduced to just those steps necessary for distributed operations. This allowed people to continue using processes they were familiar with while getting underway in the new environment. It also allowed operations people to run the mainframe and UNIX operations side-by-side for a period of time."

A migration plan should include the components described in Table 5-14.

Table 5-14 Migration Plan Component

Component	Description
Overall implementation strategy	The entire implementation strategy is described, including major milestones, task plans, and time lines. An executive summary is prepared for those not directly involved in the effort.
Assignment of responsibilities	Each task and subtask of the plan has a specific individual, business unit, or organization responsible for it. Task objectives are clearly identified along with required resources and milestones.
Detailed budgets	The budgets show where significant expenses are incurred and capital outlays required, with separate task outlines and milestones where approval is necessary. Each budgeted item is tied to specific tasks in the migration plan.
Critical success factors	All issues and events deemed critical to the migration plan's success are identified, including steps taken to ensure they are achieved.
Parallel systems efforts and switching strategy	When a new system is being implemented to replace an existing system, the two systems run in parallel until the new system passes specified criteria. Only then does switching to the new system occur; the old system is discontinued. The migration plan includes the strategy for maintaining and supporting the systems in parallel, as well as criteria for complete switching.
Critical dependencies	All dependencies among the migration tasks that affect the migration process are identified. Typically, PERT charts are used to ensure that everyone understands the dependencies.
Quality assurance strategy	Quality assurance is most critical during the migration period. Defined activities to ensure acceptable quality levels for each task are identified.
Migration support strategy	Migration plans place significant strain on organizations' support infrastructure. Not only are new processes being implemented, but the current system also must be maintained until the switch is complete.
Fallback strategy	The worst-case strategy includes fallback steps, or alternatives. These are identified in the migration plan so that everyone is aware of what will happen under certain circumstances. Fallback steps range from simply delaying the next step in the migration plan to a full return to an existing system.

Table 5-14 Migration Plan Component (Continued)

Component	Description
Training requirements	Training and education are always critical and are completed before implementation. The plan assesses current IS staff skills and the skills necessitated by the new IS technical architecture. Assessments are compared to identify any skill gaps within the current IS organization. A combination of specific skills training, new hires, and outside consultants addresses these gaps.

Acquiring Technological Expertise

IS staff usually require immersion in any new technologies used in the technical architecture, including client-server computing, RDBMS, GUIs, LANs, and network computing and programming languages. Use skills assessments to provide primary input to the resulting IS training plan. Where appropriate, execute full pilot training sessions during this phase prior to full implementation.

"We use outside trainers whenever possible. Outside trainers are typically taken more seriously, and their use indicates to employees that the company is truly investing in the transition. An additional subtle benefit is that employees tend to be more demanding and critical of outside trainers, which helps build the "demand push" necessary to jump-start rightsizing projects."

"We use outside trainers only for the basics: UNIX, C programming, and user interfaces."

"We trained our programmers all at once with an intense set of courses on tools, client-server application development, and UNIX. We then tested and sorted our programmers according to abilities."

"We trained our development staff on a just-in-time basis by giving them the training they needed only when they were ready to do something valuable with it. We also had our training classes focus on actual development projects to help accelerate the process."

A typical practice is to hire full- or part-time outside consultants and then seed them into the project teams. You can also establish a small group of technical experts—their primary purpose, to support the project teams—in specific products to emphasize knowledge transfer from experienced staff members to those less experienced. This transfer is particularly important when you employ expert consultants. Consultants seeded onto project teams are often explicitly chartered to provide ad hoc training rather than simply to be responsible for part of the project.

> *"If you use outside consultants to perform any part of the project, it is critical to set up time for the consultant to perform a technology transfer back to the IS department. If you do not allow for this, you will lose the intellectual capital or have to keep calling the consultants back."*

Determining the Mainframe's Role

During the migration phase, you should assess your mainframe's long-term role. In rightsizing, you have a wide variety of options for the mainframe. In some cases, the mainframe functions as a data repository. The large financial commitments typical of mainframes lead some companies to outsource their mainframe, while others pursue a rapid migration strategy complete with complex "financial engineering" practices.

Outsourcing Mainframe Processing

A common practice of companies is to outsource mainframe processing to a service bureau. A benefit of this approach is that mainframe expenses are smoothly downscaled by "metering" the service bureau, whereas in-house mainframe costs can only be reduced in large increments, each of which has a substantial impact on operations.

If you are moving off the mainframe but cannot move to a timesharing bureau, typical interim measures can be to:

- Freeze all mainframe software releases unless they become absolutely essential
- Discontinue all mainframe capacity monitoring software
- Devote substantial attention to tuning the current environment and maintaining it while retraining systems programming staff

"To help the staff move forward with the migration efforts, we made an effort to show specific examples of how the mainframe systems (people, equipment, processes, and procedures) had been built up to conform to the weaknesses of the mainframe. Showing and discussing these examples helped the staff look for more examples of unnecessary processes."

Rapid Mainframe Migration

Once you make the decision to move off the mainframe, it is best to move as quickly as possible (typically in less than three years but preferably in as few as two) for the following reasons:

- Longer-range efforts are easily derailed, leaving your company "partly migrated" (considered to be the worst outcome).

- Shorter time frames force your IS staff to focus on the end objective and address problems quickly.

- Shorter time frames demonstrate IS commitment to your end-user community and to top management.

"We found that setting dates for the startup of its new organization's jobs and charters is critical to the transition. We noted a problem in getting people to stop maintenance on mainframe programs, so we held a meeting with IS managers and programmers and set a date by which all mainframe maintenance would be shut down. On that date, 65 of the 75 programmers switched over to their new organizations and new responsibilities."

5

Phase V: Implementing the New IS Model or Process

The rightsized solution is brought online during Phase V according to the migration plan you developed in Phase IV.

Phase V has two objectives:

1. Implement the rightsized application or business process.
   The implementation should include performance tuning and quality assurance. For new business processes, the implementation should include continual evaluation against objectives and fine-tuning the process.

2. Discontinue use of the existing system and switch to the new application or business process.

The following examples show how other companies set their implementation strategies.

Application Migration

If you are scaling, your primary focus during the implementation phase should be on tuning to achieve desired performance objectives and on validating results with the current systems that are running in parallel until validation is completed. As each rightsized system is validated, formal acceptance should be necessary to discontinue the existing system.

\\

> *"To help with the implementation, our company borrowed UNIX expertise from the technical departments (geology and exploration). They had recently made the transition of their applications to client-server and had a working knowledge of the process and problems."*

\\

Implementing a New Business Process

If you are re-engineering, your primary focus should be on conforming to redesigned process specifications and achieving performance objectives. This frequently requires some adjustment of the new process once it is brought on line. Sometimes it is as simple as additional training or form redesign.

Application Development

When new applications are created to support new business processes, the majority of Phase V consists of application development.

Many companies embrace rapid application development (RAD) principles despite deploying several development tools. RAD principles include the aspects described in Table 5-15.

Table 5-15 Aspects of RAD Principles

Aspect	Description
Emphasis on the User Interface	Focuses on the user interface.
Systems in Less Than 90 Days	Identifies the need to develop RAD systems in less than 90 days.
Daily User Involvement	Enables end-users to critique progress made (however limited) in the previous 24 hours.
Accelerating Failure	Emphasizes "rapid failure" by encouraging the project to identify quickly what is not working.
Separating the Business Rules	Stresses the use of RDBMSs to allow stored procedures. Stored procedures support the organization's business rules, thus separating general business rules from application-specific coding, as illustrated in Figure 5-8.

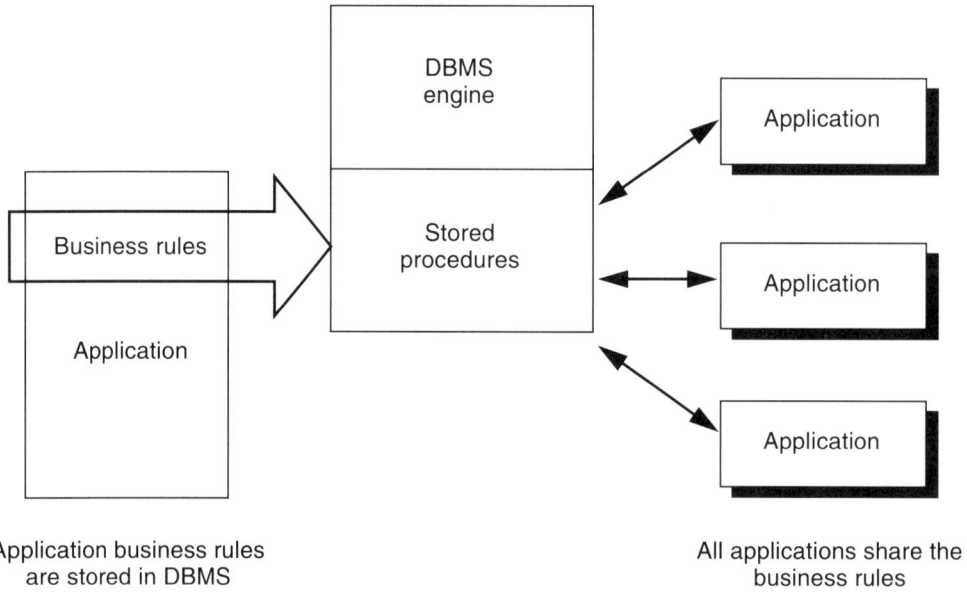

Application business rules
are stored in DBMS

All applications share the
business rules

Figure 5-8   Business Rules Are Shared by All Applications

Establishing an Enterprise Data Model

Companies are using many different approaches toward developing an enterprise data model (EDM); however, two distinctly different approaches are consistently being used:

1. Information engineering approach

   In this approach, a full EDM is created before any rightsizing efforts begin. In these cases, substantial time, effort, and user involvement are needed to define and validate the EDM.

2. "Back into" the EDM

   In this approach, a single, standard RDBMS that supports stored procedures is selected. The consistency of a single RDBMS is relied on to create the EDM. To use this approach, you need to acquire an EDM tool early in the process, establish naming conventions, and create a rough model of how the EDM evolves as applications are rightsized. You should train staff in EDM principles and consider using your DBAs to support the individual development teams to ensure consistency.

\\

"We did establish an IS architecture and plan. We did not, however, attempt to build a complete enterprise data model (EDM). This would have taken too long with little to show for the effort. Knowing that an EDM was going to be critical in the future, we focused on building standard application interfaces and portable databases that would enable us to make modifications to the data accesses in the future."

\\

Phase VI: Evaluating and Assessing the New IS Model or Process

In Phase VI, conduct a broad review and evaluation of the project and then bring it to a close. Companies are finding many benefits in the evaluation and assessment phase of the project. Phase VI objectives are:

- Reviewing the project
  Determine the lessons learned, determine whether the project met its original objectives as established in the project vision and end-user satisfaction levels, and assess the project ROI.

- Determining future potential
  Are there further rightsizing opportunities within the organization?

"There are significant benefits to be realized from evaluation and assessment. In our first rightsizing project, we overlooked this step because we were too busy. We realized afterwards the costs of not evaluating and critiquing the process—namely, duplication of mistakes, longer product cycles, and lack of controls."

Post-implementation Review

Once the new IS model or business process is implemented and accepted, perform a broad-based project review: interview and survey end-users as well as corporate management. Key questions to ask include:

- Were the project goals and objectives met?
- Where did process breakdowns occur and why?
- What can be done to avoid these in the future?
- Are end-users satisfied with the scaled application or new process?
- Did these rightsizing processes work? How can they be improved?

An important review goal is to determine other potential opportunities for rightsizing. Based on experience with the current project, what leverage exists for other rightsizing initiatives? Use the review phase to recommend any changes needed to the new process or application. Then, establish a plan to implement these modifications.

Final Project Documentation

The evaluation and assessment phase is often a critical time to go back to original documentation—designs, goals, time lines, resource plans—and assess actual results versus targets. Final project documentation should include a review of what worked and what did not. This exercise can help to retune the planning skills needed by the team before they embark upon another project. This phase was cited by several companies as one in which the executives needed to be involved with the project team to project an ongoing commitment to change—taking risks, making mistakes, and learning from them—and to keep moving forward.

"This phase is a time for celebration."

≡ 5

Rightsizing for Corporate Survival

Case Studies Summary

This appendix contains a summary of each case study presented in *Rightsizing for Corporate Survival*. See Chapter 3, "Rightsizing Opportunities," and Chapter 4, "Economics of Rightsizing," for detailed information about each individual company and its rightsizing project.

ADCO

Headquartered in Dusseldorf, Germany, Attwoods Dixi Corporation (ADCO) is a subsidiary of Attwoods, one of the world's leading international waste management companies. With its portable sanitation business, ADCO serves more than 90 percent of the German population. ADCO also provides portable accommodation and waste management, which includes disposal of residential, commercial, and industrial waste.

Old Configuration

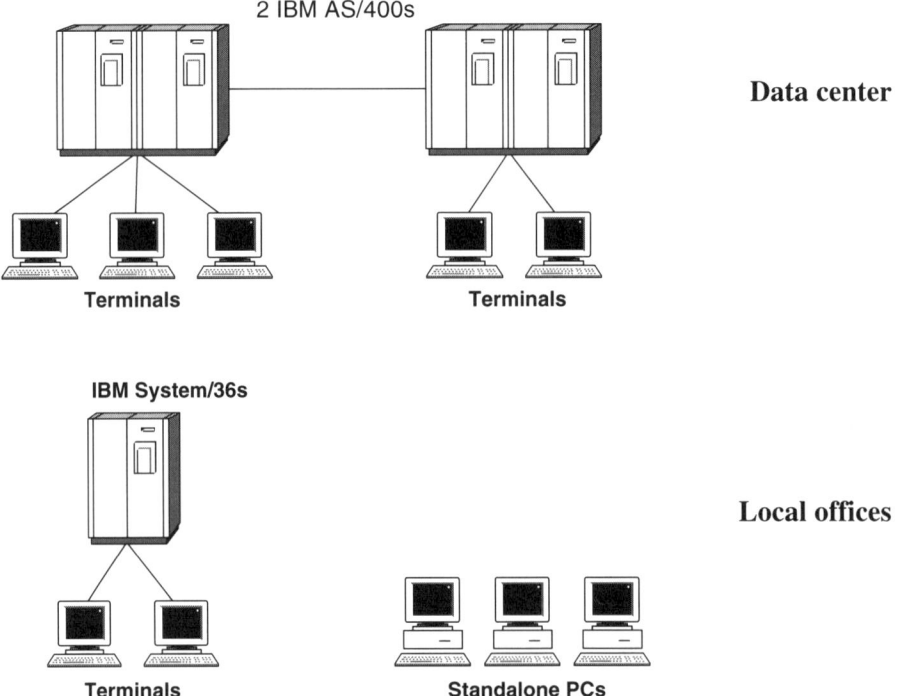

Problems Encountered

❏ Although ADCO was growing, the current system lacked the flexibility and scalability to grow with it.

❏ The company was attempting to decentralize its operations, yet it lacked a central network to communicate information effectively between corporate headquarters and the local offices. As a result, many business processes had to be performed manually.

❏ To make up for the absence of a network, the company would have to purchase courier services to transport diskettes from one location to another.

❏ The current applications, which were more than five years old, were not meeting the company's business requirements.

New Configuration

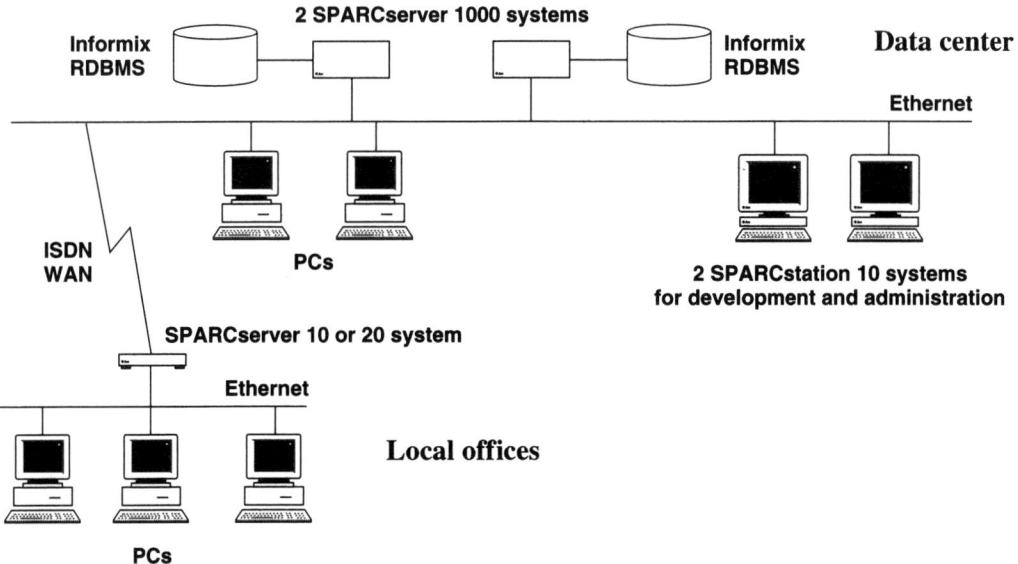

A

Business Benefits

- ❑ The ability to provide daily updates of critical data.
- ❑ Decentralization of much of its operations, moving the company closer to its customers.
- ❑ The placement of additional business units on the network.
- ❑ Automation of several manual business processes.
- ❑ Improved flexibility and scalability.
- ❑ Reduction of travel costs for IS staff visiting remote locations to manage systems.

Banc One

The Risk Management department of Bank One Columbus, a subsidiary of Banc One, is responsible for all strategic and tactical decisions regarding risk or profitability of credit card accounts.

Old Configuration

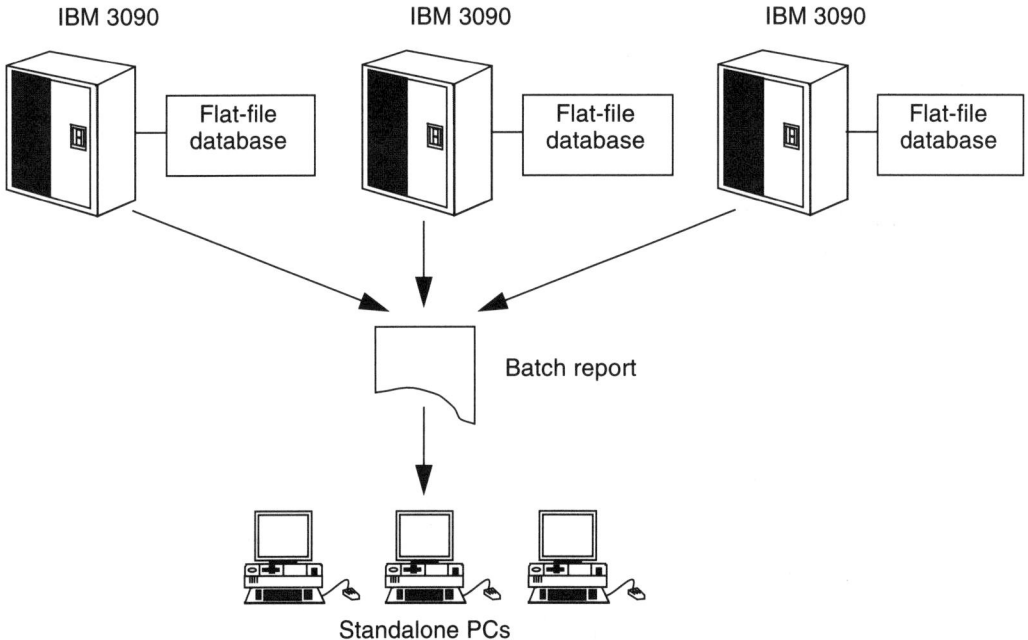

Standalone PCs

Problems Encountered

❏ Inability to effectively analyze data.
❏ Lack of timely access to information.
❏ Excessive computing costs.

New Configuration

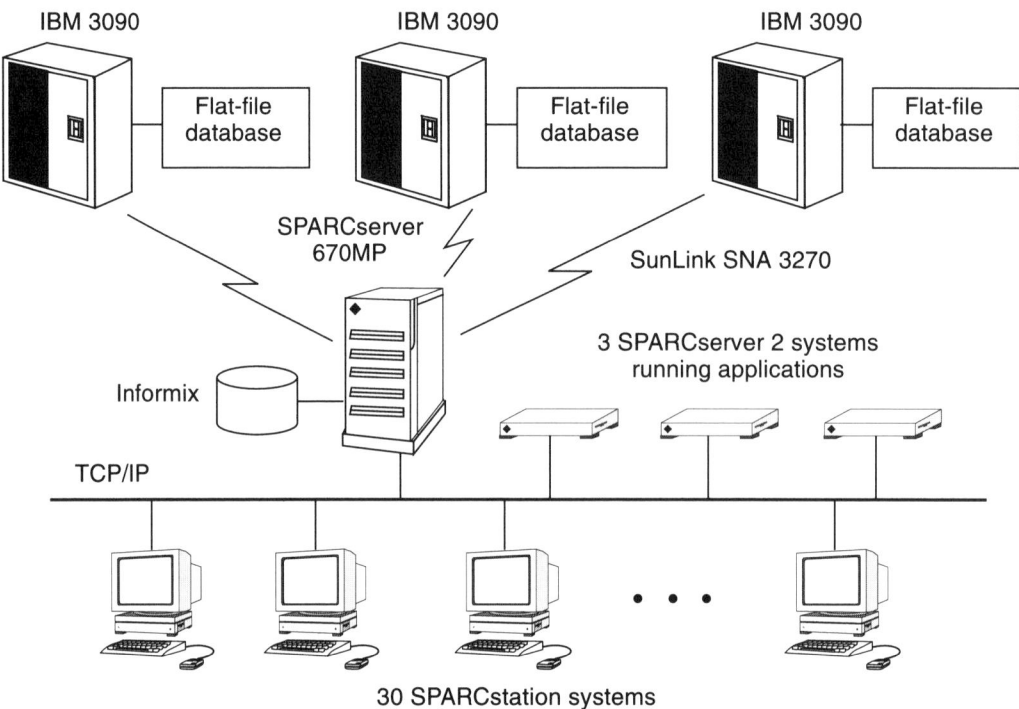

Financial Benefits

❏ Savings of $1.8 to $2.7 million achieved in annual operating expenses.

❏ Net present value of the total savings is $9,214,000.

❏ Initial costs recouped in four months.

❏ Elimination of the need for temporary data entry workers saves $870,000 over five years.

Business Benefits

❏ Improved access to account information has resulted in better, more-informed, risk management decisions, increasing business profits by $6 to $7 million annually.

❏ Enhanced analytical capabilities have reduced delinquency write-offs, resulting in an additional projected savings of $4 million.

❏ The quality and enhanced presentation of information provided to management has led to more responsive decisions.

❏ Existing departmental staff is able to handle greatly increased departmental workload.

New Zealand Inland Revenue Department

New Zealand Inland Revenue Department (IRD), the nation's central tax collection agency (comparable to the U.S. Internal Revenue Service), is responsible for collecting NZ$27 billion (US$15 billion) each year from 3.5 million people. IRD is responsible for collecting a broad range of taxes including income, fringe benefits, goods and services, estate, and gaming (gambling).

Old Configuration

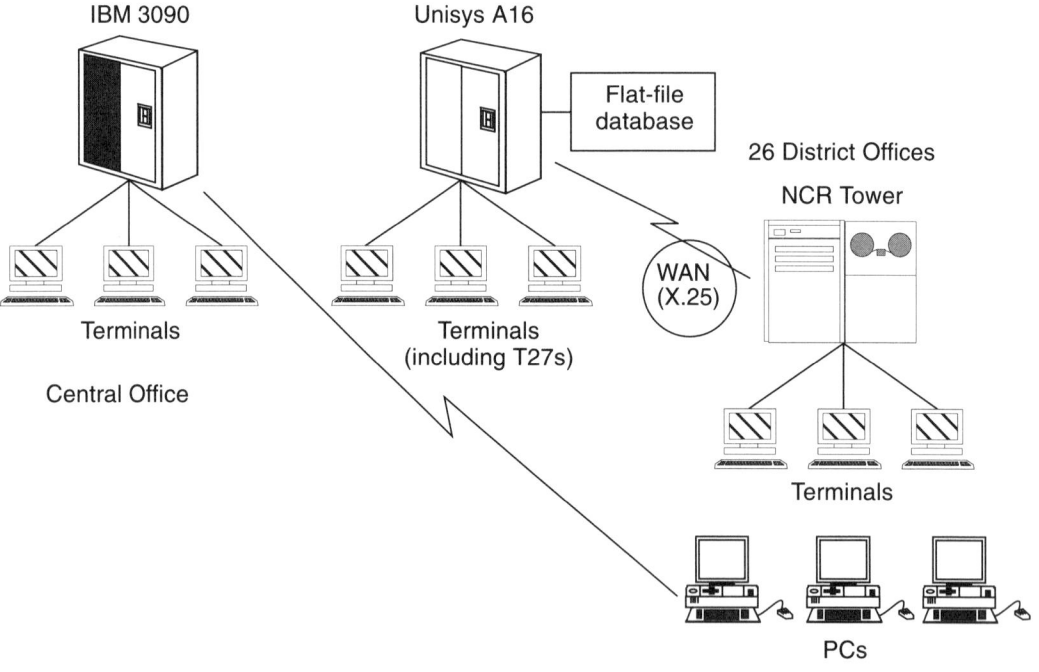

Problems Encountered

❑ Tax return backlogs.

❑ Slow response to taxpayer inquiries.

❑ Unautomated office tasks.

New Configuration

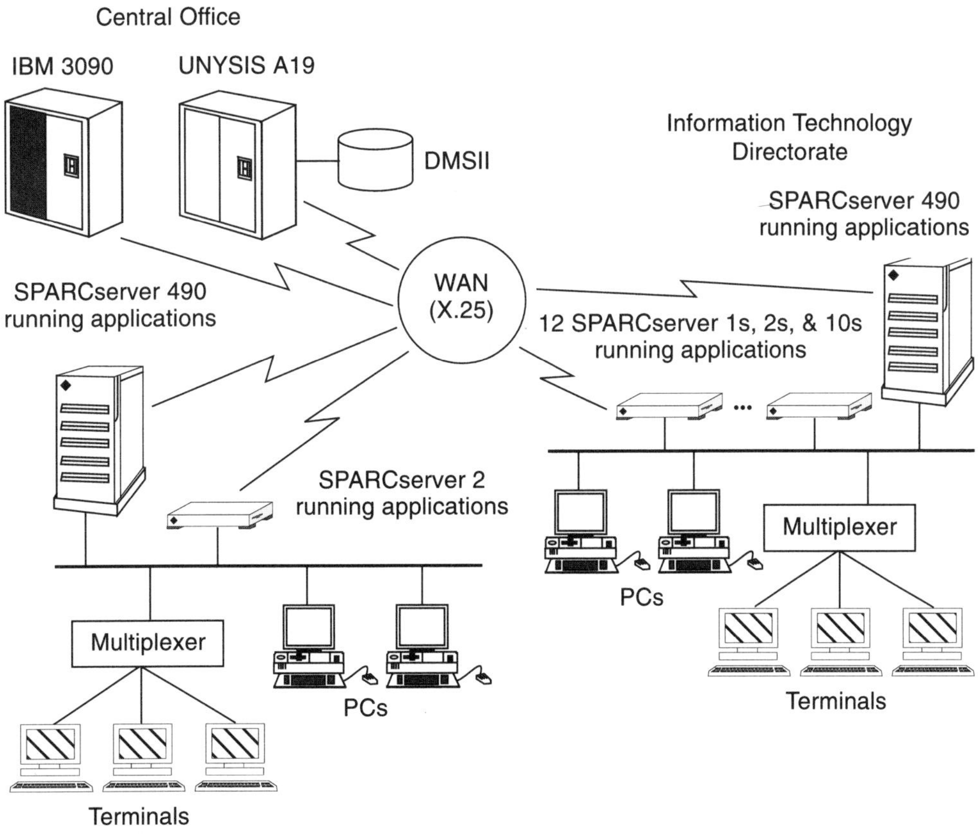

Central Office

IBM 3090   UNYSIS A19

DMSII

Information Technology
Directorate

SPARCserver 490
running applications

SPARCserver 490
running applications

WAN
(X.25)

12 SPARCserver 1s, 2s, & 10s
running applications

SPARCserver 2
running applications

Multiplexer

PCs

PCs

Multiplexer

Multiplexer

Terminals

Terminals

A

Business Benefits

❑ Faster processing of tax returns.

❑ Quick response to inquiries.

❑ Automation of office activities.

❑ Cost-efficient operation.

WorldCorp

WorldCorp is a $400-million air transportation and transaction processing enterprise based in Herndon, Virginia. It consists of three companies, including World Airways, a leading provider of air transportation for commercial and government customers, and US Order, a developer of patented automated ordering services.

Old Configuration

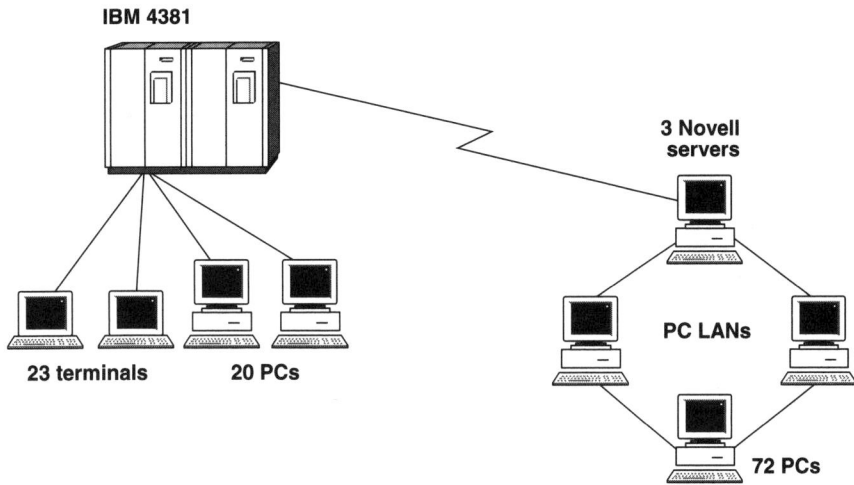

Problems Encountered

❑ Lack of reporting flexibility and timeliness.

❑ Limited access to application functions.

❑ Inadequate turnaround time.

❑ High maintenance costs.

New Configuration

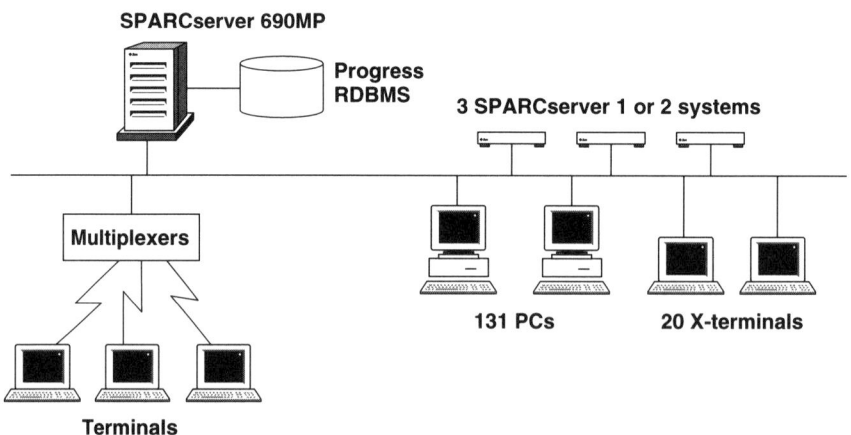

Financial Benefits

❏ Per-year costs for the UNIX client-server solution are approximately $500,000 less per year than the per-year mainframe costs over the five years.

❏ Software maintenance fees for WorldCorp's accounting software have dropped from $120,000 to $18,000 annually, far exceeding the project's goals.

❏ The new system saved significant hardware and software operating costs from the first year onward.

❏ Minimal cutover time to the new system has eliminated the expense of operating the old and new systems simultaneously.

Business Benefits

❑ Downtime for the company's financial systems has decreased by 90 percent.

❑ The learning curve of moving to the new financial system has been shortened from days to hours.

❑ Separate WorldCorp divisions can run their payrolls and financial reports at any time, regardless of what the other divisions are doing, overcoming the old system's biggest operational roadblock.

❑ Programmer productivity is up by an estimated 300 percent.

❑ Faster ad hoc report generation has improved decision-making.

A

Application Scoring Model

Scoring potential applications can be useful to determine which applications are the best candidates for initially rightsizing. The scoring criteria differs, depending on the project objective; that is, whether you are "scaling" or re-engineering the application. This appendix summarizes information contained in Chapter 5, "The Rightsizing Process."

Scaling Projects

In scaling projects, information about the current application environment falls into three categories: *application characteristics*, *usage characteristics*, and *cost*. Your team should rate each application to determine the ease and estimated payback from moving to a rightsized environment.

Application Characteristics

Application characteristics determine the ease or difficulty of moving the application to a new environment. Some applications may be impossible to move because of the language or tool in which they were developed (for example, 360 assembler Mark IV, MODEL 204); other applications require significant retooling (for example, IMS). However, many mainframe-based applications are portable. Table B-1 shows sample application characteristics.

Table B-1   Application Characteristics

Characteristic	Examples
Programming language	COBOL, PL/1, Assembler
Tools	IBI Focus, Software AG Natural
Data format	IMS, DB2, ORACLE
Subsystems accessed	CICS, DEC Forms
Machine dependence	System calls
Inter-dependencies	HR system updates payroll system with wage and employee information

Usage Characteristics

Application usage characteristics determine the new environment's size and influence the new technical architecture. Characteristics you should determine and evaluate include:

- CPU usage
- Data management (average and total working set size)
- DASD requirements
- End-user community (location, devices, network configuration)
- Transaction volume
- Number of read/write operations per transaction
- Number of users (total and concurrent)
- Peak usage characteristics

Cost Information

Application cost information is particularly important to assess if IS cost reduction is your overall goal. For a complete discussion on the type of cost information you will want to collect, see Chapter 4, "Economics of Rightsizing."

Once you have collected cost information, you can evaluate alternative, rightsized architectures. Use the model provided in Appendix C, "Cost/Benefit Model," to perform a cost/benefit analysis for each application and assess the business impact of rightsizing.

Application Scoring

Once you have evaluated application characteristics, usage characteristics, and cost, you can then score applications for ease of migration. Table B-2 identifies some sample scoring criteria (applications are rated from high 5 to low 1). Applications with the highest point totals become the best candidates for further examination. Be wary, however, of applications with high point totals but low ratings (1) in any specific area.

Table B-2   Sample Application Scoring Criteria

Characteristic	Scoring Criteria
Interdependencies with other application systems	5 – Simple interdependencies (read-only, batch-file oriented) with other applications. 1 – Complex interdependencies (read/write) with other application systems.
Percentage of mainframe CPU use	5 – Uses more than 12 percent of the mainframe CPU during prime shift. 1 – Uses less than 3 percent of the mainframe CPU during prime shift.
Payback period	5 – Payback period six months or less. 1 – Payback period more than two years.
Ease of migration	5 – Port to a UNIX environment requires few changes. 1 – Port to UNIX environment requires substantial rewriting of portions of the application.

Application Selection

Scoring applications facilitates the sorting of candidates at a high level. It is not intended to be a single measure to determine the order of application migration. Besides rating, there are several application selection criteria that you should evaluate before making a final decision. Examples of application selection criteria are listed in Table B-3.

Table B-3   Application Selection Criteria

Characteristic	Description
Technical Architecture	The entry application uses the core technologies and platforms defined by the vision statement and matches the skill set of the project team.
High Visibility	The entry application has sufficient visibility; its success will increase management's commitment to the strategy and can increase resource availability.
High ROI/Impact	The entry application provides a strong ROI or has a major impact on the business.

Re-engineering Projects

In business process re-engineering projects, you should confirm the critical business issues to ensure that everyone understands them. Then obtain and assess information about current business processes. Your result from this research, at a minimum, should be a detailed process flowchart and productivity/cost measurements for each task in the process. Table B-4 describes the assessment process.

Table B-4   Business Process Assessment

Category	Information to Obtain
Task description	Identify and describe: • Each discrete task in the process • All forms or electronic systems used within each task • Data elements used in each task • Documentation • Informal undocumented shortcuts
Task relationships	Identify and describe: • Relationship between each discrete task • Controls • All forms or electronic systems used among tasks • Documentation • Informal undocumented shortcuts
Task resource requirements	Identify and describe: • Time each task takes • Time between tasks • Jobs of people performing each task • Current productivity measures and any productivity history • Types of events that create delays in processing • Full-time equivalent (FTE) staff requirements • Costs associated with each task
Value added	Does the task add value? What new data is added during the task? How much of the task is associated with controls built into the process?
Duplicate/redundant effort	What data is entered onto a form or into a computer system more than once in the process? How many points of contact are established with customers/suppliers?

Table B-4   Business Process Assessment (Continued)

Category	Information to Obtain
Processing time	How much time does the process take from beginning to end? How much time is spent performing each task? How much wait time exists between tasks? What is the estimated time spent performing value-added effort within each task and throughout the process?

After reviewing all business processes, choose the first process to re-engineer. The characteristics of the ideal first process are similar to those used to determine entry applications in scaling efforts. Considerations for selecting the application include:

- Envision the entire business process and select applications with the fewest inter-dependencies with other application systems

- Where possible, focus on applications that are read-only

- Where possible, concentrate on applications with broad management visibility and representing a high payoff to the enterprise

- Focus on applications that gain leverage from the new IS architecture

Cost/Benefit Model C

This section provides a cost/benefit model framework for you to perform your own cost/benefit analyses for potential rightsizing projects. This model's objective is to create a side-by-side comparison of all the relevant costs and benefits of your current and proposed systems. The model is divided into the following four sections:

1. Current system costs
Use this section to analyze the total cost of ownership associated with the existing system.

2. New system costs
Use this section to analyze the total cost of ownership associated with the new, rightsized system.

3. Business benefits
Use this section to analyze the business benefits resulting from implementation of the new system.

4. Economic analysis
Use this section to analyze the net effect of the new system, determining the net annual cash flows and measuring project returns and payback periods.

The model is intended to be a starting point—you will need to customize it for your own particular situation. For example, you may want to provide more or less detail by subdividing or combining line items, respectively. Some line items may not apply to your situation, or you may need to add other line items.

Current System Costs

The Current Systems Costs section assesses the costs associated with the current system you are considering rightsizing. When completing this section, fill in all the costs that are relevant to your environment, starting with the current year as Year 1 and proceeding for as many years as the expected life span of the *new* system under consideration. Typically, this life span will be three to five years.

♦ **Hardware-Related Annual Costs**
Include all hardware-related costs for those systems the rightsizing project will replace or off-load. As a guideline, the model contains line items for each of the major equipment categories. For each equipment category, identify two cost items:

a. Ownership cost
The cost of purchasing or leasing the equipment, including any upgrades or additional equipment purchases expected during the analysis period.

If the equipment is purchased and fully expensed in a particular year, enter that cost; if the equipment is purchased and depreciated over several years, enter the annual depreciation amount. For example, if the equipment was purchased for $500,000 and is depreciated over five years using straight-line depreciation, then enter $100,000 as the annual purchase cost.

If the equipment is leased, enter the annual lease payment.

You may want to consult with your accounting department regarding depreciation schedules and amounts.

b. Maintenance cost
The annual maintenance expense for the equipment.

In the maintenance cost line, enter the annual maintenance fees.

If your department or division does not own the hardware, your computing costs are most likely assessed as chargebacks. In this case, enter your annual chargebacks on the appropriate line.

♦ **Software-Related Annual Costs**
Include all software-related costs for the systems the rightsizing project will replace or off-load. Include the ownership costs and the maintenance costs.

♦ **Development-Related Annual Costs**
Include all personnel costs for developing new applications or maintaining existing ones. These line items are subdivided into lines for in-house staff and outside contractors. Line items are also included for outside consulting and training.

♦ **Operations-Related Annual Costs**
Include all costs related to system operations, administration, and management. The operations and communications/network staff line items are subdivided into lines for in-house staff and outside contractors or outsourcing. Line items are also included for outside consulting and training. Facilities costs are subdivided into several components.

New System Costs

Use the New System Costs section to assess the costs associated with the new, rightsized system. When completing this section, fill in all costs that are relevant to your new environment, starting with the current year as Year 1 and proceeding for as many years as the expected life span of the new system.

Note – Most of the line items in this section are the same as those in the Current System Costs section.

♦ **Hardware-Related Annual Costs**
Include all hardware-related costs for the new system. Be sure to include not only new equipment purchases but also any hardware costs for the current system that will continue to be incurred, for the appropriate number of years. For example, if you are replacing a system, include its costs throughout the transition period while the new system is being implemented. If you are off-loading but not replacing a system, include its cost for the duration of the project.

Include ownership and maintenance costs and handle expensed purchases, depreciated purchases, leases, and chargebacks in the same manner as you did in the Current System Costs section.

♦ **Software-Related Annual Costs**
Include all software-related costs for the new system. Again, be sure to enter not only new software purchases but also any continuing software costs for the current system for the appropriate number of years.

♦ **Development-Related Annual Costs**
Include all personnel costs for application development, which covers new development as well as re-engineering or redeploying existing systems. Ongoing application maintenance refers to maintenance of existing systems over time. In the consulting and training line items, include all costs associated with new skills acquisition for the development staff.

♦ **Operations-Related Annual Costs**

Include all costs related to system operations, administration, and management for the new system; remember to enter costs for any remote or distributed sites. In the consulting and training line items, indicate all costs associated with new skills development for operations staff. Include any facilities modifications required by the new system in the Facilities modifications line item.

♦ **Transition Annual Costs**

Include all additional transition costs not covered elsewhere in the model. Transition costs such as new hardware/software purchases, parallel operations, and retraining costs should have appeared elsewhere, but if they have not been fully addressed, then add these costs to this section. In addition, include costs for:

- Training of end users on the new system
- Depreciation write-offs on replaced systems that have not been fully depreciated
- Lease termination fees on replaced systems that have unexpired leases
- Other consulting services that have not been covered elsewhere, such as architecture planning or design

Business Benefits

Use the Business Benefits section to assess the business benefits that may derive from the operation of the new system. These benefits can result from increases in business revenues, reductions in the cost of running the business, or both.

Business benefits are often the most difficult to quantify, but they can also be the most important reason for implementing new systems. Therefore, you should develop the most effective method of quantifying these benefits.

First, identify those business processes that will be most directly affected by the new system. Working with end-users, determine the appropriate way to measure the positive effects you expect the new system to have on the business. The model includes some sample business result line items. Because benefits can vary widely from business to business, you will probably need to add line items appropriate to your particular organization.

Economic Analysis

Use the Economic Analysis section to analyze the net effect of the new system, determining the net annual cash flows and measuring project returns and payback periods. We suggest using a spreadsheet to perform these calculations. Calculate the net annual cash flows by subtracting the new system costs from the current system costs and adding the business benefits. A positive result represents the net saving in a given year, and a negative result represents the net loss.

The model employs discounted cash flows to factor in the time value of money. Use your company's cost of capital as the discount rate, and use the discount rate to convert future cash flows into their current value.

Finally, the model employs several financial analysis techniques to determine the value or return of the project:

- Net present value (NPV) uses discounted cash flows to determine the total value of the project in today's currency. Future cash flows are reduced because their value is less.

- Internal rate of return (IRR) uses discounted cash flows to determine the rate of return for the project in today's currency. This calculation is more complex but also more accurate than the ROI technique because it discounts future cash flows when you calculate the project's return.

- Return on investment (ROI) is a simple ratio of the total benefits divided by the total costs for the duration of the project. This calculation does not factor in the time value of money.

- Payback period is the time required to recoup all the project investments. After this time, all savings become the project's return. This calculation does not consider the time value of money, but it is often used to figure out when the project will start producing payback.

Using one or more of these techniques, you should be able to determine if the proposed rightsizing project is financially attractive to your company.

Current System Cost of Ownership					
Hardware-Related Annual Costs	Year 1	Year 2	Year 3	Year 4	Year 5
Mainframes/minicomputers/servers					
Maintenance					
Terminals/PCs/workstations					
Maintenance					
DASD/disk subsystem					
Maintenance					
Tape and other secondary storage					
Maintenance					
Printers/peripherals/controllers					
Maintenance					
Data communications/networking					
Maintenance					
Chargebacks					
Other					
Hardware subtotal					
Software-Related Annual Costs	Year 1	Year 2	Year 3	Year 4	Year 5
Operating systems and utilities					
Maintenance					
Databases and TP monitors					
Maintenance					
System management tools					
Maintenance					
Applications					
Maintenance					
Development tools					
Maintenance					
Other					
Software subtotal					

Development-Related Annual Costs	Year 1	Year 2	Year 3	Year 4	Year 5
Application development staff					
In-house					
Contractor					
Ongoing application maintenance staff					
In-house					
Contractor					
Consulting					
Training					
Development subtotal					

Operations-Related Annual Costs	Year 1	Year 2	Year 3	Year 4	Year 5
Operations staff					
In-house					
Contractor or outsourced					
Communications/networking staff					
In-house					
Contractor or outsourced					
Consulting					
Training					
Facilities					
Normal production					
Disaster recovery or backup					
Transmission or leased lines					
Facilities modifications					
Utilities					
Supplies and consumables					
Other					
Operations subtotal					
Current System Total Cost					

New System Cost of Ownership					
Hardware-Related Annual Costs	**Year 1**	**Year 2**	**Year 3**	**Year 4**	**Year 5**
Mainframes/minicomputers/servers					
Maintenance					
Terminals/PCs/workstations					
Maintenance					
DASD/disk subsystem					
Maintenance					
Tape and other secondary storage					
Maintenance					
Printers/peripherals/controllers					
Maintenance					
Data communications/networking					
Maintenance					
Chargebacks					
Other					
Hardware subtotal					
Software-Related Annual Costs	**Year 1**	**Year 2**	**Year 3**	**Year 4**	**Year 5**
Operating systems and utilities					
Maintenance					
Databases and TP monitors					
Maintenance					
System management tools					
Maintenance					
Applications					
Maintenance					
Development tools					
Maintenance					
Other					
Software subtotal					

Development-Related Annual Costs	Year 1	Year 2	Year 3	Year 4	Year 5
Application development staff					
In-house					
Contractor					
Ongoing application maintenance staff					
In-house					
Contractor					
Consulting					
Training					
Development subtotal					

Operations-Related Annual Costs	Year 1	Year 2	Year 3	Year 4	Year 5
Operations staff					
In-house					
Contractor or outsourced					
Communications/networking staff					
In-house					
Contractor or outsourced					
Consulting					
Training					
Facilities					
Normal production					
Disaster recovery or backup					
Transmission or leased lines					
Facilities modifications					
Utilities					
Supplies and consumables					
Other					
Operations subtotal					

Transition Annual Costs	Year 1	Year 2	Year 3	Year 4	Year 5
End-user retraining on new systems					
Depreciation write-offs					
Lease termination fees					
Consulting					
Other					
Transition subtotal					

New System Total Cost					

Business Benefits

Business Revenue Contribution	Year 1	Year 2	Year 3	Year 4	Year 5
Improved time to market					
Improved customer service					
Increased sales productivity					
Improved order fulfillment					
New products or services					
Other					
Revenue contribution subtotal					

Business Cost Reduction	Year 1	Year 2	Year 3	Year 4	Year 5
Reduced departmental staffing					
Reduced departmental consumables					
Reduced travel or transportation					
Reduced business transaction cost					
Reduced product development cost					
Reduced service delivery cost					
Other					
Cost reduction subtotal					

Business Benefits Total					

Economic Analysis

Enter discount rate: _____ %

Current System Total Annual Cost	Year 1	Year 2	Year 3	Year 4	Year 5
Hardware subtotal					
Software subtotal					
Development subtotal					
Operations subtotal					
Current System Total Cost					

New System Total Annual Cost	Year 1	Year 2	Year 3	Year 4	Year 5
Hardware subtotal					
Software subtotal					
Development subtotal					
Operations subtotal					
Transition subtotal					
New System Total Cost					

Total Annual Saving/Loss	Year 1	Year 2	Year 3	Year 4	Year 5
Hardware subtotal					
Software subtotal					
Development subtotal					
Operations subtotal					
Transition subtotal					
Cost Saving/Loss					
Business Benefits Total					
Net Saving/Loss					
Cumulative Net Saving/Loss					
Discounted Net Saving/Loss					
Cumulative Discounted Net S/L					

C

Rightsizing for Corporate Survival

Open Systems Checklist

To benefit from open systems, you can use a checklist to isolate and define the criteria by which technologies meet your goals of openness. This appendix contains an example checklist.

❑ Published interface
At a minimum, an open specification must be well-written and published to allow other vendors to easily create their own value-added implementations of the interface. For example, the published specification for UNIX System V Release 4, which is being used by more than 250 companies.

❑ Multi-vendor
Implementations of the interface must be available from multiple vendors.

❑ Reference of the Implementation
This is not actually a requirement of openness; however, it is easier to build an implementation if you first have seen an example of one.

❑ Free or inexpensive
The specification should be accessible without exorbitant royalties or fees for its use.

❑ Legally clean
You should be able to access and use the specification without fear of being sued.

❑ Supported by independent organization
Ideally, the interface is supported by an independent organization that conducts branding and compatibility testing of implementations.

❑ Portable
The software should be able to run on multiple hardware architectures without having to be recompiled.

❑ Scalable
The software should be able to run on any system—from PCs to mainframes to supercomputers. True scalability allows developers to write one application that runs on a wide range of systems, which enables IS to equip the production facilities with a system that meets the users' needs.

❑ Inter-operable
  A system should seamlessly share data and applications with systems made by different vendors.

Note – Inter-operability and connectivity are *not* the same. Although both elements are required, interoperability requires a higher level of communication than connectivity.

Vendor-Selection Criteria

When selecting rightsizing vendors, there are several criteria which you should consider. This appendix contains an example list of criteria.

❑ Open systems commitment
Does the vendor have a commitment to openness?

❑ Commitment to standards
Does the vendor implement standards in its products and participate in standards bodies and committees to aid the shaping and direction of standards evolution?

❑ Robust operating environment
Does the vendor have a 32-bit operating environment?

❑ Portability and scalability
Are the products offered by the vendor portable and scalable to meet the future needs of your company?

❑ Commercial off-the-shelf application availability
Does the vendor port to volume platforms? The larger the volume, the larger the range of choice of commercial off-the-shelf applications.

❑ Development productivity
What is the breadth and depth of development tools from the vendor and its third-party offerings?

❑ Inter-operability
With what other producst do the products offered by the vendor inter-operate?

❑ Integrated desktop vision
How open and standard is the vendor's solution?
How does the vendor's solution play with emerging industry solutions?

❑ Secure computing
What type of computing security does the vendor offer?

❑ Data availability and integrity
Many IBM installations support mission-critical applications. For these applications, issues such as availability and integrity are of paramount importance.

❑ Spectrum of service offerings

Does the vendor provide a tiered service offering in order to customize the service level as required by your installation and the degree of autonomy desired?

Sun's Perspective of Rightsizing

Sun Microsystems is in the process of rightsizing its entire business to run on UNIX servers and workstations. Today, Sun runs its business on more than 3000 servers, 23,000 workstations, 300 UNIX applications, and one remaining mainframe. When this last mainframe is replaced, Sun, as a Fortune 120 company, will be the largest company in the world to be running its entire business on a UNIX client-server environment.

A "War Story"

In June of 1993, Scott McNealy, CEO of Sun Microsystems, related the story of how Sun began its rightsizing initiative that was spearheaded by Sun's CIO, Bill Raduchel. McNealy's version of the story is as follows:

> When Sun was started in 1983, we bought some HP 3000s. Two or three years later, these machines had about a 70-second response time—that is, it took 70 seconds from a keystroke to when the prompt came back. This 70-second delay in response time would occur at the end of the quarter, when we were trying to fundamentally book all our revenue—absolutely the worst time to have this problem arise.
>
> Recognizing that our HP 3000s were not going to meet our needs, we had to make a decision about moving to Phase Two of our computing environment. We had two options:
>
> - Option 1 was to go mainframe. Buy Cullinet and buy this big mainframe environment.
>
> - Option 2 was to invent a commercial computing environment based upon RISC and UNIX on our own computers.
>
> The software for Option 2 did not exist in 1984-85 because no one had done that type of environment before. Our vote to go with one of these two options came out 11 to 1: I voted to do it on RISC and UNIX with our computers; my other 11 managers voted to do it on a mainframe. So we did the mainframe.
>
> We got all trained and were moving forward, but just as we were about to turn on this mainframe, my CIO came into my office and said, "Remember when I told you that we only needed one mainframe and it would last us for years and years because it is so big and expensive and powerful and wonderful? Well, we need another one."

I replied, "You have got to be kidding me. Another one? Why do we need another one?"

"We certainly do not want to do development on our production machine because if we touch a piece of the application over here, we might break the application over there," he answered. "If we touch the database over here, we might break the application over there. So we have to do all of our testing on a separate machine that is away from the production environment."

The bottom line of the story is: In the history of Sun, we have only lost money in one quarter. Guess which quarter it was?

When we threw the big switch and turned the mainframe on, there was a brownout in San Jose, California and there was a blackout of information. The mainframe was not working right—the whole thing did not work—and no one seemed to know how to make it work. That quarter we had record bookings, we had record inventory—and we lost money!

Well, we finally did get the mainframe going, but then, only a few months later, my CIO comes in again and says, "By the way, we need three more mainframes over the next two years."

I then did the best thing I probably have ever done for Sun Microsystems. I had about a 38-second, one-way conversation with my CIO, which basically said, "Read my lips: No more mainframes."

I did a good thing for my CIO. As the CEO, I took the blame for every problem of every operating business within Sun. Under this directive, my CIO could say, "McNealy has gone crazy—we are not allowed to buy any more mainframes. But I am here to help us solve the problems he is causing." It allowed him the leeway to determine how to rightsize and get off the mainframe environment.

That decision turned out to be critical in the history of Sun. Today, Sun has grown to nearly a $5 billion company. It has made money every quarter except the one in which the mainframe computing environment was deployed. The company has decreased its quote-to-collection cycle time (that is, the time from when a purchase order is received until the time it collects payment for a shipment) from 273 days to about 140 days, resulting in a cash increase for the company of $700 million over three years. Sun leads its industry in such measures as revenue per employee (over $300,000/employee) and annual inventory turns (over 11/year). Furthermore, during the transition to distributed computing, Sun increased its ratio of users to system administrators from 50:1 to over 125:1.

Sun is somewhat different from most companies in that most companies would not be able to reach agreement on one common environment. Nonetheless, Sun's achievements are noteworthy. The section "Sun's Ten Commandments of Information Technology" presents lessons learned by Sun during its rightsizing process.

Sun's Ten Commandments of Information Technology

Sun has shared its rightsizing story and internal experiences with numerous companies around the world. During these sessions, companies always want to know what Sun has learned from its rightsizing experiences. Throughout this book, we have presented many lessons learned by other companies that have successfully rightsized. In this section, we list Sun's top ten lessons learned about information technology with respect to rightsizing.

1. Engineer Simplicity—Do Not Manage Complexity

When you look at client-server computing, you find an enormous number of technology options relative to mainframe-based environments. These options give you flexibility in:

- How you implement your hardware and software environments
- How you set up your network
- How you manage your environment
- How you develop your applications

While flexibility is good, it also can produce a real concern: a very complex environment that may be beyond anyone's ability to manage. Open systems provide lots of choices, but if you execute all of them, you will have an environment that is too complex to manage.

Sun took advantage of the capabilities, functionality, and flexibility of open systems to re-engineer its business, but it also restricted technology options to a limited number of choices, creating an environment that was simple: simple to manage, simple to run, and simple to operate. It is critical to limit technology options and enforce these decisions to minimize complexity.

2. Closely Align IT Activities with Business Needs

Client-server computing enables you to re-engineer your systems and to operate in a different manner. It gives you the capability and the flexibility to closely align your IT activities (that is, your information systems) with your business needs. This alignment is of critical importance and is perhaps the number one issue of most corporations today. Make sure you take advantage of one of the key benefits of rightsizing: the ability to organize your computing in a way that aligns very closely with your business needs. In many cases, the mainframe has been the major obstacle to achieving this goal.

3. Large Outcomes Require Architecture—Not Large Projects

Most corporations are used to big mainframe projects: large projects that take many years, require millions of dollars, lots of resources, and lots of planning. If you have the right architecture *and* client-server computing, you can use small projects—small projects that can be self-managing and that can connect closely to users. Many software development studies have shown that small projects can be a factor of 10—and sometimes as much as a factor of 100—more effective at delivering results than large projects. At Sun, the "rule of thumb" is 10 people, one year, $1 million. Any larger projects have to be broken down into smaller projects.

4. Functionality Is Cheaper than Freedom

Sun has found that a centrally administered network, operated much like a production environment with a lot of management control and discipline, can drive down costs. Using structured, disciplined architecture standards, you can achieve far lower costs per seat in the network. In the most extreme cases, you can lower your costs by as much as a factor of 10.

This type of network and associated cost reduction provides the ability to implement a lot more functionality than you had before, which can make users much happier. The user sees a great trade-off, the company comes out ahead, and the IS department looks very good in the process.

5. Run One Homogeneous (As Possible) Network

Run one network backbone and keep it as homogenous as possible. This commandment is important because Sun could never operate its system as effectively if it had to run all of the multiple network protocols available in the market today. Sun has reduced operational costs significantly by running one homogeneous network backbone.

6. A Computer System Is ... a Computer System

This message often gets lost in people's misconceptions about UNIX. Amazingly enough, they believe that computer systems based on a microprocessor and that run UNIX do not require the rules, procedures, and people that are required to operate other computer systems. Many companies are conditioned to think that moving to a UNIX environment means changing everything. This is not true.

Sun runs a computer system like any other computer systems. The fact that the system is a UNIX system, the fact that it is the Solaris operating system, and the fact that it runs on SPARC microprocessors, does not change the way Sun manages the system. Sun changed the least amount possible while moving to UNIX and did not "throw away" the knowledge, the procedures, and most importantly, the people used to manage the mainframe.

7. Employees and Knowledge of Your Systems Are Your Greatest Assets

Your greatest asset going forward will be your employees and their knowledge of your systems. While rightsizing, Sun did not get rid of its mainframe designers. It is important to understand that most of the skills of your IS professionals will transfer easily. The fundamentals behind how to build an information system do not change. Not surprisingly, the people who built the best applications on the mainframe, usually build the best applications in UNIX environments. If you change the operating system and you change the microprocessor, the skills of these people are not going to be affected. People need to understand that they have an enormous base of talent in their existing organization that they can apply as they go forward with implementing client-server computing.

8. Implement Business Practice Change, Not Systems

Within nearly every major rightsizing project at Sun, you will find a business practice change. It is critical to involve your users when you are implementing business practice changes. Your users are committed to you. They want you to be successful. They want to support you, and they can give you the help you need to make the project happen. If users do not benefit from the change, it will be hard for them to be enthusiastic supporters. Concentrate your limited investment dollars where you can get a business practice change instead of where you are only implementing a systems change.

9. Keep Peak Loads Local and Network Loads Flat

In some ways, this commandment is a repeat of the first commandment, but it is so important that it is worth repeating. Keeping your peak loads local and your network loads flat is actually an important part of engineering simplicity and not trying to manage complexity.

As the network becomes the point of greatest complexity in your environment, you need to make everything else simpler. To give yourself the opportunity to effectively manage your network over time, keep your network loads flat and your peak loads local. This rule may require you to duplicate data, but you will benefit by maximizing processing where you have the most capacity (local servers and desktops) and minimizing traffic over your network.

10. Target Writing a Fixed Percentage of Your Application Source Code

No IS organization can survive long-term unless it writes some source code. You must write code to make your systems better and to obtain competitive advantage. However, you want to write as small a portion of that source code as possible because it is time-consuming and costly. Once you have implemented your business practice change, you do not want to do anything more.

Recommended Reading

Other Books on Rightsizing

Business Re-engineering: The Survival Guide by Dorine C. Andrews and Susan K. Stalick; Prentice Hall, Englewood Cliffs, NJ, 1994; ISBN 0-13-014853-9.

A look at the end-to-end process of re-engineering a business. Presents proven tools, techniques, and real-life examples.

Business Re-engineering with Information Technology by John J. Donovan; Prentice Hall, Englewood Cliffs, NJ, 1994; ISBN 0-13-125907-5.

Presents a re-engineered information architecture: a three-tiered client/server, an architecture based on open systems, and Open Distributed Environment tools.

Mainframe Downsizing to Upsize Your Business: IT-Preneuring by James Grosvenor; Prentice Hall, Englewood Cliffs, NJ, 1994; ISBN 0-13-102708-5.

A guide through the process of downsizing from mainframes to intelligent networks.

Re-engineering the Corporation: A Manifesto for Business Revolution by Michael Hammer and James Champy; HarperCollins Publishers, Inc., New York, NJ, 1993; ISBN 0-88730-640-3.

An authoritative guide to creating a new kind of company for the world of business based on how re-engineering was approached by leading companies.

Rightsizing the New Enterprise: The Proof, Not the Hype by Harris Kern and Randy Johnson; SunSoft Press/Prentice Hall, Englewood Cliffs, NJ, 1994; ISBN 0-13-132184-6.

Discusses the "how-tos" of rightsizing a mainframe data center to support a heterogeneous client-server distributed environment based on the actual experience of Sun Microsystems.

G

Books on Various Technologies

The following is a list of books on some of the various technologies you may want to consider when planning your rightsizing strategy.

Multiprocessor System Architectures: A Technical Survey of Multiprocessor/Multi-threaded Systems using SPARC, Multi-level Bus Architectures and Solaris (SunOS) by Ben Catanzaro; SunSoft Press/Prentice Hall, Englewood Cliffs, NJ, 1994; ISBN 0-13-089137-1.

    A comprehensive survey of the technology used to design high-performance multi-processing systems.

Object Data Management by R. G. G. Cattell; Addison-Wesley Publishing Company, Reading, MA, 1991; ISBN 0-201-53092-9.

    Introduction to the latest and most promising database technologies—database systems that manipulate "objects."

The Object Database Standard: ODMG-93 by Tom Atwood, Joshua Duhl, Guy Ferran, Mary Loomis, and Drew Wade; Edited by R. G. G. Cattell; Morgan Kaufmann Publishers, 1994; ISBN 1-55860-302-6.

    An important industry standard on component technology for database products and languages.

Solaris International Developer's Guide by Bill Tuthill; SunSoft Press/Prentice Hall, Englewood Cliffs, NJ, 1993; ISBN 0-13-031063-8.

    How to create global applications that run on the Solaris environment

Solaris Porting Guide by SunSoft ISV Engineering: Robert A. Massoudi, Michelle Ann Goodman, and Manoj Goyal; SunSoft Press/Prentice Hall, Englewood Cliffs, NJ, 1993; ISBN 0-13-030396-8.

    Provides a comprehensive technical overview of porting to the Solaris environment.

Stacks: Interoperability in Today's Computer Networks by Carl Malamud; Prentice Hall, Englewood Cliffs, NJ, 1992; ISBN 0-13-484080-1.

    Discusses inter-operability and high-speed networks.

ToolTalk and Open Protocols: Inter-Application Communication by Astrid Julienne and Brian Holtz; SunSoft Press/Prentice Hall, Englewood Cliffs, NJ, 1994; ISBN 0-13-031055-7.

    Discusses how to design, write, and implement "good" open protocols.

The ToolTalk Service: An Inter-Operability Solution by SunSoft, Inc.; SunSoft Press/Prentice Hall, Englewood Cliffs, NJ, 1993; ISBN 0-13-088717-X.

    Describes ToolTalk and its functionality in depth.

Papers Available on Rightsizing Technologies

The Common Object Services Specification, Volume 1, Object Management Group; OMG Document Number 94.1.1, January, 1994.

The Common Object Request Broker: Architecture and Specification, Object Management Group; OMG Document Number 91.12.1, December, 1991.

Rightsizing: Strategies, Tools & Markets, Ovum Research, Ltd. (1 Mortimer Street, London W1N7RH, England).

UNIX Systems V Product Catalog, UNIX International, Fall 1992.

Papers Available from Sun on Rightsizing Technologies

Business Application Development on Sun Systems by Sun Microsystems Computer Company, Mountain View, CA; Part Number FE389-0.

Desktop Integration Solutions Guide, The Desktop Evolution by Sun Microsystems Computer Company, Mountain View, CA; Part Number SE267-0.

Developing OpenStep Applications Using NEXTSTEP 3.2 by SunSoft Inc., Mountain View, CA; Part Number 94080-001.

Enterprise Integration Solutions Guide by Sun Microsystems Computer Company, Mountain View, CA; Part Number SE263-0.

Fourth-Generation Languages: Unleashing the Power of Client-Server Computing by Sun Microsystems Computer Company, Mountain View, CA; Part Number FE341-0.

Introduction to the ToolTalk Service by SunSoft Inc., Mountain View, CA; Part Number 91031-0.

Managing a Distributed Environment: Alternatives for Data Distribution by Sun Microsystems Computer Company, Mountain View, CA; Part Number SE 291-0.

ONC™/NFS: A Technology Guide to Distributed Computing by SunSoft Inc., Mountain View, CA; Part Number 92015-001.

Open Systems Interconnection by Sun Microsystems Computer Company, Mountain View, CA; Part Number FE298-1.

OpenStep and Solaris by SunSoft Inc., Mountain View, CA; Part Number 94081-001.

Rightsizing: An Economic Analysis by Sun Microsystems Computer Company, Mountain View, CA; Part Number SE281.

Rightsizing: Case Studies by Sun Microsystems Computer Company, Mountain View, CA; Part Number SE270.

Rightsizing: IS Manager's Guide by Sun Microsystems Computer Company, Mountain View, CA; Part Number SE269.

Rightsizing: Tools and Services Guide Version 2.0 by Sun Microsystems Computer Company, Mountain View, CA; Part Number SE286.

Solaris Distributed Computing Foundation, Federated Services by SunSoft Inc., Mountain View, CA; Part Number 92197-001

Solaris ONC: Design and Implementation of Transport-Independent RPC by SunSoft Inc., Mountain View, CA; Part Number 91028-0.

Solaris ONC: Network Information Service Plus (NIS+) by SunSoft Inc., Mountain View, CA; Part Number 91027-0.

Solaris ONC+: Network Information Service Plus (NIS+): An Enterprise Naming Service by SunSoft Inc., Mountain View, CA; Part Number 92245-001.

SPARCserver MP Systems New Technology for Flexibility, Scalability, and Growth by Sun Microsystems Computer Company, Mountain View, CA; Part Number FE345-0.

The SuperSPARC™ Microprocessor by Sun Microsystems Computer Company, Mountain View, CA; Part Number FE344-0.

The ToolTalk Service and Project DOE Relationship by SunSoft Inc., Mountain View, CA; Part Number 94078-001.

Glossary

administration

See *system administration* and *network administration*.

AIM

A set of character-based benchmarks used to measure hardware/OS multi-user performance. The AIM-III benchmark is commonly used to fairly compare systems of all architectures.

AIX

IBM's version of SVR3.1 UNIX that runs on the RS6000 hardware.

American National Standards Institute (ANSI)

An organization that reviews and approves product standards in the United States. In the electronics industry, its work enables designers and manufacturers to create and support products that are compatible with other hardware platforms in the industry. Examples are PHIGS and GKS. See also *International Organization for Standardization (ISO)*.

American Standard Code for Information Interchange (ASCII)

The standard binary encoding of alphabetical characters, numbers, and other keyboard symbols.

ANSI

See *American National Standards Institute (ANSI)*.

API

See *application programming interface (API)*.

application

A software program designed for a particular task or the specific use of a software program.

application programming interface (API)

(1) The interface to a library of language-specific subroutines (called a graphics library) that implement higher-level graphics functions.

(2) A set of calling conventions defining how a service is invoked through a software package.

architecture

The specific components of a computer system and the way they interact with one another.

ASCII

(Pronounced "as-kee.") See *American Standard Code for Information Interchange (ASCII)*.

Asynchronous Transmission Methodology (ATM)

One of the new protocols being utilized to support different network packet structures and higher network bandwidth requirements.

backup

A copy on a diskette, tape, or disk of some or all of the files from a hard disk. There are two types of backups: a full backup and an incremental backup. Synonymous with "dump."

bridge

A device that connects two or more physical networks and forwards packets between them. Bridges can usually be made to filter packets, that is, to forward only certain traffic. Related devices are: *r*epeaters which simply forward electrical signals from one cable to another, and full-fledged routers, which make routing decisions based on several criteria. In International Organization for Standardization's open systems interconnection (OSI) terminology, a bridge is a data link layer intermediate system.

CDE

The Common Desktop Environment that will be shipped by all major UNIX vendors this fiscal year.

central processing unit (CPU)

The part of the computer in which calculations and manipulations take place.

client

(1) In the client-server model for file systems, the client is a machine that remotely accesses computer server resources, such as compute power and large memory capacity.

(2) In the client-server model for window systems, the client is an *application* that accesses windowing services from a "server process." In this model, the client and the server can run on the same machine or on separate machines.

client-server model

A common way to describe network services and the model user processes (programs) of those services. Examples include the name-server/name-resolver paradigm of the domain name system (DNS) and file-server/file-client relationships such as *NFS* and diskless hosts. See also *client*.

client system

A system on a network that relies on another system, called a *server system*, for resources such as disk space.

closed architecture

Any computer design with specifications not freely available. Such proprietary specifications make it difficult or impossible for third-party vendors to create ancillary devices that work correctly with a closed-architecture machine; usually, only its original master can build peripherals for such a machine. Contrast with *open architecture*.

CORBA

The multi-vendor Object Management Group's specification for object interoperability.

CPU

See *central processing unit (CPU)*.

data server

Relational Database Management System, or a distributed system that stores or houses data.

database management system (DBMS)

A software system facilitating the creation and maintenance of a database and the execution of programs using the database.

dataless

A hybrid mode of operation offering the cost advantages of diskless mode without the performance penalty. Dataless mode keeps the OS and swap space on the local disk, but stores all other data on an NFS server.

DBMS

See *database management system (DBMS)*.

DCE

OSF's Distributed Computing Environment, providing the world's most advanced set of heterogeneous networking and middleware. Based on TCP/IP, DCE provides four main services: security (kerberos authentication), distributed filing and data management, naming (cell directory service) for administrative control, and execution/data exchange, providing the infrastructure for distributed subroutines.

device-independent

Software that has been written expressly for portability across dissimilar computer systems. An industry-standard graphics library, such as PHIGS, is a device-independent interface.

diskless

A mode of operation in which a system and applications run without a disk by using remote NFS servers. Allows systems to boot and run entirely via the network, saving a bit on hardware costs, and forces a centralized administrative model, saving a lot on labor.

disk mirroring

Keeping consistent, redundant copies of disk data to automatically "fail around" a disk or controller crash. Redundantly records all data, keeps track of all disk failures, and automatically reads from only the valid copies of data.

distributed file system

A file system that exists on more than one server, enabling each user to access files on it or on other servers.

environment

The conditions under which a user works while using the UNIX system. A user's environment includes those things that personalize the user's login and how the user is allowed to interact in specific ways with UNIX and the computer. For example, the shell environment includes such things as the shell prompt string, specifics for backspace and erase characters, and commands for sending output from the terminal to the computer.

Ethernet

A type of local area network that enables real-time communication between machines connected directly through cables. Ethernet was developed by Xerox in 1976, originally for linking minicomputers at the Palo Alto Research Center.

FDDI

An emerging, high-speed networking standard. The underlying medium is fiber optics, and the topology is a dual-attached, counter-rotating token ring. FDDI networks can often be spotted by the orange fiber cable.

global

Having extended or general scope. For example, a global substitution of one word for another in a file affects all occurrences of the word. In networking, global refers to worldwide connectivity.

graphical user interface (GUI)

The graphical user interface, or GUI, provides the user with a method of interacting with the computer and its special applications, usually via a mouse or other selection device. The GUI usually includes such things as windows, an intuitive method of manipulating directories and files, and icons.

hardware

(1) The mechanical and electrical components of a computer system.

(2) The components of a computer system responsible for user input, display, and mathematical processing. Often the term hardware is used in specific reference to the computing power of the CPU or the graphics accelerator, or both. Another term for the collection of compute hardware is *platform*.

heterogenous network

A network composed of systems of more than one *architecture*. Contrast with *homogeneous network*.

homogeneous network

A network composed of systems of only one architecture. Contrast with *heterogenous network*.

HP/UX

The Hewlett-Packard version of SVR3.2 UNIX that runs only on the HP Precision Architecture RISC platforms.

infrastructure

The functions that perform utility services, such as networking, data center, and system administration. Each organization should have an architecture statement defining the organizational structure and operational procedures.

International Organization for Standardization (ISO)

An international agency that reviews and approves independently designed products for use within specific industries. ISO is also responsible for developing standards for information exchange. Its function is similar to that of *ANSI* in the United States. Also known as "International Standards Organization."

internet

A collection of networks interconnected by a set of routers that enable them to function as a single, large virtual network.

Internet

(Note the capital "I.") The largest internet in the world, consisting of large national backbone nets (such as MILNET, NSFNET, and CREN) and a myriad of regional and local campus networks worldwide. The Internet uses the Internet protocol suite. To be on the Internet the user must have IP connectivity, that is, be able to Telnet to—or "ping"—other systems. Networks with only email connectivity are not actually classified as being on the Internet.

Internet Protocol (IP)

The cornerstone of the TCP/IP architecture. The main tasks of IP are the addressing of the computers and the fragmentation of packets; it contains no functions for end-to-end message reliability or for flow control. IP makes the best effort to forward packets to the next destination, although the forwarding is not guaranteed.

ISO

See *International Organization for Standardization (ISO)*.

ISV

Independent software vendor, provides binary applications or toolkits for customers wanting off-the-shelf product.

Journaling File System

Also known as logging file system, provides transactional logging of file writes to disks. A Journaling File System has two key benefits: higher performance for database and NFS servers, and faster system recovery from crashes.

LAN

See *local area network (LAN)*.

load sharing

A protocol that can switch network packets between connections.

loading

Putting the machine-language instructions of a program into memory.

local

Having limited scope. Contrast with *global*.

local area network (LAN)

A group of computer systems in close proximity that can communicate with one another via some connecting hardware and software.

Local Bisync 3270

IBM or compatible character-based, bi-synchronous, dumb terminal.

MAE

The AppleSoft Macintosh Application Environment.

mail gateway

A machine that connects two or more electronic mail systems (especially dissimilar mail systems on two different networks) and transfers messages between them.

message

Information generated by a process that informs users about the status of that process.

modem

Short for modulator/demodulator. A device that enables a machine or terminal to establish a connection and transfer data through telephone lines.

modem pool

One central server with up to 32 modems attached and a rotary of telephone access numbers.

Motif

The windowing environment and programming libraries for standard UNIX desktops. Motif provides the display widgets and window-managment facilities needed to exploit the X11 distributed windowing system.

Multi-Processing (MP)

The ability to exploit the processing power of symmetric MP hardware. MP operating systems let user processing and operating system "housekeeping" work run concurrently on all CPUs, providing better performance and lowering latency. MP implementations are judged on the "fairness," efficiency, and linearity with which resources are allocated across a wide range of workloads. A system with a linear MP factor is said to be scalable, in that system resources are not wasted and performance is predictable, given the workload and hardware resources.

Multi-Threading (MT)

The availability of multi-threaded programming interfaces. All modern MP implementations use some sort of MT technology in the kernel, but the key differentiator among implementations is the scalability of the performance and the "weight" or "granularity" of the threads available to user programs.

multi-tasking

The ability of an operating system to handle many user and housekeeping jobs simultaneously, providing the illusion to users that they have a system dedicated to their work even though the system supports several users concurrently. Memory, disk, network, and CPU resources are allocated and managed to give the best possible performance. Multi-tasking systems are judged by their ability to handle a wide range of workloads with minimal waste and with security and robustness from isolated failures.

multi-user system

Any computer system that can be used concurrently by more than one person. Although a microcomputer shared by several people can be considered a multi-user system, the term is generally reserved for machines that are accessed by several or many people through communications facilities or via network terminals.

MWM

The Motif Window Manager. See *Motif.*

network

Technically, the hardware that connects various distributed or remote systems, enabling them to communicate.

network administration

Tasks of the person who maintains a network, such as adding systems to a network or enabling sharing between systems.

network administrator

The person who maintains a network.

Network File System (NFS)

The Sun NFS distributed computing system provides distributed heterogeneous data sharing. NFS, in conjunction with NIS+, AutoFS, CacheFS, and Volume Management, provide the user with automatic data location, navigation, and access over wide-area networks. The data appears to be instantly available on the user's desktop, even if it is stored on a mainframe in another state. NFS is licensed to more than 300 computer hardware and software companies worldwide.

Network Information Service (NIS)

A distributed network database containing key information about the systems and the users on the network. The NIS database is stored on the master server and all the slave servers.

Network Management Station (NMS)

The system responsible for managing a (portion of a) network. NMS communicates with network management agents that reside in the managed nodes, via a network management protocol.

network management strategy

Defines guidelines for making the transition through the various stages of development in the implementation of the tools, structure, and protocols that directly relate to the management of the network.

network management tool

Software responsible for managing the network and with the capacity to decentralize operations; for example, SunNet Manager.

network router

(1) An Ethernet connection that connects different locations over a leased circuit or satellite.

(2) The hub connectivity between cities, campuses, and buildings.

NFS

See *Network File System (NFS)*.

Network Information Service Plus (NIS+)

Used as a data repository for network and system management information. NIS+ has record-level security, on-line updates, and is extensible online.

OMG

The Object Management Group, consisting of Sun, HP, IBM, DEC, and 200 other system- and application-software vendors. This group specifies inter-operable technologies for object-based computing.

ONC+

The Sun Open Network Computing services, facilities and APIs, including the Network File System (NFS). ONC+ includes file and printer sharing, data exchange, remote procedure call, naming service (administrative data repository), and several other file-system technologies.

open architecture

A term used to describe any computer or peripheral design that has published specifications. A published specification enables third parties to develop add-on hardware for an open-architecture computer or device. Contrast with *closed architecture*.

open system

In communications, especially with regard to the ISO open interconnection model, a computer network designed to incorporate all devices—regardless of manufacturer or model—that can use the same communications facilities and protocols. See also *open architecture*.

operating system

A collection of programs that monitor the use of the system and supervise the other programs executed by it.

OSI

A set of protocols and network services for Open Systems Interconnect. Popular with EEC customers, OSI provides basic WAN connectivity (X.25), naming (X.400) and mail (X.500) services.

PC-NFS

SunSoft's implementation of the TCP/IP stack and NFS for the DOS/Windows PC. Provides remote print and file sharing, Berkeley mail tools, and Telnet access for PCs that are not configured as full Solaris clients. Fully supports heterogeneous data and service access.

platform

The foundation technology of a computer system. Because computers are layered devices composed of a chip-level hardware layer, a firmware and operating-system layer, and an applications program layer, the bottom layer of a machine is often called a platform, as in "a *SPARC* platform." However, designers and users of applications software view both the hardware and systems software as the platform because both provide support for an application.

plug-compatible

An adjective describing hardware equipped with connectors that are equivalent both in structure and in usage. For example, most modems having DB-25 connectors on their rear panels are plug-compatible; that is, one can be replaced by another without the cable having to be rewired.

port

(1) In computer hardware, a location for passing data in and out of a computing device. Microprocessors have ports for sending and receiving data bits; these ports are usually dedicated locations in memory. Full computer systems have ports for connecting peripheral devices such as printers and modems.

(2) In computer programming, to change a program in order to run it on a different computer.

(3) To move documents, graphics and other files from one computer to another.

(4) The abstraction used by Internet transport protocols to distinguish among multiple simultaneous connections to a single destination host.

POSIX

The Institute of Electrical and Electronic Engineers (IEEE) specifications for Portable OS Interfaces. A series of specifications (for example, 1003.1, 1003.2, and 1003.4) that state detailed requirements.

PPP

Point-to-Point Protocol for Internet access via modems and serial lines. Similarly to SLIP (serial line internet protocol), provides users with the full set of Internet and ONC services via low-cost modems and phone connections.

processor

A hardware device that executes the commands in a stored program in the computer system.

program

A sequence of instructions telling a computer how to perform a task. A program can be in *machine language* or it can be in a higher-level language that is then translated into machine language.

protocol

A formal description of messages to be exchanged and rules to be followed for two or more systems to exchange information.

prototyping

Analyzing multiple vendors to determine the best implementation to meet an architecturally defined solution.

RDBMS

Relational Database Management System, often called just "DBMS." Products from CA/Ingress, Informix, Oracle, Progress, and Sybase all fit in this category.

server

In the client-server model for file systems, a machine with compute resources (sometimes called the compute server) and large memory capacity. Client machines can remotely access and make use of these resources. In the client-server model for window systems, the server is a process that provides windowing services to an application, or "client process." In this model, the client and the server can run on the same machine or on separate machines.

server system

A system that is on a *network* and provides resources, such as disk space, software services, and file transfers, to other systems.

Simple Network Management Protocol (SNMP)

The open network protocol of choice for TCP/IP-based network management systems.

SMP

Symmetric Multiprocessing. See *Multi-Processing (MP)*.

SNMP

See *Simple Network Management Protocol (SNMP)*.

Solaris

SunSoft's complete 32-bit virtual-memory, multi-tasking, multi-processing, operating environment for RISC and CISC systems. Solaris provides a complete distributed window environment for commercial and technical users, based on X-windows, Motif, Open Look, ONC/NFS, TCP/IP, and SunOS (SVR4 UNIX).

SPARC

The 32-bit Scalable Processor ARChitecture from Sun. SPARC is based on a reduced instruction set computer (RISC) concept. The architecture was designed by Sun and its suppliers in an effort to significantly improve price and performance. SPARC is a registered trademark of SPARC International, Inc.

SPX/IPX

The NetWare proprietary protocol stack.

subnet

See *subnetwork*.

subnetwork

A collection of International Organization for Standardization's open systems interconnection (OSI) end systems and intermediate systems under the control of a single administrative domain and using a single network access protocol. Examples: private X.25 networks, collection of bridged LANs.

SVID 3

The UNIX System Five Interface Document, version 3. The basic compliance specification for System Five Release 4, the merged AT&T and Berkeley UNIX.

system

A computer that enables a user to run computer programs.

system administration

The tasks of a person who performs maintenance to systems, servers, or desktop machines attached to a network. Also manages and supports the LAN with control of the building-level gateway down to the desktop.

system administrator

The person who performs system administration functions.

TCP

See *Transmission Control Protocol (TCP)*.

TCP/IP

The protocol that provides OSI levels 2-4 of network connectivity. TCP/IP is the most proven "transport stack" in the world, with more than 1 M nodes "internetworked" in a single logical network. TCP/IP provides dependable messaging with automatic retries and routing around failures, subnets for location transparency and administrative efficiency, and an address space that has recently been expanded to millions of nodes.

terminal

A process running on a machine that originates with the physical device called a terminal, or as the software representation of such a physical device, like a window.

tool

A package of compact, well-designed programs designed to do a specific task well. Several tools can be linked to perform more complex tasks.

toolkit

A set of programs and predefined routines that a programmer can use in writing a program for a particular machine, environment, or application.

Transmission Control Protocol (TCP)

(1) A protocol of the transport layer, lying above the IP. Its main task is the reliable transportation of data through the network.

(2) The major transport protocol in the Internet suite of protocols providing reliable, connection-oriented, full-duplex streams.

User Datagram Protocol (UDP)

The User Datagram Protocol is a connectionless transport protocol. Its attributes are connectionless, addressing via port numbers, data checksums, very simple, best-effort forwarding.

user interface

See *graphical user interface (GUI)*.

uucp

UNIX-to-UNIX copy program. A protocol used for communication between consenting UNIX systems.

virtual memory

The ability of an operating system to create "memory spaces" well beyond the available RAM hardware.

volume management

The automatic cataloging and mounting of removable storage such as CD-ROM and diskette.

Wabi

SunSoft's Windows-application execution environment that runs under OpenWindows. Allows popular windows application binaries to run within a UNIX system unmodified, presenting the Windows look and feel as a "window" on the Solaris desktop.

wide-area network (WAN)

A network consisting of many systems that provide file transfer services over a large physical area, sometimes spanning the globe. A WAN can span between different locations, regions (for example, cities or states), and countries.

X11

The industry-standard distributed windowing protocol, providing high-performance interaction with remote and local computer systems. Provides the APIs and intrinsics underlying OPEN LOOK and Motif.

X.25

Wide-area packet network support, usually provided via telephone or leased lines.

xhost

The ability to display windowed applications and graphics running on a remote CPU. The xhost technique allows hardware resources to be used or shared more effectively and can be used with X-terminals, Solaris systems, or PCs (running X-window terminal software such as Hummingbird).

XPG

The X/Open Portability Guide, specifying commands, functions, and APIs for writing portable applications.

Rightsizing for Corporate Survival

Index

Covia Technologies' Communications Integrator, 41
cross-development environments, 51
customer management, 69
customer management applications, 56
Customer Service Representatives (CSRs), 70

D

data access technology, 41
data availability, 209
data integrity, 209
database gateways, 40
database integration and synchronization, 160
database models, 35
database replication technology, 38
"dataless" desktop systems, 103
DB2, 145
de facto industry standards, 25
decision support, 57
decision-support applications, 56
DECnet, 16, 46
Deskset Productivity tools, 25
desktop standards, 158
development approaches, 48
disposing, of old equipment, 106
distributed database, 156
distributed database management system, 37
distributed database technology, 36
distributed enterprise management tools, 47
Dynamic Business Systems (DBS), 89

E

Eastman Kodak Company, 101
economic analysis, 97
EcoTools, 47
electronic imaging, 51
enterprise data model (EDM), 171
enterprise management, 44, 46
   components of, 44
enterprise management tools, 44
enterprise networking, 42

enterprise-wide distributed systems, 3
executive sponsor, 134

F

file sharing, 160
Financial Dynamics, 89
4th Dimension, 47

G

gateway technologies, 40
graphical user interfaces (GUI), 30
Gulf Canada Resources Ltd., 8, 10, 96

H

hardware acquistions, new, 106
hardware ownership, 97
Hewlett-Packard, 24
high-impact applications, 136
high-payoff applications, 136
human resources, investment required, 143

I

IBM COBOL, 51
IBM Corporation, 24
IDE's Software through Pictures, 49
imaging technology, 51
IMS, 40, 144, 189
incompatible networks, access to, 16
Information Builders' EDA/SQL, 41
Information Builders' FOCUS, 51, 145
Information Engineering, 49
Integrated CASE (I-CASE), 49
integrated desktop vision, 207
integration issues, 160
integration standards, 160
International Standards Organization (ISO), 23
inter-operability, 209
inter-process communication, 43
IPSYS's ToolBuilder, 49
IS architecture, typical, 154
IS infrastructure, 17